Daughter of Independence

Lived by Wenny Achdiat
Written by Bryce Alcock

Echidna-Fox Publishing

Copyright © 2013 Wenny Achdiat and Bryce Alcock

This book is copyright. Except for private study, research, criticism or reviews, as permitted under the Copyright Act, no part of this book may be reproduced, stored in a retrieval system, photocopied, or transmitted in any form or by any means without prior written permission.

Every effort has been made to acknowledge and contact the copyright holders for permission to reproduce material contained in this book. Any copyright holders who have been inadvertently omitted from *Permissions and Credits* (at the back of this book) should contact the publisher and omissions will be rectified in subsequent editions.

Enquiries to:
Echidna-Fox Publishing
PO Box 1791
Toowoomba Qld 4350
Australia
Email: bryce@brycealcock.net

Cover and layout by Lucy Robertson-Cuninghame

The authors acknowledge the assistance of the Australian Society of Authors Mentorship Program, which is supported by the Copyright Agency's Cultural Fund.

ISBN:	Soft Cover	978-0-9875837-0-3
	Ebook	978-0-9875837-1-0

This book is dedicated to
the children of Wenny and Dahlan
Cheddy Marvian Nuradil
Shanti Febrianti
Dian Dianawati
Ira Yuliarti
Ari Irawan

Table of Contents

Prologue 7
1. Cherished by the Moon 8
2. Revolution 18
3. Refugees 28
4. Jakarta 41
5. The Mango Tree 47
6. Merdeka 52
7. Fearsome Mother, Wayward Father 57
8. Taking Charge of My Education 61
9. The Presidential Painter 65
10. September in the Rain 69
11. Fissures and Tensions 73
12. Childhood's End 77
13. Crisis 85
14. Judgement Days 90
15. University 98
16. Exile 106
17. Back to the Revolution 114
18. A Sundanese Wedding 125
19. The Baby with Perfect Ears 140
20. Guests and Ghosts 151
21. Departure from Chaos 166
22. Working with White People 175
23. The Scattered Dust of Love 185
24. Tears and Laughter 199
25. Crunch Time 210
26. Standing Up For Myself 220
27. Dahlan 228
28. Ibu and Bapak 235
29. Achdiat Karta Mihardja, My Father 241
Glossary 250
Appreciation 256
Permissions and Credits 259
Works Consulted 261

Prologue

The day after he turned ninety-eight my father asked me a question I did not want to answer.

His birthday dinner the previous night had been quiet, unlike the surprise party for his ninetieth birthday. For that earlier event my children and I flew to Canberra. Members of the organising committee had met us at the airport and driven us to the restaurant where more than a hundred people were waiting. The Indonesian Ambassador paid tribute to my father's achievements as a writer and teacher, and as a respected elder of the Indonesian community in Canberra. That time, an incident the next morning destroyed the happiness I had felt for my father.

Now, eight years later, the mood was different. While my mother dozed on a couch nearby, my father and I talked quietly. I felt close to him. We reminisced about how our family had survived the Japanese occupation and the Revolution, how my mother had tricked the Dutch, and about our flight to the mountains.

When I told him about writing my life story, he said, 'To a writer there are no secrets. You must be honest as long as you don't hurt people.'

Then he asked the question. 'And now it is time to be honest with each other. How have I been as a father to you? Tell me if I have done anything to hurt you.'

'Oh, Bapak,' I said. 'Let's not talk about that.'

'I would like to know how you felt as my daughter.'

'That's all in the past. Let's talk about something else.'

'Wenny, I don't have long to live. If we don't open our hearts now, we never will.'

'Bapak, if I answer you honestly, will you do the same? Will you tell me how I have been as a daughter?'

'Of course.'

At first I could not speak. There were so many things I wanted to say but I knew they would hurt him. Bapak watched me, his eyes bright.

CHAPTER 1
Cherished by the Moon

> I saw my titles as nonsense. It's just something that divides mankind. So at the age of 11 or 12, still in the lower school, I stopped using my title, erased it from my name.
> —Achdiat Karta Mihardja, *On the Record: Indonesian Literary Figures*

Two trucks full of men with rifles drove into the street. We stopped playing hopscotch and watched as the soldiers jumped down.

'*Jepang*,' said one of my playmates. Japanese.

The soldiers fanned out, going to nearby houses. I ran to Nini, my grandmother, who was weeding pot plants on her terrace. 'Nini,' I cried. '*Jepang*.'

She ran inside and called her two teenage daughters. She put a chair on a table and my aunts stood on it and climbed up through the manhole into the ceiling. 'Go outside,' she told me. 'Keep playing. Don't say anything to the soldiers.'

I rejoined my friends in the street. We stared at the men as they went from house to house. Four came to my grandparents' place, and one patted me on the head. I looked at the shiny bayonet on the end of his rifle and held my breath. They went inside, and I waited, thinking of my aunts. My father and mother had talked about how cruel the soldiers could be. When they came out, I ran inside and asked Nini what the men did. 'They went into every room and opened all the wardrobes and cupboards,' she said. 'But they didn't look above their heads.'

My aunts stayed in the ceiling until the trucks had gone from our street.

Neighbourhood children often came to the big yard in front of my grandparents' house to play hopscotch in squares that we scratched in the dirt. Sometimes we would make mud biscuits or pretend *gado-gado* salad from flowers and leaves, and set up market stalls to sell them to one another.

But better than playing games was helping Aki, my grandfather. When the carp were big in the fishponds beside the house, the ponds were drained and his workers caught the fish while Aki counted them. I wanted to help, so I waded into the mud and reached down for the biggest fish I could see. As I held it to my chest it flapped furiously, covering my playsuit with slime. I carried the fish to Aki and nearly burst with pride and happiness when he said, 'Clever girl.'

Then the fishmongers from the market came to buy the carp, and while they haggled with Aki I noticed my long gold chain necklace was lost – it must have happened as I was catching the fish. Knowing Mamih, my mother, would be angry, I ran crying to Nini, and one of the workers helped me comb through the mud. When we couldn't find the necklace I grew terrified about what would happen when Mamih came home. Then Nini brought out the food: *ikan goreng,* fried fish, *lalap,* steamed vegetables and sambal, *krupuk udang,* prawn crackers, and *nasi timbel*. I loved nasi timbel and the way the rice smelt of the banana leaf it was wrapped in. I sat down beside the pond with my grandparents and the workers, and we had a big feast. It was fun being with all the grown-ups, laughing and eating, and I forgot to be scared that Mamih would be angry with me.

And even better than playing games or helping Aki was being with my father. When I was little I called him Papih and he never got angry with me. Sometimes he took me for walks through the streets of our suburb, and one evening as we walked through the town square, my hand in his, I saw the soldiers again. They were sitting at tables outside a restaurant and had girls with thickly powdered faces, pink cheeks and bright red lips sitting on their laps. Everyone was laughing. I asked Papih about the soldiers and the girls, but he ignored my questions and made me walk faster.

Another evening when we were walking we saw a man in hessian lying beside the road. It was a time when many people wore hessian sacking, but this man was covered in flies. 'What's wrong with the man, Papih?' I asked.

Again my father hurried past, pulling me along with him. I thought of the soldiers with their guns and shiny bayonets. Perhaps they had hurt the man in hessian. I hoped they would not hurt my Papih.

Achdiat Karta Mihardja, my father, was born into a family of Sundanese nobles who lived in Pakuwon, a small exclusively aristocratic suburb in the city of Garut in West Java. Achdiat's father, Kosasih Karta Mihardja, worked as a manager in a government-owned bank.

Achdiat (left) with his father, mother and siblings.

While still at primary school Achdiat read all the books in his father's huge collection, and developed a passion for literature and philosophy. His exam results made his family proud, but his ideas troubled them. At the age of twelve he decided that feudalism was divisive and, arguing that God created all people equal, stopped using his titles, shocking his parents, who valued their nobility. After finishing junior high school in Bandung, he attended the Dutch senior high school in Solo in Central Java, studying Asian literature for three years. He had actually been too old to be accepted into this school but, as birth certificates were not issued at that time, he was able to qualify by shifting his date of birth from 1910 to 1911. For the rest of his life his official year of birth was 1911.

During his schooling in Solo Achdiat became active in the anti-colonial movement. Nationalist feeling had been boosted when the 1928 All Indonesian Youth Congress adopted the "Youth Pledge", a resolution proclaiming the ideals of one motherland, one nation and one language. Subsequently all the provincial youth groups began uniting into one national group, Young Indonesia, and Achdiat helped found the Solo branch, becoming secretary. He rejected provincialism, and worked to rid himself of his Sundanese-ness.

The first great love of Achdiat's life was Arini, a fellow student at Solo. They planned marriage but Arini's family forbade it because of the ethnic difference – Arini was Javanese. The two young lovers were heartbroken.

Achdiat continued to question traditional ways of thinking, especially after another incident when his father ordered Achdiat to accompany him to an audience with the Bupati, the head of Garut Regency, the local government. The Bupati was a high status Sundanese man, the official through whom the Dutch administered the Regency. Achdiat's father followed the tradition of paying obeisance to the Bupati at certain times.

When Achdiat saw what he must do – crawl on his hands and knees to a position before the Bupati, keeping his eyes always on the floor even while raising his clasped hands in the gesture of respect, addressing the Bupati as his lord – he refused. His father was enraged at the embarrassment Achdiat caused him. A rift opened between father and son with the devout Kosasih angered by the way Achdiat questioned everything, even his religious beliefs. Their arguments began to cause tension in the family.

After high school Achdiat wanted to study philosophy and literature at university, but his father could not afford the fees, so Achdiat became a teacher at Taman Siswa, a nationalist private school, and joined the editorial staff of a newspaper and a journal. Then Kosasih lost his job due to the depression and received a lump-sum payment with which he bought an auction shop for Achdiat who tried to interest himself in the business so that he could earn enough to attend university.

Near the shop was Restaurant Bandung where Achdiat began to have lunch every day because he had noticed the beautiful and self-assured young woman who worked in the kitchen.

Tati (second from right) with her father and siblings

The scholar M A W Brouwer said that God was smiling when He created Parahyangan, the heartland of Sundanese West Java, a realm of active volcanoes, lush forest, vegetable gardens, terraced rice fields, citrus orchards and serene tea plantations. Haji Noor and his wife owned some of those fields, as well as businesses in Garut such as a large hotel with a popular café and billiard room. Their first child, born in 1917, was Suprati, my mother.

Tati, as she was known, was nine when her mother died from tuberculosis. She took over responsibility for the household, looking after her father and four siblings. Haji Noor passed on his management expertise to Tati, and she became confident and quick-thinking. When she was twenty, he arranged for her to learn the art of restaurant cookery and, while working at Restaurant Bandung, Tati Suprati Noor met Achdiat Karta Mihardja.

Achdiat and Tati at their engagement

The couple began courting. Achdiat introduced Tati to his family, and she and Achdiat's sister Ipit became close friends. Ipit sometimes accompanied the couple to the cinema as chaperone. But when they planned marriage, both Achdiat's and Tati's parents refused permission because tradition dictated that nobles and commoners must marry within their own class. The aristocrats believed that their blood would be diluted by mixed marriage, while Haji Noor was more concerned about the dilution of his wealth.

Achdiat's experience at school in Solo had hardened his resolve – having lost Arini through ethnic prejudice, he would not allow class prejudice to separate him from Tati. The couple threatened to elope and, although such a catastrophe would ruin each family's good name, their parents still resisted. Then Tati left home and went to stay with her aunt in Bandung and this, the first step towards elopement, forced both sets of parents to consent to the marriage.

The wedding took place in June 1938. Achdiat and Tati were pioneers, among the first Sundanese to marry outside their social class. Others followed their example until gradually such unions became common.

I was born in April 1939. Haji Noor asked that his first grandchild be named after the rice goddess Sri Anggrawati in the hope that I would develop her refined and feminine qualities. He could not have anticipated how events in the coming years would frustrate this wish. My father added "Wennie" to my name as he liked its sound, despite its Dutch flavour.

Achdiat and Tati struggled to survive in the first years of their marriage. The auction shop failed, and they moved to Bandung, where they converted half their tiny house into a *warung*, a small shop selling basic necessities. Achdiat wrote short stories and articles for news services, and had a growing reputation as a journalist and writer. In 1941 we moved to Jakarta, where Papih became an editor at Balai Pustaka, the publishing house set up by the colonial government to provide appropriate reading matter for the "natives".

A year later Achdiat was diagnosed with the first stage of tuberculosis, the disease which had killed Tati's mother. He needed cooler mountain air so we moved back to Garut and stayed with Achdiat's family in Pakuwon.

In March 1942, Japanese forces occupied Java, and my earliest memory is the coming of the soldiers to our street. My sister Ati Asyawati was born at this time, and in choosing her name, Achdiat was influenced by larger events. He had observed the rapid succession of Japanese victories, and believed that the age of European imperialism was ending, that Asia's time had come, so he included 'Asia' in Ati's name, changing it to 'Asya' so that it would not be too obvious in case of a resurgence of Dutch power.

Achdiat's health quickly improved and a few months after the Japanese invasion we moved back to Jakarta and rented a house in the suburb of Menteng. Papih joined the staff of the News and Information Service of Radio Jakarta, and one of his duties was to translate Indonesian into Sundanese for listeners in West Java. Later I found out that at the same time as he was working for the Japanese administration, he had also joined the anti-Japanese underground movement and was involved in black market operations.

I rode pillion on my father's bicycle while Ati sat on Mamih's bike. Ati and I wore our going-out-on-Sunday clothes – frilly dresses instead of our usual playsuits.

As he peddled, Papih told a story, making me laugh. 'So the mouse deer fooled the crocodiles,' he said, '*and* escaped from the tiger. Hey, Ati, wake up.'

My sister was nodding off.

'Here, Papih,' I cried. 'Let's eat here. I want saté.'

I was four years old when the best thing in the world was riding pillion behind my Papih, listening to his funny stories, stopping at roadside stalls for saté, or calling on friends where I would play with the children.

And the really best thing, I thought, was Papih's special name for me – "Nyenyen". Mamih only ever called me "Wennie" but I knew my father had made up another name to show his extra love for me.

At night we listened to him on the radio. 'You're so big,' I said to him. 'How can you fit inside the radio?'

'I say a magic word, and poof, I'm this small,' he answered, holding up his finger. 'Then I can crawl inside.'

I laughed and wrapped my arms around him, and he let me stand on his feet as he waltzed around the room.

But better than anything else in the world was when Papih took me for a walk, late in the afternoon when the house was hot, just the two of us with my hand in his as we explored the streets of Menteng.

Once, when we passed a footpath vendor, I wanted fried peanuts and asked Papih to buy me some. But he never carried money – that was Mamih's job. Then I remembered that I had money and I pulled from my pocket a note of the smallest denomination.

'That's not enough, Nyenyen,' said Papih. 'You need two of them.'

I ripped the note in half. 'This is two,' I said.

The peanut vendor laughed. 'It's no good now. You can't buy anything with that. But I'll give you some.' He twisted a piece of paper into a cone and filled it with peanuts. 'Here,' he said, 'for you.'

Darkness began to fall and, walking along the street, I watched the moon rolling over the tops of the houses. 'Look, Papih. The moon is following me.'

'That's because the moon loves you, Nyenyen.'

Wenny with her father

CHAPTER 2
Revolution

Proclamation
We, the Indonesian people herewith proclaim the independence of Indonesia. All matters pertaining to the transfer of power etc. will be carried out correctly and in the shortest possible time.
Djakarta, 17 August 1945
On behalf of the Indonesian people
Soekarno – Hatta
—The Indonesian Declaration of Independence

Before Japanese occupation in 1942 the Indonesian archipelago had been a Dutch colony since 1800. A mass nationalist movement had been agitating for *kemerdekaan*, independence, since 1908. When Japan surrendered in August 1945, Sukarno and Hatta, the main nationalist leaders, proclaimed Indonesia's independence. A republican government was formed with Sukarno as President and Hatta as Vice-President.

British forces arrived to take over from the Japanese and keep order until the Dutch could return. Months of chaos followed with clashes between militias and the British, attempted takeovers by groups such as the communists, and massacres of civilians.

By December 1945 the republican government had formed an army, which Achdiat joined. Then the British assisted the Dutch to land their own forces, and to recapture Jakarta, forcing the Indonesian government to transfer its capital to Yogyakarta in Central Java.

Our family moved back to Garut, where Indonesian authorities had taken over from the Japanese. Achdiat established his own newspaper, *Gelombang Zaman*, "The Wave of the Times", employing two editors and several journalists.

Between Garut and Jakarta lay the capital of West Java, Bandung, which was now divided. British troops occupied the northern half of the city while Indonesian authorities remained in control south of the railway line. Europeans and Eurasians who had been in the Japanese internment camps sought refuge in the northern half, while Indonesians from the north fled to the southern zone. By January 1946, the north was an isolated and besieged European enclave protected by Gurkha battalions, while the south became a centre for the *pemudas*, revolutionary youth groups.

On 23 March 1946, the British announced that all armed men must leave the southern half of the city by midnight the following day. The pemudas and the Indonesian army knew that they would lose many of their best fighters and their limited stock of munitions if they were to try to resist an invasion by the superior British force. By the afternoon of the next day, the decision was taken to evacuate the Indonesian zone and burn it to the ground – a scorched earth policy that would deny resources to the enemy. Dynamite was distributed, pemudas were assigned to each area and, by dusk, half a million civilians were moving into the countryside with the city exploding into flames behind them.

My mother's aunt, Ma Lengkong, lived in a big house in the centre of Bandung with her husband and two sons and their families, and she had decided that they would not join the evacuation. My parents were frantic with worry until they heard that Ma's family had survived, huddled in their house listening to the explosions. There had not been enough time for the pemudas to destroy all buildings, and those in Ma's area were among those that survived.

Bandung Lautan Api, the Bandung Sea of Fire, was celebrated as an act of defiance that showed how far Indonesians would go to defeat the imperialists.

Achdiat had joined the Siliwangi Division of the Indonesian army but his health precluded a combat role, so he served in the Intelligence Section, providing information to the forces operating around Garut. My father now seemed to spend all his time writing, publishing his newspaper and meeting with guerrilla fighters and Indonesian army soldiers. I felt that I was no longer important to him, and wished he would pay me more attention. But there was one demand on his time I had not known about.

I rode pillion on Mamih's bicycle, hanging on tightly as we sped over the rough road on the way to Papih's office. When we arrived I ran after her as she stamped inside. Everyone stopped the work they were doing to look at Mamih, and a young woman called Dewi half rose from her seat behind a desk, a look of terror on her face.

'Witch!' Mamih screamed at her. 'Stay away from my husband!'

'No, no, Ibu, not me,' cried Dewi and backed away. 'I'm not bothering your husband.'

'Don't lie to me,' yelled Mamih as she advanced.

My father was now between them, trying to calm Mamih who was still shouting. I held onto her dress, peering around her, and suddenly I understood. Dewi was trying to steal my father. I watched as she stood shaking, looking from side to side, her mouth open, and I was gripped by a fierce hatred for her.

'Tati, it's my fault, not hers,' said Papih, keeping in front of Mamih as she tried to get around him. 'I'm sorry, Tati. Please be calm.'

'Sorry, Ibu, sorry, sorry,' pleaded Dewi.

'I'll kill you,' screamed Mamih, lunging toward Dewi with raised fists.

Papih wrapped his arms around Mamih and tried to hold her back. She struggled free and thrust him away but Dewi ran to the door and escaped into the street. Mamih turned to my father.

'Sorry, Tati, a thousand times sorry,' he begged. 'It meant nothing. It won't happen again. I promise. It's finished.'

But my mother wasn't finished. For months she went on and on about it. 'How could you fall in love with Si Hideung? She's so ugly,' she would taunt.

Mamih had lighter skin than Dewi, so she called her *Si Hideung*, Blackie, even though Dewi's skin was not as dark as mine, or my father's.

'Okay, okay,' Papih would reply. 'It's over now. It's behind us.'

In 1946 I began primary school in Garut. Each day after school I played with my cousin, Bi Momi, who was always sitting on the steps of her house next door, waiting for me. She was deaf and mute, an attractive teenager with curly hair, but very lonely as no one else wanted to be with her. When she saw me coming she jumped up and down, her eyes shining. We hugged and then had a big conversation – somehow we understood each other perfectly using our own made-up sign language. We shared our snacks and played *bekelin,* a game similar to knucklebones.

I may have had a gift for communicating with Bi Momi but I was a poor student at school. Mira, the other pupil at my desk, became a good friend and we chatted or played together during breaks. Her mother, single and poor, struggled to bring up several children, so Mira always wore simple clothes and no shoes. I admired her cleverness – she had quickly learnt the alphabet and had begun to read, and she knew her times tables. So, because I hated school and never did any work, I paid Mira to help me. When we did exercises in class she would show me her answers under the desk in return for some of my lunch money. I also paid her to do my homework. As my parents were very busy, they relied on my report cards, which were always good, and I was too young to think about what might happen if Papih found out that the only thing I had learnt in Grade One was how to be devious.

At the end of the year the teacher recommended I advance to the next grade.

When we first went to Garut we moved in with Papih's parents in Pakuwon. I loved Aki Karta, Papih's father. I snuggled into him while he told me exciting stories of his aristocratic family. When Nini, my grandmother, told me such tales they became long and boring.

Later we moved into the manager's quarters of a hotel owned by my other Aki, Mamih's father. One night there was loud banging on the door, waking us all. I saw Papih leaving with his cousin. Mamih, crying, sent me back to bed.

In the morning she told us that Papih's father had become ill and had died during the night. This was the first time someone I loved had died, and I couldn't understand what it meant. At the funeral later that day Aki's wrapped body was placed on a bamboo framework draped with seven batik cloths. Bearers held the bier on their shoulders and first my father and his brothers and sisters passed beneath the body, then the grandchildren. As I walked under Aki, I understood, and my tears came.

It was not until I was older that my father told me what had happened that night.

After his cousin had woken us at the hotel, Achdiat had gone to find a doctor to take to his father. The doctor could do nothing – Aki was dying. His children gathered at his bedside. Aki opened his eyes and looked at Achdiat. 'Get out,' he croaked. 'You always try to upset my beliefs. I need to be at peace with God.'

Then Aki raised his hand and gestured his son away. Stunned, Achdiat left the room. He sat just outside the door, grief-stricken at how much suffering he must have caused his father by challenging his beliefs. Whereas Aki's other children had accepted Islam without doubt, Achdiat always asked questions that made his father angry. How do we know that the teachings of Islam are true? Is Marx right about religion? Now he was tortured by regret. He waited outside the room for several hours until his father passed away.

Three years later Achdiat would publish his first novel, in which a major turning point occurs when the main character's father orders him away from his deathbed.

Now I had only one Aki, Mamih's father Haji Noor. Ati and I loved our visits to Pasir Wangi, his plantation in the mountains. We would giggle as Aki's servants piggy-backed us from the main road to the house. There we shouted 'Ibu Gunung, Ibu Gunung' before rushing into the arms of our step-grandmother. We should have called her Nini, the word for grandmother but, as she was younger than our mother, we used Ibu instead. And because she was from the mountains, *gunung*, I had given her the full name of Ibu Gunung with Ati and our cousins following my lead.

In the house at Pasir Wangi Ibu Gunung kept our toys in a special cupboard. We sometimes played make-believe afternoon tea with our favourite miniature porcelain tea set. We also loved playing with our goats. As Aki had many goats he had given one to Ati and one to me and I called mine *Si Putih*, because he was pure fluffy white. As I cuddled Si Putih I could see how much he had grown since our last visit.

'What would you like to eat?' Aki teased. 'Goat saté or fish?'

'Fish! We want fish!'

Although I was seven I still loved catching fish. 'Pick a big one,' said Aki, holding me as I leaned over the pond filled with carp. When I grabbed one he said, 'Clever girl,' just as my other Aki used to.

After dinner we watched our grandfather comb Ibu Gunung's hair, which reached all the way to her thighs. I wanted hair like hers. When Mamih cut my hair she left it looking like half a coconut shell which I hated so much that she had to chase and catch me on hair-cut day.

In bed at Pasir Wangi Ati and I would talk about the day. 'The best thing,' I said, 'is that Ibu Gunung doesn't give us cod liver oil.'

Mamih believed in cod liver oil. When she forced the slimy liquid down our throats, she told us it was to keep us healthy. She said it was because there wasn't enough good food. Luckily there was plenty of good food at Haji Noor's farm.

Everybody spoke of *merdeka*, freedom. During the time we lived at Haji Noor's hotel it was a key meeting point for guerrillas and pemudas. I was in awe of the many young fighters who came to the hotel, where my grandfather provided free meals and a place to sleep. They were rough, spirited men who often raised their fists and shouted 'Merdeka!' Ammunition belts crossed their chests and grenades hung at their waists. All had rifles and some carried swords. They were not afraid of dying and many belonged to a special unit called *Pasukan Berani Mati* or Suicide Squad. Their hair was long and tangled because they had sworn not to cut it until after independence had been achieved. Some of the most fearless fighters were Batak men from Sumatra and they told stories about the legendary guerrilla Maulana who would decapitate any enemy he captured with his sword and then lick the blood from the blade to increase his *kesaktian*, his supernatural power.

The fighter's stories were terrifying, but I felt safe among them. I made friends with a handsome Batak man, Pak Tjo Ibrahim, a member of the Suicide Squad but a gentle giant with long curly hair who often gave me a few coins.

As well as the guerrillas, Indonesian army soldiers came to the hotel and talked for hours with my father, who had gathered information about the strengths and weaknesses of the Dutch. NICA, the Netherlands Indies Civil Administration, was sending parties of Dutch soldiers into West Java to raid guerrilla bases and capture Republican leaders. We lived in fear that spies would tell NICA about the hotel. Papih was suspicious of Syahrul, a friendly man who often visited the hotel and mingled with the fighters, and he was convinced that Syahrul was responsible for what happened next.

It was night when they came for my father.

The waiter appeared at our quarters behind the hotel to tell us Dutch soldiers were outside. My parents were ready. Papih put a chair on the table and used it to climb through the manhole to the ceiling. Mamih grabbed my hand and we walked across the dark courtyard to the reception lobby. There was loud banging from outside. She nodded to the staff who were huddling in the shadows, and one came forward to open the double doors.

White men in uniform stamped into the lobby. Behind them more men with long rifles jumped down from a truck and came up the stairs.

'Where's Achdiat?' one demanded in Indonesian.

Mamih answered in Dutch. 'I don't know, Sir. We haven't seen him for weeks.'

The man told the other soldiers to search the hotel, and they began pounding on the doors of the guest rooms on each side of the lobby, inspecting the frightened people who opened the doors and pushing past them into the rooms.

I thought, now they'll go to our quarters. They were so tall I imagined them stretching up and looking through the manhole. They'll drag Papih away and we'll never see him again. And they'll take Mamih too, for concealing him. I clung more tightly to her housecoat.

The commander came back to Mamih. 'Where is he?'

'We've had no news. I don't even know if he's still alive. You can ask the staff. They'll tell you we haven't seen him.'

The soldiers gathered around us as the commander glared at Mamih. She pointed to some tables and chairs. 'Would you like to sit down?'

The commander did not move.

Mamih took a step towards a table and indicated a chair. 'Please,' she said.

The commander frowned, hesitated, and then sat down with two of his soldiers. 'Mrs Achdiat, if he is not here, where is he?'

'He just disappeared,' said Mamih, and sat opposite the commander. I stood beside her, hanging on to her housecoat, her arm around my shoulders. 'One day he didn't come home. We've been searching for him, but no one's heard anything. We're so worried. It's a hard time for families. I keep waiting for news. I'm sure something's happened to him, otherwise he would have sent us a message.'

There was a catch in her voice, and I looked up to see tears running down her face. My hand shook as I clutched her.

'Look at my children, they are suffering,' she said. 'My youngest is always crying for her Papih. This one keeps asking when he is coming home.'

The commander was nodding as he looked at me.

'My poor children,' said Mamih, 'they miss him so much. I don't know what to do.'

The commander sighed, then reached over and patted my head, and murmured gentle words. He seemed to feel sorry for us. His face had softened, and his soldiers lounged back in their chairs.

'Would you like supper?' Mamih asked, and gave instructions to the staff to prepare *nasi goreng,* fried rice, and *kopi tubruk,* strong black Indonesian coffee.

The soldiers ate their meal quickly. I watched them, holding my secret knowledge inside me, staying glued to Mamih as she continued to sit opposite the commander and speak quietly with him. After the meal he shook Mamih's hand and thanked her. He patted her on the shoulder, and stroked my hair. All the soldiers smiled as they called 'thank you' and waved goodbye. They left without searching our quarters at the back of the hotel.

The hotel was no longer safe, so we moved back to Papih's mother's house. My father now expected a full-scale invasion by the Dutch to re-establish their control over West Java. Many people were evacuating from Garut, and the rest of my father's family had departed. We stayed because Achdiat believed that his newspaper and his work as an intelligence officer were important to the independence cause. And Mamih was pregnant, so my parents wanted to stay close to medical help. But Mamih kept our bags packed.

When we had moved back to the Karta Mihardja house the first thing I had done was hide my red handbag behind the dressing table Mamih was using. Whenever Papih travelled to conferences or meetings he always brought back *oleh-oleh,* gifts for everyone. Once, after a literature conference in Solo, he had given me a beautiful deep-red handbag made from hemp. I loved that bag, and used it to store tokens for *congklak,* a game in which the tokens are moved between holes in a wooden board. I became an avid collector of the small black shiny seeds of soursop, perfect for playing congklak. When anyone ate the fruit,

I pounced on the seeds and cleaned the pulp from them, soaking, washing and drying them many times before adding them to my collection. The red bag became my greatest treasure and I loved counting the seeds, so whenever we moved to a new home I always found a safe place for it.

Two days later I was playing in the yard, and looked up to see planes flying towards us with bombs falling from them like rain. The siren sounded but we didn't have time to run to the shelter. Our parents pulled Ati and me into a bedroom where we all hid under the bed. I lay on my tummy, my whole body shaking, my legs and buttocks shuddering up and down. In my heart I prayed to God that a bomb would not fall on our house.

When the siren sounded again, we emerged to see buildings destroyed or on fire. Papih said we must leave immediately. We grabbed our bags and ran out of the house, but at the gate I remembered the red bag, and started to run back.

Papih grabbed my arm and shouted 'Nyenyen! Where are you going?'

'I have to get my red bag.'

'No, it's too dangerous. You could be killed.' He wouldn't let me go and pulled me out through the gate. 'When the war is over we'll get you another bag.'

I struggled and screamed. I wanted my bag, *that* bag.

When we came to the main road Papih somehow managed to find a *delman*, a horse and buggy, and he lifted Ati and me up beside Mamih. He climbed in and we rode through thick black smoke past factories, shops and houses in flames, but I did not care. Tears streamed down my face. I had lost my red bag.

'I will never ever forgive him,' I told myself.

CHAPTER 3
Refugees

> [Anwar] reached the orchard fence in a few strides and in another stride ... he was over the fence, brazenly picking the mandarins as if he owned them ... A moment later Anwar returned with his hands, shirt and trouser pockets bulging with mandarins. ... "Don't worry! They're only owned by capitalists!" he said as he peeled the biggest mandarin.
> —Achdiat Karta Mihardja, *Atheis*

The delman driver took us to where the road ran out at the edge of the city and we walked to the village of Karang Pawitan where we stayed with a local family. The spirit of independence was strong, and people everywhere welcomed refugees into their homes. During the few days we stayed there, guerrilla fighters with shoulder-length hair often came to get information from Papih.

One night my father heard that trucks with Dutch soldiers had been to nearby villages, so the next morning we left the house and began walking east towards Telagabodas Volcano. We followed tracks where we could, or walked through rice fields, along rivers, and through the jungle. We were always on the move, staying for a night or two in villages, then on the road again at sunrise. Because Mamih had been so well prepared she had brought all her jewellery, which she kept hidden in a pouch under her clothes above the mound of her pregnancy. She used pieces of the jewellery to barter for food with villagers. Her planning helped us survive.

We did not stay in any one place for long in case we came to the notice of informants. Ati and I had always called our parents Mamih and Papih, Dutch words, but now these names could betray my father's status as an intellectual so we had to call him *Ajengan*, as he was pretending to be an Islamic teacher, while Mamih became *Ibu*. We kept forgetting the new rule.

Papih tried to hide his identity by wearing a sarong and

a *kopiah*, a rimless Muslim cap. But these efforts at fitting in amongst local people were somewhat spoiled by the battered brown leather briefcase from which he would not be parted as it was full of notebooks for his writing.

Village people made us welcome. Food was scarce but they shared the little they had, usually very basic meals – rice, sambal and steamed vegetables, with occasional salted fish. No one ate well. Walking all day, eating little, I was always hungry and susceptible to temptation. Knowing theft was wrong, I struggled in my heart when hunger made me think about stealing food from farmers.

One night a *Lurah*, a Village Chief, made room for us in his brick house. He had an orchard of *jeruk garut*, large sweet mandarins. I stared at the ripe fruit weighing down the trees, thinking how easily the skin would come off, imagining myself stuffing the segments into my mouth, the juice running down my chin. It was so long since I had eaten fruit.

The Lurah said, 'Please don't pick the jeruk as they are almost ready for market. You can take any that have fallen to the ground.'

That night I dreamt of sweet mandarins, so the next morning I woke early when I thought everyone else would still be asleep and tiptoed out into the orchard. There was no fruit on the ground but, when I took hold of a branch and shook it, mandarins cascaded all around me. I stuffed them into the deep pockets of my playsuit.

As I crept back towards the house I saw the Lurah through the window, sitting at the table with a glass of coffee, rolling a cigarette. He watched me as I walked in and stopped in front of him, trembling. 'You picked the jeruk,' he said, using the word '*memetik*', meaning to pick from the tree with a twisting motion.

'I didn't pick them. I only collected the ones on the ground.'

'Impossible. That many?'

'Well, I did shake the branch. But I didn't memetik.'

He laughed. 'Enjoy your jeruk. Share them with your sister.'

I told Papih what I had done, and he apologised to the Lurah for both of my crimes – theft, and for being a smart aleck. But the Lurah said 'Don't worry. Your daughter is very clever.'

After the success of that first theft hunger drove me to steal food many more times. As I feasted on corn I'd taken from a farmer's garden, happiness overcame guilt. Mostly I did not get caught, but if Papih found out he was always angry.

As we walked into the mountains our progress was slow because Mamih often vomited and needed frequent stops to rest. As she walked she leaned against Papih. At the village of Cisempong a farmer took us to his *dangau,* a tiny windowless hut in the rice field, in which workers took their rest breaks. It was isolated, a half-hour walk to the village, and so a perfect hiding place from Dutch patrols and spies. The dangau was cool, with a roof of coconut leaves and walls of woven bamboo, and it contained a narrow kitchen with a dirt floor and a raised sleeping platform made from bamboo, just big enough for the four of us to lie down.

After the farmer left us at the dangau, Papih spread a sarong over the sleeping platform and both Mamih and Ati went straight to sleep. Papih and I sat with our legs hanging over the edge of the platform and ate bananas, and I began to think about food. In the kitchen was a fireplace. Who would cook? Mamih was too sick; Ati, at five, was too young; and I knew men never went near the kitchen, so Papih couldn't do it. That left me, but I was only eight, and I had never cooked anything.

Mamih had been nine when she took responsibility for the household after her mother died. Now it was up to me to care for my family.

'I have to cook, don't I?' I said to Papih.

'Do you think you can do it?'

There were too many things to think about. Papih had bartered his coat for rice and bananas, and we had salt, sugar, coconut oil and tea, but nothing else. I didn't even know how to boil water, let alone cook rice. And what could we eat with the rice? I looked down at the fireplace and the axe the farmer had left for us.

'How will we light the fire?' I asked Papih.

'Go to the farmer's house in the village, and ask for an *obor*, a bamboo torch.'

The next morning I set out in the dark to walk to the village. At the farmer's house his wife Bu Mimin, a cheerful tiny woman with a pretty face, took me into her kitchen and gave me a snack – *nasi ketan*, steamed sticky rice topped with grated coconut.

'What will you cook?' she asked.

'We have only rice.'

She smiled and stroked my hair. 'You need vegetables,' she said, and showed me plants to collect in the field, and told me which ones to boil, which to stir-fry, and which could be eaten raw. She taught me how to stir-fry vegetables in coconut oil. The farmer gave me an obor, a length of bamboo plugged with a burning piece of coconut husk. As I left, Bu Mimin gave me two *pisang goreng*, fried banana fritters, one for me and one for Ati.

Back at the dangau Papih had found firewood and made kindling with the axe. We lit the fire and I boiled water to make tea. Feeling happy at what I had achieved I went into the field to collect the plants Bu Mimin had shown me.

From the sleeping platform Mamih gave me directions for cooking the rice. Then I prepared the vegetables following Bu Mimin's instructions, boiling *genjer*, a chewy plant, stir-frying *gelang*, pigweed, and chopping *antanan*, a herb eaten raw. Smoke filled the dangau.

While I cooked, my father wrote and Mamih showered under the *pancuran*, a large bamboo pipe in front of the dangau from which water always gushed, part of the irrigation system in the rice fields. After the meal had been prepared I helped Ati shower. Then we sat down to eat together. It was just rice and weeds and salt, but I was excited and proud that I had cooked a meal.

'This is really nice, Nyenyen,' said Papih.

Mamih was still sick, but she had eaten a little, and managed a smile. 'It's good,' she said.

Afterwards I put away the leftover food for another meal

in the afternoon, and I washed the dishes under the pancuran, using the ashes from the fire as detergent.

Every morning I walked to the village for the obor, and stayed a while with Bu Mimin as she gave me cooking tips and treats such as *serabi*, pancakes made with rice flour and coconut milk, cooked in a clay pot and eaten with palm sugar syrup. As I left she always gave me a snack to eat on the way and another to take back for Ati.

After a few days Bu Mimin asked if we had sambal.

'No, just salt.'

'Can't eat without sambal,' she said. She gave me chillies and a block of *terasi*, shrimp paste, and showed me how to make raw sambal.

Bu Mimin always asked what ingredients we needed and sometimes gave me tamarind and tomatoes from her garden, or peanuts and limes to make the spicy peanut sauce for *lotek*, a Sundanese vegetable salad. Occasionally she spared some salted fish.

Sometimes I gathered *tutut*, the small edible snails from the rice fields, or caught some of the tiny, fast-moving fish that hide among the rice plants. But on most days our meals still only consisted of rice and weeds and salt with a little sambal.

After our meal on the first day, Papih opened his briefcase and took out a slate and some Grade One reading books. I looked at them with dread. 'Now,' he said, 'you must practise every day so that you don't forget your lessons.' He handed me a book, open at the first page. 'Read it to me, Nyenyen.'

I looked at the page. The marks on it meant nothing. I could not speak.

'Just start,' he said.

'I don't know how.'

'What? Of course you do. You passed Grade One. You're doing Grade Two.'

Papih pointed to the page. 'What is that word?'

I began to cry. 'I don't know.'

'What is this letter?'

'I don't know.'

He stared at me, his eyes wide. 'Didn't you have homework? Didn't the teacher check your homework?'

'No, I didn't do it.'

'Didn't you do any tests at school?'

'Yes.'

'How did you do them?'

'I cheated.'

'Cheated! How?'

'The daughter of the Tukang Lotek showed me the answers under the desk. I gave her my lunch money. She did my homework too.' I cried harder and admitted everything.

Papih's eyes opened wider and wider. He sat staring at me until my sobs became whimpers. Then he set out the new rules.

Every day, after I had washed the dishes, my father would sit with me and teach the alphabet and the times tables. I wrote the letters and the numbers on the slate. I hated these lessons and became very slow at cooking the meal and cleaning up. He often looked out to the pancuran and called me to hurry. After the lesson he set homework to do before going to bed at night. Mamih and Ati went to bed early, but my father and I sat on the edge of the sleeping platform, Papih writing while I struggled with my homework. Our light consisted of a dish filled with coconut oil, with a wick made from a piece of cloth twisted through the hole in a Dutch cent coin. Papih kept a diary, a tattered notebook with a soft brown cover, and he wrote in it every night. Before we went to sleep, my father often played Sundanese tunes on his bamboo flute and I would creep outside to look at the rice fields in the moonlight. The only sounds were my father's flute and the water flowing from the pancuran. How different it was from the city of Garut. Serenity and peace filled me, and a deep love for my country grew inside me. For the first time I felt in my heart the beauty of my motherland.

One day after lunch I was slowly washing the utensils at the pancuran, dreading the next lesson from my father. I squatted facing the water spout with the dirty wok and dishes on my left, moving them to my right as I cleaned them with the ashes. I heard my father call in a soft voice, 'Nyenyen, don't move.' I looked up and froze. There was a huge yellow and black python staring straight at me from less than a metre away. Papih crept out carrying the axe. The python and I remained perfectly still. Papih raised the axe and with one stroke cut off the head. As the snake's body twisted and writhed, I screamed and ran sobbing to the dangau and into my mother's arms.

Pythons had been known to take children, and my father later said that if I had tried to run away, it would have attacked. Farmers saw them as an enemy because they stole chickens and goats. I had not thought of snakes while gathering vegetables or walking by myself to collect the obor. The mountains of my homeland held danger as well as beauty.

The moon was full and after finishing my homework in the evening I walked to the farmer's fish pond, not far from the dangau, and peered at the large carp swimming close to the surface. I knew from helping my grandfather that these fish were fully grown and would soon be harvested. I thought how wonderful it would be to eat one and I had to tear myself away to return to the dangau to join my parents and sister on the bamboo platform. But I could not stop thinking about the fish and while the others were asleep, I took a knife and crept back to the pond. The moon seemed to draw the fish – their fat silver bodies shone in the water. I stepped into the mud of the shallow pond, reached in and grabbed a big fish. Then I caught another one. I scaled and cleaned the fish, took them back to the hut and seasoned them with salt. By then it was time to walk to the village to get the obor.

I was back at the dangau frying the fish when my father woke. 'You stole the farmer's fish,' he said.

'I'm bored with eating weeds and rice.'

He gave me a big lecture, but then he ate the fish. Mamih and Ati were delighted and Ati wanted me to steal more. We picked the bones completely clean. There was not even flesh left on the heads.

Later the farmer came. 'Ajengan,' he said to my father, 'last night an otter stole fish from my pond. But the otter has a big head with long black hair.'

Papih put his hand on my head. 'This is the otter with the big head and the long black hair.'

I was ashamed. 'I'm very sorry, Pak,' I said. 'I know it's wrong to steal but I was fed up with eating antanan and genjer every day for weeks. I wanted to have a special dinner.'

The farmer chuckled and said, 'Next time, don't steal, just ask. But if you do steal you should learn to be a better thief. You left a mess where you cleaned the fish, and I just followed your muddy footprints here. You were lucky you chose last night to steal them, because today they are to be harvested.'

Next day, the farmer and his wife brought us two large fried fish, cooked rice and bananas. For many people, helping refugees was a way of supporting the Revolution.

After several weeks we left the dangau and walked through the foothills of Telagabodas Volcano to the village of Sagara, where my father had arranged to meet his colleague Pak Saleh. Mamih was about to need the assistance of Bu Saleh, who was a midwife. Pak and Bu Saleh were temporarily staying in a humble village house, and we moved in with them.

Bu Saleh prepared the meals and looked after our family, and I felt a burden lift from me. Ati and I made friends with the village children, who came to our yard to play congklak, hide and seek, and skipping-rope games. We danced and sang and made mud biscuits. My childhood had returned.

Two weeks after we arrived in Sagara, Mamih started having pains and Papih told Ati and me to stay in the yard while he and Bu Saleh looked after her. We could hear Mamih screaming as we played with the village children. Then a street peddler came past and we ran to look at the snacks she was selling – layer cakes, cupcakes, serabi pancakes, fried sweet potato and my favourite, pisang goreng, fried banana fritters. All the village kids were pointing to what they wanted and calling out, 'I'll have this'; 'I'll have that.' The pisang goreng looked so warm and tempting that hunger seized me and I called out, 'Papih, can I have some money for pisang goreng?'

No answer.

Ati said she wanted to eat pisang goreng too. Again I yelled to Papih for money, and then again, louder.

Suddenly the curtain on the window upstairs was yanked back and my father appeared, his face red and his eyes blazing, his voice loud and harsh. 'Don't you understand your mother is in pain?'

The village children went quiet and then scattered. The peddler left. I shivered, feeling very small and frightened because my father had yelled at me. Papih was much angrier than when he found out I couldn't read. He could reduce me to tears when he looked at me with his eyes wide, but he had never before raised his voice to me. I realised that Mamih was in danger, and that some things were more important than eating pisang goreng. In that moment I grew up a little.

When we heard the baby crying, Ati and I ran up the steps. We saw Mamih lying on a mat on the floor, with the baby wrapped in cloth beside her, and Bu Saleh on her knees cleaning up with a towel.

'This is your new sister,' said my father. 'Her name is Nurpatria.'

Ati and I knelt beside the baby and I reached out my hand to stroke her head. Ati was holding back so I took her hand and placed it on our sister. My father knelt on the other side of Mamih, his face shining with a broad smile.

Mamih went to sleep and Papih left the house with Pak Saleh. Ati and I sat quietly, looking at the baby. When the men returned, Papih gathered us by Mamih's side. 'Dutch forces are coming,' he said. 'Pak Saleh and I have to get away.'

He kissed and hugged each of us. 'I will always love you,' he said. 'When the war is over and we are free we will have a good life. Nyenyen, you are the oldest child. If you don't see me again, you must care for your mother and your two sisters.'

I followed Papih and Pak Saleh out to the street. When Papih hugged me again, I felt it was for the last time. 'Nyenyen, don't forget you are in charge while I am away,' he said. 'Keep studying, keep reading, practise your times tables. Every day you must read the books. Read them over and over.'

I watched the two of them walk away, terrified that I would never see Papih again, that he would be killed by the Dutch. I now carried an even heavier burden than at the dangau because my father had passed his role on to me. I felt that my childhood was over.

In the house Mamih was still lying down, unable to stand up. I helped Bu Saleh give Mamih a sponge bath by bringing warm water from the kitchen. By the next day, Mamih was well enough to get up, but still very weak. Every day I helped Bu Saleh prepare meals and clean up. I drew water from the well to give Ati a dipper bath and when I put her to bed I told her stories from Sundanese legends that Papih had told me. I did not read the two books or practise the times tables.

Mamih often cried, and every night before we went to bed she asked Ati and me to pray that Papih would be safe and that we would all be together again. I begged God to send him back to us. Then, about a week later, there was a knock on the door and when I opened it Papih was standing there. He hadn't shaved and he was smelly, but I didn't care and jumped into his arms. My parents held each other for a long time, crying.

That night I thanked God, then slept, carefree again and, for the moment, unaware of the dilemma with which my parents were grappling.

We were in a war zone, no place for a family with a new baby and a mother who had not yet recovered from the birth. Clashes between guerrillas and the Netherland Indies Civil Administration were frequent, and NICA spies were everywhere. My father knew he would be arrested if he returned to Garut to try to publish his newspaper or continue his intelligence work. As his priority was to care for his family, he decided that the safest place to do that would be Jakarta. The city had been peaceful since Allied forces captured it nearly two years previously and, after the initial fierce battles, there had been little fighting there. NICA tolerated the nationalists who lived in Jakarta provided they were not active combatants. Importantly, Papih thought Jakarta offered the best prospect for finding work.

At the time I understood none of this. All I knew was that we were to leave Sagara with Papih. He gave Mamih his diary to hide under her *gurita*, the corset that women wore after childbirth to make their abdomen small. We said goodbye to Pak and Bu Saleh and set off, Papih in front carrying the baby in a sling made from a Javanese shawl, then the two village men Papih had hired to carry Mamih in a *tolombong*, a large bamboo basket tied to a pole which the men bore on their shoulders, and then Ati and me, holding hands. We were barefoot, our shoes having long ago fallen apart.

After a week we reached a village near Garut, where a family invited us to stay in their house. During the night the sound of sobbing woke me. Light flickered across the ceiling and I smelt something burning. I crept out to the front room and saw my parents, both in tears, Mamih holding Papih as he threw a sheet of paper into a fire in a large enamel bowl. When my father saw me he pulled me to him. From his tattered brown diary he tore out a page, examined it, and dropped it into the flames. I knew how important the diary was to Papih – he had written in it every day since the hotel became the meeting place for guerrilla fighters. Mamih and I held Papih as he fed more pages into the fire, all three of us crying. 'I must do this,' he said. 'My notes are too dangerous.'

Mamih's housecoat had fallen open, and Papih pointed to the broken, red and raw skin on her tummy where the diary had been hidden. 'I'm sorry, Tati,' he said, and she hugged him tightly. When the whole diary had been destroyed, Papih sent me back to bed, where Ati was still asleep.

Several days later we arrived at Rancaekek, a small town near Bandung where Mamih had been born. Because Haji Noor owned extensive rice fields there we were able to stay with one of his sharecroppers, Mang Udin. As soon as we arrived Mang climbed the tall palms to pick fresh coconuts for us, and Bu Udin brought out my favourite – pisang goreng. The next morning

Mang slaughtered a goat and the whole family joined with us in a feast to celebrate our survival. There were not enough chairs, so we sat on the floor while Bu Udin spread a tablecloth on a mat and covered it with dishes of food we had not seen for months – goat saté, fried chicken, and steamed carp in banana leaf. I felt a great wave of happiness, and began to eat – and eat. 'Not too much,' said Mamih. 'You'll be sick.'

But I ignored her. I ate and ate, until I could not rise from the floor.

Staying with the Udins was like being on holiday. Although Mamih was still not strong and spent her time resting, Nurpatria, or Nuy as we called her, was a happy baby. My father just kept writing. Ati and I made friends with the Udin children and Kang Nana, the oldest boy, taught me how to thread worms onto a hook. Every morning I fished in the pond – I didn't have to be a thief or an otter. We collected edible snails in the rice fields, but I refused to gather genjer, the weed we had eaten at the dangau. As I fished and explored the fields with Kang Nana, it was easy to imagine that heaven might be as peaceful. I was sad when, after several days, my father said it was time to move on.

We didn't have to walk this time but took the train to Bandung, then rode a delman to the home of Mamih's aunt, Ma Lengkong, who had survived the Sea of Fire and remained in the city with her husband, her sons, and their families. When we arrived people came running from all over the house, all asking questions at the same time, crying and excited to see us alive. Ma fussed over Mamih and baby Nuy, and worried that Ati and I were thin, barefoot and black from the sun. She sent the servants to buy the best food available from stalls and peddlers for a big dinner in honour of our return from the mountains. An air of celebration reigned in the house.

My grandmother, who had died many years previously, was Ma Lengkong's sister and Ma had taken on the role of grandmother to Ati and me. The day after we arrived she took us shopping for dresses and shoes and, after months without entering a shop, we were excited, especially as Ma said we could choose what we wanted. Usually Mamih selected our clothes for us. That day I chose green *kelom geulis*, traditional Sundanese shoes with the sole and sides made of wood and carved with flowers, like Dutch clogs but open at the toes. Ati bought bright red kelom geulis, and we each chose two dresses. I was so happy to have the unaccustomed privilege of making my own choice and delighted that my dry and cracked feet were now shod. After shopping Ma took us to a restaurant and again said we could choose whatever we liked. Ati and I ordered *nasi ramas*, rice with side dishes, and *es cendol,* a crushed ice drink of coconut milk and palm sugar. I asked Ma if we could take nasi ramas home for my parents as I knew we would only have a short time in Bandung and I didn't want them to miss out on all the treats.

    But back at Ma's house Mamih ignored the food and pointed to my feet. 'Wennie,' she said. 'What vulgar shoes! They're too bright, they hurt my eyes!'

The next day we departed for Jakarta as my father wanted to leave the war zone quickly. At Bandung station Papih sat quietly, looking down. I think he was trying not to be noticed, and I felt his anxiety. As we boarded the train Ma slipped some money into my pocket and said, 'Every school holiday you must come to Bandung and stay with me.'

    In Jakarta we went straight to the home of my parents' friends, Mochtar and Hally Lubis.

CHAPTER 4
Jakarta

[Lebaran] is a day for showing each other's love by forgiving each other's sins ... [and] to remind us that, now that one is reborn as innocent and sinless as a baby, one should carry on to be like that, and make life beautiful.
—Achdiat Karta Mihardja, Speech on Lebaran Day, Athens, Ohio, 1981

When Allied troops had taken Jakarta, Republican politicians, government officials and citizens left the city and set up their capital at Yogyakarta in Central Java. But there was still a strong nationalist community in Jakarta, promoting independence, publishing newspapers and magazines, and debating ideas about the shape of a future Indonesian nation. NICA sometimes cracked down on the nationalists, but mostly they were tolerated. Of greater danger were violent pro-Dutch vigilantes from the island of Ambon.

A prominent member of the nationalist community was a young journalist called Mochtar Lubis who worked in the Jakarta office of ANTARA, the Republican news agency. Mochtar often wrote about the international context in which Indonesia would become a free country, especially after he had accompanied the Republican Prime Minister, Sutan Sjahrir, to a landmark Conference of Asian Nations in New Delhi, where he was inspired by Nehru and Gandhi. In late 1947, the United Nations was trying to establish meaningful Dutch-Indonesian negotiations and, to cover these meetings, Mochtar was often away from home. He was fluent in Indonesian, Dutch and English, enabling him to interview all the main players.

Staying with Mochtar and Hally, my parents became devoted members of the Jakarta nationalist community. This was a time of noisy meetings with writers, journalists and activists gathering to argue fiercely about ideas, literature and politics. Should literature instruct and inform the reader? Should Indonesia embrace Western values and political ideas? Achdiat was an enthusiastic participant in these debates. My mother stayed on the sidelines, preparing snacks.

If Mochtar was at one of these meetings I liked to watch him – he was polite and charming, and always treated Hally lovingly. But I hated Chairil Anwar, whom everyone described as Indonesia's greatest poet. He was red-eyed, wild-haired, disorganised and ill-mannered, with a loud rough voice. 'Achdiat,' he once called to my father. 'Your wife is so beautiful. I cannot resist her.' He turned to my mother. 'Tati, I'm in love with you.'

Both my parents laughed, but I felt a surge of anger. How dare he?

Only later did I realise that my father had been observing Chairil Anwar, and was turning him into one of the main characters, an artist and anarchist, in the novel he was writing. He was also taking note of his friend Cucun Rusni, who often visited us and stayed all night, talking politics with my father. He was an adventurer with no job, wandering from friend to friend, often asking people for money, especially those with ready cash such as gamblers who had won, and using such funds not only for himself but to help in the struggle against the Dutch. Writing his novel, my father was transforming Cucun Rusni into a persuasive Marxist.

Both my father and Cucun Rusni joined the PSI, the Indonesian Socialist Party, and sometimes took me with them to meetings at the home of its founder, Sutan Sjahrir, who had been the Republican Prime Minister from 1945 to 1947. Achdiat supported Sjahrir's attempts to counter the Communist Party's growing influence and was drawn to Sjahrir's vision of a democratic, egalitarian, and industrialised Indonesia.

We stayed with Mochtar and Hally for several months, then moved in with HB Jassin, a noted critic and essayist. Eventually Achdiat rejoined Balai Pustaka publishing house, and his salary enabled us to shift into a rented house in Jalan Rasamala.

Bapak had burned his diary because it contained all the details of his work for the Republican forces and was therefore too dangerous to carry into the Dutch-controlled zone. For him the tragedy was that he had intended to use the notes in his diary as the basis for a future novel. In Jakarta he began to rewrite what he could remember from the burnt diary, describing the events of the Revolution, especially those in which he was involved.

Although we were no longer in the war zone, there were still dangers. One day Bapak had a visitor – Syahrul, the man he suspected of having informed on him to the Dutch in Garut before the raid on the hotel. Now Syahrul was in Jakarta and came to our house several times. Bapak had to be careful – if Syahrul was a spy he was a threat to our safety. Then, during one visit, Syahrul proudly showed Bapak his membership card for the Dutch intelligence agency. After Syahrul left Bapak shook his head. What sort of spy shows off his credentials? But then he was enraged to discover that the rewritten diary of his part in the Revolution was missing. Now we were frightened that the soldiers would come as they had in Garut. But nothing happened, and later we heard that guerrilla fighters had killed Syahrul in Purwakarta and thrown his body into the river.

During our time as refugees I had become used to calling my mother *Ibu* but I hated calling my father *Ajengan*. 'Can we call you Papih again?' I asked.

'No, we have to be free of the Dutch,' he said. 'But now that we're in the city you can call me Bapak.'

Bapak is the Indonesian word for Father, just as *Ibu* means Mother.

Ati and I attended Taman Siswa, the private primary school at which Bapak had once taught. It was a nationalistic school, and there was a strong feeling against anything Dutch. My name was spelt in the Dutch fashion, ending in "ie", and the other children teased me with taunts that I was trying to be Dutch. Without telling my parents, I changed the spelling of my name so that it ended in "y". The teasing stopped.

Months later Bapak noticed my name on a school exercise book and said in surprise, 'That's not how your name is spelt.'

When I explained the reason I had changed it, he had to agree because of his own nationalist beliefs. But whenever he wrote my name he continued to use 'Wennie'.

At school, my class was from 11 am to 2 pm, and Ati's 7 am to 10 am. When Ati began Grade One she was too timid to go by herself, so I took her to school and sat with her in class. During the breaks she stayed close to me, not wanting to play with the other children. When her class ended Ibu picked her up, and I went to my lessons.

    One day Ati remade herself. Her class had finished and Ibu was late, so I told Ati to wait at the gate. A little later, our mother appeared at the door of my classroom. Ati was missing and Ibu blamed me for not staying with my little sister. We searched the school with no success. Across a busy street was Pasar Senen, the open-air market. 'She must be there,' said Ibu, and pulled me across the road and into the market. We pushed through the people thronging the narrow walkways between the stalls of fruit, vegetables, fish and meat, but could not see Ati. Weaving our way between the small shops selling dried food I glimpsed bamboo cages hanging ahead. I tugged at Ibu's arm. 'The bird market!' I yelled.

    There was Ati looking up at the cuckoos and doves. As we cried and hugged her, Ati remained calm. What was the matter? She had just been admiring the birds.

    Ati had proclaimed her own independence. From then on she became an adventurer who always went her own way. We thought, she will travel the world – and she did, many times.

We expected many friends, family and neighbours to visit at *Lebaran*, the end of the fasting month so, during the last days of Ramadan, Ati and I helped Ibu prepare an enormous feast of cakes and snacks. First we made the biscuits. Ibu gave Ati and me some of the mixture and with our hands we created biscuits in shapes we liked – fishes, flowers and dogs. When they were cooked we looked longingly at them. 'Can we have one now?' we pleaded.

Ibu held up her finger. 'No! Not until Lebaran.' But she let us lick the beaters while she stored the biscuits in large glass jars.

The next big project was *kue lapis legit*, spiced layer cake, traditional Lebaran food, usually made once a year and so rich that we could only eat a tiny piece at a time. It required an expert touch so we watched as Ibu mixed flour, sugar, butter, vanilla and about thirty egg yolks. She added the spice blend of cloves, cinnamon, mace, nutmeg and cardamom. Then she poured enough cake mixture into the base of a Dutch oven to form a thin layer, and heaped coals below the pot and on the lid so that the heat cooked the layer from above and below. When the first layer was done Ibu poured more on top of it, and cooked that. She repeated this process with about twenty more layers. All the while Ati and I fanned the coals to keep them alive and after three hours the cake was complete. We looked at this magnificent creation knowing that not one crumb of it could be eaten before Lebaran.

On the last day of Ramadan, we made *ketupat*, rice cakes cooked in woven palm leaf pouches. Then it was time for *rendang*, beef cooked for several hours with spices and coconut milk, the dish I was most excited about because meat was scarce during the Revolution. My job was to stir the rendang. I wielded a wooden spoon, watching the pieces of meat slowly shredding in the turmeric-yellow mixture, and breathed in the spices – ginger, garlic, chilli and the pine tree aroma of galangal. Most of all I loved the smell of the beef – it made my mouth water.

When the rendang was cooked, I asked, 'Can I have a tiny bit now?'

Again Ibu held up her finger. 'No! Not until tomorrow.' But she let me scrape and eat the crust from the saucepan.

That night we arranged all the dishes we had made on the dining table and protected them with bamboo food covers. Ibu planned to rise early the next morning and make *sayur lodeh*, mixed vegetables in coconut milk, to eat with the *ketupat*, and *sambal goreng ati ayam*, fried chicken liver sambal, another Lebaran treat.

I lay awake for hours thinking of all the things that would

happen tomorrow. We would finally wear the new dresses Ibu had made, and the new shoes she had bought. Everything had to wait for Lebaran. I thought about each of the dishes sitting on the table – tomorrow we would have such a feast! But time was moving so slowly and it seemed tomorrow would never arrive.

I woke when a piercing scream filled the house. Ati and I ran to the dining room. Ibu was still screaming and we couldn't understand her. But we looked at where she was pointing and saw with horror that all the food had gone. Bapak held Ibu, trying to calm her. In the doorway was a pile of human faeces.

'What's that?' I yelled.

Bapak said, 'Thieves think it protects them from being caught.'

Now the full force of the catastrophe hit, and Ati and I began to sob. Bapak dealt with the robbers' visiting card at the door, while Ibu screamed curses on them as she cleaned up the mess they had left when they took the food. 'How could they do this on a holy day?' she cried, and began to add up the costs. Ati and I sat in a corner and cried.

It took a long time for Bapak to calm the three of us. Then he sent us to have our baths and put on our new Lebaran dresses and shoes. Instead of waiting for neighbours and friends to come, we visited them first, and told them of our disaster. Then we came back to a house without food.

Bapak said, 'Don't be sad. Let's go to a restaurant.'

Few Indonesian restaurants were open on Lebaran but, as we loved Chinese food, we chose Chungsan, famous for its cuisine. Bapak said Ati and I could select the meals. When I studied the menu I ignored the names of the dishes and just picked the ones with the highest prices. I needed a remedy for my disappointment.

CHAPTER 5
The Mango Tree

Arguments and misunderstandings are the 'spice' of love, without which life would be boring ... the peace after an argument is always blissful; tenderness and understanding grow stronger with every reconciliation.
—Achdiat Karta Mihardja, *The Scattered Dust of Love*

There were seven mango trees at the house at Jalan Rasamala and I had spent a lot of time climbing them. When Ibu said we were moving to another rented house in Jalan Meranti I knew I would miss the trees. But the first time I walked out the back door at the new house, I looked up in wonder at an enormous mango tree which covered the whole yard, from the kitchen to the fence. Feeling happy with our new home, I sat down under the tree and admired the canopy.

I had no idea how much that tree would mean to me.

Ibu always had total control of the household and the family budget. Bapak's salary was small but Ibu was creative at doing a lot with little, especially when food and other goods were scarce during the Revolution. The Dutch administration imposed rationing, providing families with coupons for basic necessities such as rolled oats, bread, butter and sugar. Sometimes we could get *hagelslag*, chocolate sprinkles that were used as a topping on bread for breakfast. Hagelslag was a luxury, a welcome change from bread with sugar.

One afternoon Ibu came home from the coupon shop carrying a roll of material with grey and white stripes, and after dinner that night she went to her sewing machine. There were no curtains on the windows of our new home and Ibu wanted privacy from the neighbours. She was still making the curtains when I went to bed, and in the morning the curtains had been hung. Then Ibu told Ati and me to try on our new dresses – made from the same material! I should have been grateful, but at nine I was old enough to feel embarrassed about wearing a dress which had the same pattern as our curtains. I wanted to rip it but was frightened by the thought of what Ibu might do.

There was good reason to be scared of Ibu, and most people were. She was often described as *galak*, fierce, and she would not tolerate disagreement. Her father Haji Noor always accepted whatever she said, nodding his head and saying, 'Ya, ya, ya.' My father, for the sake of a quiet life in which to write his novel, never questioned Ibu's rule of the household and, although he believed all humans to be equal, Ibu maintained a rigid class structure in our house. We ate the best quality rice while our servant, Bi Tasiah, ate the lowest and Ibu terrified Bi by screaming abuse when our food wasn't perfect or she found a speck of dust on the furniture.

Ibu also screamed at Bapak, often accusing him of paying attention to some other woman, or angry that his brother had asked for a loan. At first Bapak quietly defended himself, but then Ibu would hit him and shove him around the room and he begged for her forgiveness. He tried to hug her to calm her down, and sometimes she did stop fighting, but often she got wilder and thrust him away. After the fights they always made up, hugging and kissing and talking lovingly to each other.

While they were fighting I would squeeze myself into the narrow space between the food cabinet and the dining room wall and hug my knees to my chest. I thought I had done something to cause the fight, and I always felt sorry for Bapak. It was so unfair that my kind and gentle father was being attacked.

One day I returned from school, took a pisang goreng from the food cabinet, and sat down on the floor to play bekelin, knucklebones, with Ati. Ibu told me to change out of my school dress. I was eating and playing and didn't listen. Suddenly Ibu pulled me up from the floor and slapped me hard on my bottom. Then she was hitting me all over my body, again and again.

'Stubborn disobedient child,' she yelled as she whacked into me. 'You never listen to me. You rude naughty girl.'

'Sorry, Ibu. Sorry, Ibu,' I cried, but she hit me again,

pinched my arm and twisted my ear.

'Stop crying,' she yelled.

I tried to choke back my tears but, whenever I gasped for breath, she slapped me again.

After the beating she turned back into a loving mother. She took me to the bathroom, shampooed my hair and gave me a dipper bath. She dressed me in newly ironed clothes and gently brushed my hair, all the while speaking tenderly to me.

'What would you like?' she said. 'Do you want to come to the shop and I'll buy you something nice? I'll cook your favourite food.' Then she sat me at the dining table and cut pieces of cake for Ati and me.

That was the first time. Before, when I had been naughty, she had pinched me, not hard, but had never hit me. Now she often beat me, sometimes with her hand, at other times with whatever was nearby – the rattan mattress beater, or the *sapu lidi*, a broom made from a bundle of dried coconut-leaf spines.

Later, while others took their afternoon naps, I would creep out to the backyard and sit under the big mango tree and cry, feeling utterly alone.

Sometimes Bi Tasiah, the servant, brought out a snack. 'Don't cry,' she would say. 'Go back to your bed.'

But I always shook my head. The mango tree became my refuge. Its branches spread over me as if to offer comfort.

We stayed in Jalan Meranti for almost two years. In a house across the lane from us lived a large family belonging to the Minangkabau ethnic group, originally from Padang in West Sumatra. Oom and Tante Syaiful had three boys of their own, as well as looking after five nieces and nephews and Tante's mother. Caring for nieces and nephews is an important obligation in Minangkabau culture. Their house was full of love and laughter where everyone had a good time sharing the work and there were always delicious snacks to eat. Tante and Oom Syaiful treated me as one of their own and I became good friends with their niece Antje.

Antje and I shared our deepest feelings. When I told

her about my mother's beatings she felt sorry for me – her aunt never treated her in that way – but I felt sorry that she had never known her mother. Even though Ibu was galak and beat me, she was my mother, and I did love her.

In the Syaiful household the family cooked and ate real Padang food, more flavoursome and spicy than Sundanese meals and with a greater variety of dishes placed on the table for people to share. I loved *gulai pakis*, fern tips in coconut milk. Every day the family prepared a feast, whereas in our house we only ate a special meal once a month, after payday when Ibu had a chicken slaughtered. She insisted that the breast would be for Bapak, while we could only have a drumstick or a wing, so I always looked forward to being invited to join the Syaifuls. Oom Syaiful ran a successful business, which meant his family could afford meat and chicken dishes every day, and anyone could select whatever portions they wanted. At Lebaran, the end of fasting month, their house overflowed with food.

Our small street contained many cultures. A Chinese family lived on one side of us, a Batak family on the other, and just up the lane a Javanese man lived with his Japanese wife. I sometimes saw her at the door, but never outside the house. Neighbours said her husband brought food home from the market and did not allow her to go out, so that she was like a prisoner. She must have been sad living so far away from her own family and country.

Mpok Ayamah, a widow with two adult daughters, lived next to the Syaifuls across the lane. One daughter had tuberculosis and sometimes sat out in the sun, as skinny as a skeleton. Mpok had rented the front room of her house to an *Indo*, a Eurasian woman, who was often visited by Dutch soldiers during the afternoon and evening. When I climbed the Jambu tree in front of our house to wait for Bapak to come home from work, it was possible to see through the transparent curtain on her window, to where she would be hugging and kissing each visitor. I didn't tell my mother what I saw.

People in the neighbourhood avoided the widow. When the neighbours held get-togethers, she was not invited. My mother and the other neighbours talked about her, wishing she would move away because she gave our street a bad name. But I thought she must be lonely and miserable so sometimes I walked across to talk to her. She told me about her sick daughter and seemed a friendly, caring person. To me it was unfair that no one wanted to know Mpok Ayamah, just as it was unfair when Ati started a fight and I was the one who was beaten.

On the day that Mpok Ayamah's daughter passed away, none of the neighbours offered condolences or help. I hoped she also had a mango tree in her backyard where she could seek comfort.

Bapak did nothing about the beatings, but I didn't know if that was because he wasn't aware of them or because he considered all household matters to be Ibu's concern. Sometimes she would not hit me for a week or more, but I lived in terror of the next thrashing. I would unthinkingly do something that provoked Ibu, such as the time I came home from school and took some hagelslag from the food cabinet for my sandwich. Because hagelslag was strictly for breakfast, Ibu belted me with the sapu lidi. After each beating I would find solace under the mango tree.

But there were better days at Jalan Meranti, usually when Bapak spared us a little time between his job and his writing. When he was due home from work, I climbed the jambu tree to wait for his bicycle to appear at the end of the lane. Then I ran to meet him, and he gave me his battered, brown leather briefcase to carry. Inside, Ati and I raced to take off his shoes. We undid his laces and pulled and pulled while he pretended the shoes wouldn't come off. Ati and I searched his head for grey hairs and for each one we pulled out he gave us a small coin. We also earned money for massaging his arms, legs and shoulders. Sometimes he brought us snacks from a meeting at work.

I was happiest when Bapak came home.

CHAPTER 6
Merdeka

> Islam and Marxism for the people in this generation were realities of Indonesian experience, of Indonesian culture, Indonesian outlooks. And yet, they were subject to interpretation under the framework of Indonesian nationalism.
> —Keith Foulcher, *On the Record: Indonesian Literary Figures*

For Achdiat the battle of ideas within the independence movement was almost as important as the struggle against the Dutch. What sort of nation would be built once independence was achieved?

The leaders of the Republican Government planned a state based upon belief in God, with all persons free to worship according to their own religion. This was not secular enough for communists who wanted no role for religion, and far too secular for fundamentalist Muslims who were calling for an Islamic state. Achdiat abhorred communism and wanted the nation to follow religious rather than atheistic values but, like many Muslims, he believed the state should respect the rights of everyone and be pluralist.

The ideological battle had become bloody. The Dutch invasion, from which we had fled in 1947, had conquered the western and eastern ends of Java forcing independence groups to crowd into the central part of the island around Yogyakarta, the Republican Government's temporary capital. Tensions rose, and leftist and Muslim militias clashed. In September 1948, groups associated with the Communist Party captured the city of Madiun and declared an Indonesian Soviet Republic. The army, supported by Muslim militias, crushed the uprising in a series of fierce battles in which thousands died.

Later in the Revolution, the army division battling Dutch forces in West Java also had to fight for territory against fundamentalist Muslim militias, who were demanding an Islamic state.

These events were the battlefield counterpart to the passionate debates that had characterised the independence movement for forty years and Achdiat put these competing world views at the centre of his first novel, *Atheis*.

The novel's protagonist is Hasan, a devout Muslim, who meets Rusli, a former classmate, and falls in love with Rusli's friend Kartini. Rusli is a Marxist and atheist, so Hasan resolves to convert him to his own beliefs. Instead, it is Hasan who loses his faith under the influence of the persuasive Rusli and Rusli's friend Anwar, an unruly artist and anarchist. Hasan is eventually destroyed because of his rejection of religious values.

When *Atheis* was published in February 1949 the book caused an immediate furore. The multiple voices in the novel – Muslim, Marxist, anarchist, merchant, civil servant – were matched by the many voices that debated it. Orthodox Muslims accused Achdiat of being an atheist because he allowed the Rusli character to present his views so forcefully. Communists attacked the book because they saw that it promoted religious values. But Achdiat's fellow writers and most critics were full of praise. With its lively language, complex structure and depth of characterisation, they saw the novel as something completely new in the development of the country's literature and described it as the first national novel of Indonesia. *Atheis* addressed a central problem, not only of the Indonesian independence movement, but also of human existence.

The novel ran to many editions and became a classic, studied by generations of students at schools and universities in Indonesia, Singapore, Malaysia and Brunei, and in Asian Studies courses in Australia where the University of Queensland Press published an English translation. In 1974 an Indonesian movie adapted from the book re-ignited controversy because of Rusli's advocacy of communism, which the then New Order regime had banned. In the twenty-first century many young Indonesians are still reading and debating the novel.

Atheis was launched when Indonesia was on the verge of independence. In December 1948 Dutch forces had invaded Central Java, where they pushed the Republican army out of

Yogyakarta and captured Sukarno and the other leaders, exiling them to Sumatra. As a result world opinion, led by India and Australia, turned against the Dutch. In the Cold War atmosphere the United States had been wary of the revolutionaries because their ranks included communists, but American support swung behind the cause of an independent Indonesia after the Republican army crushed the communists at Madiun. Continued guerrilla resistance and international pressure forced the Netherlands into negotiations that came to be known as the Round Table Conference, and finally they agreed to transfer sovereignty to the Republic. The Indonesian parliament confirmed Sukarno as President.

One day after the transfer of sovereignty, on 28 December 1949, Sukarno returned to Jakarta. Early that morning my father took me to the vast central city square which is now called Lapangan Merdeka, Freedom Square. On the north side of the square was the palace where the Dutch Governors-General and Japanese Commanders had resided. The previous day, the red and white Indonesian flag had replaced the Dutch flag above the building, which would now be the President's residence, becoming known as Istana Merdeka, Freedom Palace.

We found a position in front of the palace. The square soon filled with thousands of excited people. When the shouting became louder, we knew something was happening, and Bapak lifted me onto his shoulders. On the street between the square and the palace a milling crush of people slowly moved in our direction. The whole square erupted with cheers and shouts of 'Merdeka! Merdeka!' I too yelled as I gripped Bapak's head. The commotion moved towards us and a big black car appeared, surrounded by soldiers who pushed the crowd back. The President, in his white suit and black felt cap, stood tall in the open car, smiling and waving. When the car reached the palace, President Sukarno followed the soldiers to the top of the marble stairs. He faced us and raised his arms. The whole square became silent.

'Thanks be to God,' he proclaimed. 'We are free.'

Independence had been fought for and won mostly by the common people while many aristocrats had continued to work for the Dutch. Consequently, people lost respect for nobles, and customs relating to hierarchy began to change. Bapak had anticipated this with his belief in equality and his rejection of titles. These changes also affected the way I behaved towards my elders.

My parents' mixed-class marriage meant that I was lower in status than Bapak's family but higher than Ibu's side, and before the Revolution I had acted in accordance with this hierarchy. When visiting my father's family I made obeisance to Nini, my Grandmother. I served her with a drink as if I was a servant, keeping my head lower than hers and making the gesture of *sembah*, with hands together and fingertips upwards. In my Mother's family the position was reversed. My great-aunt, Ma Lengkong, believed that I was higher in the hierarchy than she was, so she always called me by the title '*Agan*' even though she was one of the wealthiest people in Bandung. When she served me food or drink, she addressed me as 'Agan Wenny.'

When I was eleven I noticed how the hierarchical customs were changing and I began to see the justice in Bapak's belief in the equality of all human beings. I no longer wished to pay obeisance to Nini, and when serving her with a drink I did not perform the sembah gesture. She was angry and told me I must do it, but I refused.

On my mother's side, I tried to make Ma Lengkong conform to my new views. Since the time we had sought refuge in her house and she allowed Ati and me to choose our own shoes and dresses, I had always spent the school holidays with her, while Ati stayed with Ibu Gunung. Ma prepared my favourite foods and gave me money. I slept in her bed and she would stroke my hair and massage me while telling me family stories and Sundanese legends, or making up hopeful tales for my future – that I would have a university education, buy a big car and take her driving.

One night I said, 'I don't want you to call me Agan anymore. I think of you as my grandmother. You are not a servant.'

'I have to call you Agan,' Ma said, 'because your father is a noble.'

'No. God created us all on the same level. If you call me Agan I won't come here anymore.'

Ma looked at me, her eyes glistening. 'It's not easy for me to change. But I'll try.'

Next morning at breakfast Ma said, 'Agan Wenny' as she presented the food to me. I was angry and said, 'I won't eat. I'm going home.'

Ma's husband took me aside and explained that Ma needed much longer than a day to make such a big change. I now know that her love was more valuable than my new principles, and I regret being so demanding.

During World War II, the Japanese Command had interned Europeans and Indos, who were people of mixed heritage, usually with Dutch fathers and Indonesian mothers. When the detainees were liberated from the camps in 1945, they were often attacked or even murdered because of their association with the hated colonial regime. After Independence, without Dutch forces to provide protection, many Indo and European people left the country, and those who remained continued to suffer prejudice and abuse.

My mother was sometimes mistaken for an Indo because of her light-coloured skin. Once, at the market, she bargained with one of the fish sellers who were sitting on the ground in front of large trays of fish. He snarled, 'You Indo Belanda, you want to get it cheap. Just take it all and go back to where you came from.'

'What?' yelled Ibu. She swept all the fish off the tray with her foot. 'I'm Indonesia *tulen*, pure Indonesian,' she screamed.

I was terrified that the six brawny fish sellers would gang up on her, but they all edged back. They were frightened of my mother. She was galak – fearsome – and I was proud of her.

CHAPTER 7
Fearsome Mother, Wayward Father

What have I done? ... The question haunted him. A guilty feeling weighed heavily upon his heart. ... He blamed himself for having succumbed to what he called 'devilish vexation' and for being so easily aroused. But yeah, I'm just a human being, said another voice inside him.
—Achdiat Karta Mihardja, *The Scattered Dust of Love*

In 1950 my parents used the royalties from *Atheis* to buy land and build a house at Jalan Tembaga. I often rode pillion on Bapak's pushbike when he peddled to our new house to inspect building progress. While he looked around I climbed the *belimbing* tree and ate the ripe star fruit as I watched the labourers at work and counted the days until I had my own bedroom.

When we moved to the new house I was sad to say goodbye to the mango tree that had given me so much comfort, and to the jambu tree where I had waited for Bapak each afternoon, but happy to be leaving a house where I had felt so hurt and lonely because of Ibu. The beatings had become less frequent, perhaps because I was older or because she had become pregnant again. In the new house I was never beaten.

The house had six bedrooms and large lounge and dining areas, with terraces on three sides. It was perfect for entertaining and soon filled with life – friends coming for dinner and dancing, or to play chess with Bapak and bridge with Ibu. And at last I had my own room with my own wardrobe. I covered the walls with pictures of the man I had fallen in love with – Gregory Peck. Bookshops sold photos of all the film stars and I collected every picture of him. He was my ideal – good-looking, manly and tender. I thought that if I could marry him I would be really happy. One night I dreamt that he kissed me.

I took responsibility for beautifying our new home by rearranging the furniture once a month, carefully positioning lounge chairs, tables and pot plants, and by growing flowers in the garden and placing them in vases throughout the house.

On Sundays I enjoyed watching Ibu or the servants cooking. I had been forced to cook during the revolution but now I wanted to, so I asked Ibu if I could prepare a meal. I found a recipe in *Indonesia Raya*, Mochtar Lubis's newspaper, and went with a servant to the market to buy the ingredients. I marinated meat in coconut milk and spices and made saté. Watching Ibu sample the dish, I held my breath, but she smiled, and said, 'Delicious.' From then on I often cooked Sunday meals for the family.

I missed our neighbours in Jalan Meranti, although Antje remained a good friend and sometimes came to stay overnight at our new place. I was delighted to find that Pak Tjo, one of the guerrillas who used to visit the hotel in Garut, lived nearby. Having helped achieve independence, he had now cut his long curly hair. Ati and I often visited his place after school and his friendly, talkative wife always had a special treat for us.

Relations with other neighbours were sometimes not so harmonious. Ita, a classmate who lived across the street, asked for help with her homework. I didn't help and her mother scolded me. When I told Ibu, her eyes blazed and she strode across to their house. Ita's mother was a small woman who always wore traditional *kain kebaya* and tied her long hair up in buns. She was outside her house and tried to run inside when she saw us coming, but Ibu caught her by the hair so that all her buns unravelled.

'How dare you abuse my daughter,' yelled Ibu. 'The children's problems are theirs. Don't get involved in their fights.'

'*Ampun*, Ibu, *ampun, ampun*,' cried the terrified woman.

People were always begging forgiveness from my mother. She was still galak.

In 1951 Bapak spent six months in Europe giving seminars about Indonesian literature and culture. As the head of Indonesian PEN, the writers' organisation that defended freedom of expression, he attended the international PEN conference at Lausanne as the

Indonesian delegate.

We all missed Bapak. Then Ibu changed, becoming angry all the time and often crying. To add to the misery in the house my sister Nuy caught whooping cough.

One day when I came home from school Ibu said, 'You must write to your father. You're the oldest child.'

'I've just written to him,' I said.

Ibu buried her face in her hands. I heard a sob. 'Bapak is unfaithful. He has fallen in love with a Dutch woman.' She looked up at me with her angry eyes. 'Write and tell him to come back to his wife and children.'

I was stunned. Was this my Bapak? How could he do such a thing? 'What will I say?' I asked.

'Just write in your own words.'

I wrote a long letter to Bapak reminding him of his family, blaming him for turning his back on us. How terrible it was, I told him, for his children to have a father who betrays their mother, especially when one child was very sick and another still a baby. My brother Fari had been born shortly before Bapak left for Europe.

Bapak wrote back. He said he felt very bad after he received my letter, that he knew that what he had done was wrong, and he promised to break off his relationship with the Dutch woman. He asked me to forgive him. 'I love your mother,' he wrote, 'and I love you and Ati and Nuy and Fari. I will not be unfaithful again.'

Ibu read the letter and said, 'We'll see.'

The Balai Pustaka publishing house continued paying Bapak's salary while he was in Europe, but Ibu's budget was tight, and she needed extra money to take Nuy to the doctor. On Bapak's desk she found the manuscript of a play he had been writing, *Bentrokan Dalam Asrama*, Conflict in the Dormitory. She took it to Balai Pustaka and they agreed to publish it and to give Ibu an advance payment.

'I'll kill you,' Ibu screamed at Bapak when he returned.

'Ampun, Tati, ampun, ampun,' he pleaded.

But the forgiveness he begged for took a long time. In the following months Ibu launched many blistering attacks on Bapak for his infidelity, while he insisted the affair was over and he would not stray again. Between the tirades they hugged and kissed and spoke softly to each other, and he told her how beautiful and clever she was and how much he loved her.

Bapak's remorse as a husband was mixed with his anger as a writer – his play had been published before he had finished polishing it. But he could do nothing as any mention of my mother's action precipitated another tongue-lashing from her. I was just relieved to have my Bapak back, and excited about all the gifts he had bought from Europe. The best was the big red sphere of Edam cheese, which Ibu doled out to us in paper thin slices.

Many years later I visited my parents in Canberra and slept on the couch in my father's office. There were sheets of paper everywhere, and I noticed a letter that was written in Dutch and not in my father's hand. Curious, I picked it up, and saw that it was dated 1951 and began with "My Darling Didi."

More recently, we were talking about how much he loved Ibu, and I teased him about the Dutch woman who called him Didi.

'Oh! How did you know she called me Didi?' he asked.

'I saw her letter. "My Darling Didi".'

He laughed. 'I was young and silly. Men always do that when they're far from home. It was just a fling. But Ibu is very kind. She forgave me.'

CHAPTER 8
Taking Charge of My Education

> Santa Ursula is the legendary all girls school established in 1859 by the Ursuline sisters ... Famous for having a strict and stern principal.
> —SMA Santa Ursula Facebook Page

When Bapak had fled from Sagara after the birth of Nuy he gave me, as oldest child, responsibility for the family. This was the turning point of my childhood, when I began to see that if I was to care for others, I must become capable myself, and for that I must do well at school. Time and again Bapak said that he wanted all of his children to become independent, regardless of whether they were male or female, and that the only road to independence was education. Yet now he never asked about my homework. I resolved to motivate myself, and drew up a timetable showing when to wake up, bathe, eat and study, and stuck it to the wall beside my bed. I became a disciplined student and passed each year at Taman Siswa primary school with high grades.

When I was thirteen I started at the state junior high school and hated it. The boys were the worst. As I walked past I heard them snigger, 'Look at her!' Or they leered and called, 'Hey, pretty girl, where're you going?'

When I came home Rawiah, the girl who lived next door, asked, 'How was school?'

'Terrible,' I said, 'Nothing like Taman Siswa. The boys tease the girls all the time. The building's dirty and rundown. I hate it.'

'Why don't you go to Santa Ursula? No boys there. And they've got sewing machines. You can learn dressmaking.'

That night I lay in bed thinking about sewing machines. If all the students could use them, the school must be wealthy. I was excited by the thought of making my own clothes.

The next afternoon, after more teasing from the state school boys, I rode my bike to Santa Ursula. I liked it immediately – the yard was well kept, the two-storey building had archways around the windows on the top floor, and inside was spotless. Next to the entrance vestibule was the office of the principal, who was working at her desk, a nun in full habit.

'Do you want to see me?' she asked.

'I want to enrol,' I replied.

'Where are your parents?'

'My father's at work. My mother is busy at home.'

'What's your name?'

'Sri Anggrawati Wenny.'

She took me into her office. 'Now, Sri, why do you want to come to Santa Ursula?'

'I just started at the state high school and I don't like it. I heard that this is a good school and there are sewing machines here to teach dress-making.'

'Do you like sewing?'

'I don't know. I've never done it but I want to learn. My mother is a good dressmaker.'

'What else attracts you?'

'It's an all-girls school. And the building is nice, especially with two storeys. The cathedral is beautiful.'

'What's your religion?'

'My parents say I'm Muslim. But I don't know much about it.'

'Do you pray five times a day?'

'No. I don't know how to pray in Islam.'

'Do your parents pray five times?'

'I don't see them pray.'

She studied me, a friendly expression on her face. Then she asked more questions about my parents, my favourite subjects, and my hopes for the future.

'Your father must sign this form,' she said, 'But you will be accepted. You can start tomorrow.'

That night I gave the form to Bapak and told him that Santa Ursula was much better than the state school. 'It's up to you,' he said. 'If you really want to go there we can pay the extra fees. But you must study hard. I want you to go to university.'

I loved Santa Ursula – except for sewing. The sewing teacher, a Dutch nun, was very strict and every garment had to be perfect.

'You didn't do it properly,' she pronounced once when I showed her the baby's smock I'd spent hours on. 'Pull it out and do it again.'

Everyone else was working on the next garment while I struggled nervously with the intricate folds of the smocking. My grade for sewing was written in red ink on my report cards, but in all my other subjects I received high marks.

My great-uncle Aki Sukamah often came to Jakarta to bet at the cockfights and was staying with us when I brought my report card home. He was impressed. 'I'll buy you a present for doing so well,' he said. 'What would you like?'

I closed my eyes and thought hard. The biggest luxury would be ... durian! The richly flavoured fruit was expensive so Ibu rarely bought them. When she did, the family sat on a mat while Bapak opened the durian. I ate quickly, leaving some flesh on the seeds so that I had time to take more pieces. When the durian was finished I would eat what I'd left on the seeds. But Ibu noticed and stopped me taking more than my share.

I told Aki, 'Durian's my favourite.'

'Durian it will be,' he said.

A whole durian to myself. I could hardly wait.

The next day I was in the yard and saw two *becak*, pedicabs, coming to our house. Aki was in one and the other was full of durians. He'd won a lot of money at the cockfight. Overjoyed, I ate four at once but was soon struck down by durian intoxication, with my body on fire and my head splitting open. I hurt all over, my tummy kept turning upside down, I couldn't think and couldn't stop crying. Ibu called the doctor, who emptied my stomach with a tube. Then I went to bed and slept for twelve hours.

'Serve you right for being so greedy,' said Ibu.

I would be an adult before I could again eat durian, and then only in very small portions.

My parents never came to Santa Ursula, but during my six years there Ibu supported me when I was studying. In the division of power in their marriage, Ibu was the dictator of household and financial affairs, while Bapak ruled on matters of principle, including education. Accepting Bapak's declaration that a university degree was essential, Ibu began to encourage me to do well at school. When I had a test, she stayed with me as I studied late into the night, making cups of tea and lying on my bed, just to be there for me as I worked at my desk. She would wish me luck in the morning and ask about the exam when I came home. I was grateful for Ibu's support, but disappointed that Bapak took no interest in my school work.

CHAPTER 9
The Presidential Painter

Basoeki Abdullah was famous as a portrait painter, especially of beautiful women, royalty and heads of state, and he was inclined to depict them as more beautiful than they actually were.
—Museum Basoeki Abdullah brochure

After his time in Europe in 1951, Bapak would travel overseas several more times during the 1950s. He went again to Europe to study adult education, and to America to study drama. In 1956 he spent six months in Sydney learning English under the Colombo plan.

Bapak later wrote that since childhood he had noticed in himself a feeling of inferiority, which he attributed to being taught throughout his school years to look up to Europeans as a "super-race" – clever, beautiful and powerful – in contrast to the "natives", who were dumb, lazy and ugly. Although his subsequent embrace of nationalism made him proud to be Indonesian, he struggled to overcome the colonialist conditioning and when he travelled overseas he still found himself affected by feelings of inferiority.

Achdiat's close friend, the artist Basoeki Abdullah, had also felt the pain of his low "native" status as a child, and had resolved that when he grew up he would marry a Dutch girl. The fact that this was not possible in the colony only made his resolve stronger. In the 1930s he went to Holland to study art and his passion for reading about art, history and culture drove him to stand in bookshops, losing himself in books he could not afford to buy. Most bookshops objected, but one was managed by a girl called Josephine who was happy for him to stay for hours, just reading. Basoeki and Jo fell in love and they married in The Hague.

When we had lived in Jakarta during the Japanese occupation, Basoeki and Tante Jo were our neighbours. I often visited their house to play with their daughter Saraswati, who had many more dolls and toys than I did. I was only four years old, but I still remember the Dutch treats that Tante Jo prepared.

Basoeki and Jo divorced and he married another Dutch woman – Maya Michel, a talented mezzo-soprano, known as Riet within her circle. As well as his fame as a painter, Basoeki had become well-known in Europe as a dancer, especially in the role of Hanuman, the monkey king in the Indian Ramayana epic. He also loved Western classical music and opera, and was enchanted when he first heard Riet sing.

During the 1950s we sometimes spent the weekend with Basoeki and Riet at their bungalow in the mountain resort area of Puncak. There we enjoyed the fresh air and flowers, walked up an appetite and indulged in the splendid feasts that Tante Riet always provided. She was a tall, slim woman who was even more beautiful than Tante Jo. I was mesmerised watching Basoeki and Riet as they romanced each other, and enchanted by Basoeki's beauty, with his curly hair, dark sleepy eyes and friendly smile. They were our first dinner guests after we moved to Jalan Tembaga.

Basoeki and President Sukarno were close, having first met when Basoeki was eighteen. The artist had painted Sukarno on his release from prison after the Japanese invaded in 1942, a portrait that was later used on a postage stamp. In the 1950s Sukarno appointed Basoeki to be the Presidential Painter.

One day at Santa Ursula, the Principal called me from class and asked me to follow her to her office. This only happened when I was in trouble. We had to walk from one end of the school to the other and all the way I was thinking, 'What have I done?' When we arrived at the office Basoeki Abdullah and Tante Riet were there.

'Wenny, I'm going to paint you,' Basoeki said. Apparently he had suddenly felt that he must paint my portrait and needed to act before the inspiration was lost, and knowing the painter's fame, the Principal let me go with Basoeki and Riet.

At his studio, he sketched me and then began to paint. At the end of the session I tried to look but he stopped me. 'You must not see it until it's finished,' he said.

I was disappointed but I soon forgot about the painting because Tante Riet had prepared European snacks of *poffertjes*, small Dutch pancakes, with *kaastengels*, cheese shortbread, and *spekkoek*, layer cake. How lucky, I thought, to always eat such nice food.

Basoeki needed three more sittings to complete the painting. Each time he barred my way when I tried to look. Each time Tante Riet prepared more treats, sometimes sweet snacks, sometimes a meal such as *huzarensla*, Dutch meat and potato salad.

When Basoeki showed me the finished painting I cried, 'That's not me. She's too beautiful.'

He had painted not only my portrait, but also background images of young men and the buildings of Pasar Baru, the historic market in central Jakarta. As I studied the painting I fell in love with it. Basoeki was known as a realist painter but it seemed that people became more beautiful when he portrayed them.

The painting, titled *Pasar Baru*, was hung in Basoeki's solo exhibition at Hotel Des Indes. The artist offered my parents the first option to purchase the painting but they could not afford it. Instead, the First Lady, Fatmawati Sukarno, bought it.

Basoeki later became the Court Painter to King Bhumibol and Queen Sirikit of Thailand. My father visited him when he lived in Bangkok and again when he had returned to Jakarta. Bapak's last visit was in October 1993 and a few weeks later, Basoeki was dead, murdered by robbers who broke into his home to steal his collection of wrist watches. His house in South Jakarta would be made into a museum honouring his work, with his bedroom left as it was the night he died. *Pasar Baru* is not among the paintings now hung in the museum, and I have always regretted that it was lost to me.

Both Achdiat and Basoeki had been disturbed by their status as lowly "natives" under the colonial regime, but they reacted differently. Basoeki had married a Dutch woman, confidently asserting his equality with the colonists. Achdiat knew on a rational level that he and Westerners were equal, but feelings of inferiority continued to trouble him and later would almost stop him from moving to Australia.

CHAPTER 10
September in the Rain

> How wonderful it was being in love ... I used to be as placid as water on a lake, but now I seemed to be surging like a mountain stream.
> —Achdiat Karta Mihardja, *Atheis*

I will always remember the moment I first saw Cheppy.

It was in 1955 when I was in Grade 9. I was staying with my grandmother in Bandung during the school holidays, and my uncle, Mang Entang, invited me to a birthday party for his friend Lian, a young Chinese Indonesian woman. I was excited as Mang, a famous pop singer, was good fun and had many friends. As we entered the room where the party guests were assembled, a tall, broad-shouldered, handsome man stood up and looked straight at me. Feeling a thrill of excitement, I looked down. As Lian took me around the room introducing each of the other guests, I could feel the tall man watching. When we came to him he shook my hand, holding it for a long time. I looked into his brown eyes and felt the rapid beating of my heart. His name was Cheppy.

He joined Mang Entang and me at the smorgasbord lunch and was very attentive as we selected our food. 'Of course you like *krupuk*,' Cheppy said, adding a cracker to the rice he had spooned onto my plate. He poured me an iced water.

After the meal the servants cleared the food away and shifted the tables and chairs to make space for dancing. Lian put an LP on the turntable and Cheppy immediately asked me up. I glided around the floor, secure in his confident arms. Dancing with other boys had never felt like this.

Between dances we sat and talked. A trainee pilot, he spoke of his passion for flying and the thrill of soaring high over the earth. I told him about Santa Ursula and my dream of attending university. Cheppy knew I was the daughter of Achdiat because of my connection with Mang Entang. 'My father's not famous like yours,' he said. 'He's just a postmaster, but he's a very good man. I would like you meet my mother. She's kind and loving. And my brother and sister. I feel lucky to have such a close family.'

It was a Sunday in September and outside the rain teemed down. Lian put a new record on to play, and there was Bing Crosby singing *September in the Rain*. Cheppy and I looked at each other then jumped up to dance again, my cheek next to his. I felt transformed. I was sixteen and becoming an adult.

Cheppy's friends teased him. 'Come on Cheppy, don't monopolise Wenny. Give someone else a chance.'

'No way,' he said. 'Ask Wenny if she wants to dance with other boys.'

'What happens if I do want to dance with someone else?' I asked.

'I won't let you.'

I spent the whole party with Cheppy and too quickly it was time to leave. 'I will see you again soon,' he said.

That night I couldn't sleep. I kept thinking of Cheppy, longing to be with him, to be dancing, singing and laughing with him. Never before had I felt such a strong attraction.

A few days later Mang Entang took me out to the Baltic Ice Cream Parlour in Jalan Braga. As we were eating our sundaes Cheppy appeared beside our table. What a coincidence – or was it? With a big smile Cheppy joined us and we talked for ages. Then Mang left us and Cheppy said, 'Let's go and meet my family.'

We walked the short distance to his house where his parents, brother and sister welcomed me warmly. I could see how close-knit the family was and felt the strong bond between Cheppy and his mother. As he had said, they were good people.

During the next week back at school, daydreams of Cheppy made it hard to concentrate in class. Then one day as I wheeled my bike out the school gate my heart jumped when I saw him waiting for me. 'Let's go to the movies,' he said. 'There's a Doris Day film at Garden Hall Cinema.'

I peddled home and he followed on his motorbike. In those days, when a boy asked a girl out he must first have obtained her father's permission. Bapak was still at work and I was relieved that Ibu gave her consent. I thought that would do.

I was so happy riding pillion on Cheppy's motorbike, especially if he had to stop suddenly and I was pressed against him. In the cinema he held my hand for the whole movie. When Doris Day sang *Love Me or Leave Me*, Cheppy looked at me more than at the screen. I had never known I could be so happy. I dumped Gregory Peck – now I was in love with a real man who was even more handsome than the film star. I felt so proud to be with him and could not believe how lucky I was.

After the matinee Cheppy took me home. Bapak was leaning on the closed bottom half of the Dutch door at the front of our house. His eyes blazed as we walked into the yard and he yelled at Cheppy, 'Get out! Don't come back! Don't come near my daughter again.'

I was stunned. How could my own father behave so rudely to the boy I loved? I felt humiliated and embarrassed, but Cheppy calmly apologised to my father, said goodbye and left.

I was crying and angry. 'Why?' I demanded of Bapak.

'He's a bad man.'

'How do you know he's a bad man?'

'He's a friend of my brother, and my brother is a womanising parasite whose friends are all scoundrels. And pilots always betray their wives. They have a girlfriend at every airport.'

I gasped. What had happened to my father, that he could say such things? I tried to argue, but he cut me off and I ran to my room, sobbing. My parents defied their parents to get married, I thought, but now he won't let me follow my heart.

A week later Cheppy was again waiting for me after school. We went to the Ragusa Ice Cream Parlour near Santa Ursula and I explained why my father would not let me see him.

'It's just coincidence that I know your uncle,' he said. 'It doesn't mean I'm bad. And if Bapak doesn't like me being a pilot, I can follow a different career.'

'No, flying is what you want. Even if you were not a pilot I don't think Bapak would accept you.'

'Maybe he doesn't want you to marry into a poor family.'

I thought this might be true because the reasons Bapak

had given didn't make sense. I told Cheppy about Kiki, a student who often visited our house and who had cultivated my mother's friendship. 'I think my mother's behind this,' I said. 'She wants Kiki to be my boyfriend, and he comes from a rich family. She gave me permission to go out with you, but she must have changed her mind and told Bapak to throw you out.'

Cheppy and I continued to meet after school and I felt torn between my love for him and guilt at disobeying my parents. My desire for Cheppy was the biggest thing in my life and yet I could not discuss it with my mother or father. A fissure had appeared, and I felt as if I was turning into a different person.

CHAPTER 11
Fissures and Tensions

The Second World War gave rise to the Revolution of 1945. The Revolution of 1945 gave rise to the two clashes with the Dutch. Clashes 1 and 2 gave birth to Bung Karno's new direction. This new direction culminated in the Round Table Conference.
All of this resulted in expectations rising day by day. And accompanying this was a rise in the number of muggings, beggars and prostitutes; and of motions, meetings, cocktail parties and interviews.
—Achdiat Karta Mihardja, "The Story of Leader X", *Fissures and Tensions*

In the early fifties government employees such as my father were given land in Kebayoran, a new suburb in South Jakarta, under the condition that they build a house on it within two years. Many employees did not have enough money to do this, and sold the land to businessmen who had the resources to build. My father considered this practice to be corrupt and, instead, gave the land back to the government. When Ibu found out, she was livid. 'You idiot,' she screamed at him. 'Why didn't you sell it? We could have made a big profit.'

Bapak argued back. 'I'm not corrupt. It's not right to make a profit out of the government.'

'You are stupid, stupid, stupid! We needed that money.'

Now Bapak was angry. 'Leave me alone. Principle is more important than profit.'

The land was given to another public servant, who sold it to a businessman who built a large luxury home on it. Every time we passed that house, Ibu shouted at Bapak, 'Look at that place you gave away. We could have made a lot of money. You're a fool.'

'Stop nagging me. I might be a fool, but I'm an honest fool.'

Winning independence created expectations of a better life

for a people desperately poor after years of Dutch colonialism, Japanese occupation and revolution. Yet, during the fifties, the economic situation worsened.

I now know that my father despaired at the failing economy, the increasing misery of the people, and the shambles of government, with short-lived coalitions of parties rising and falling. He blamed the corruption of the country's leaders, who were putting their own wants before the needs of their people. He poured his anger at injustice into stories defending poverty-stricken village people or satirising the selfishness of the elite. He published some of these stories under the pseudonym of Marhaen, a name with a history.

President Sukarno claimed that, as a young man cycling through the countryside near Bandung, he had met a Sundanese farmer called Marhaen. Sukarno began to use this name to designate poor peasants, vendors and becak drivers who made up the bulk of the population. Based on this archetypal character, Sukarno created an ideology, Marhaenism, a mix of socialist and nationalist ideas targeted at improving the lives of "his people", the have-nots. Marhaenism became the basis for his political vehicle, the Indonesian National Party.

The 1950 interim constitution had put government in the hands of cabinet, subject to the confidence of parliament, with the President's role mainly a ceremonial one. Having always seen himself as the saviour of his people, Sukarno resented being out-manoeuvred by the colleagues who designed this system and was working to rebuild his power. Achdiat had been a friend of Sukarno in the forties, and admired his vision but worried about any increase in the President's power, believing that Sukarno's oversized ego made his plans unrealistic. For this reason Achdiat hoped that parliamentary democracy could be made to work rather than be replaced by a presidential system.

Mochtar Lubis, the journalist who sheltered us in Jakarta during the Revolution, often came to dinner at our house and he and Achdiat would talk into the night, analysing Indonesia's politics and problems. Like Achdiat, Mochtar was writing fiction that conveyed his concern for the poor. Mochtar also used his newspaper, *Indonesia Raya*, to expose corruption and embarrass Sukarno, whom he hated. The feeling was mutual, especially after *Indonesia Raya* revealed that the President had secretly taken a second wife while still married to the popular Fatmawati, whom the people called "Mother of the Nation".

In April 1955, the first conference of Asian and African heads of government was held in Bandung, with the duel aims of promoting cooperation between their countries and resisting neo-colonialism by Cold War powers. Prominent leaders from both continents attended, including Chinese Premier Chou En-lai, Indian Prime Minister Nehru and Egyptian President Nasser. The conference focussed world attention on Indonesia, and Sukarno revelled in the glory, styling himself as the leader of this Third World challenge to the "old established forces" of imperialism.

Mochtar Lubis registered as a reporter for the conference and was given a hospitality committee card along with a list of addresses for women who would satisfy delegates' needs. He visited these addresses, interviewed the women, and published the details in *Indonesia Raya*. The tall, lanky Mochtar, who dressed in jeans when few people wore Western clothes, was accused of "cowboy" journalism, but the scandal took some of the gloss off the Government's pride in staging the prestigious gathering.

Achdiat hoped that the country's first elections, scheduled for September 1955, would resolve the chronic political instability and expected his party, the Indonesian Socialist Party (PSI), to do well. PSI policies stressed social justice and planning for economic development, and many intellectuals supported the party. Achdiat and Mochtar feared the increasing influence of the Indonesian Communist Party (PKI) because they believed it rejected religious values. However, the election result was a bitter disappointment for Achdiat, with the vote split between 28 parties and no likely coalition gaining a clear majority. Sukarno's party led the count with 22 percent, followed by two Islamic parties then the communists, while the PSI won only two percent of the vote. The elections confirmed the divisions within the country, and the political system moved towards crisis.

In 1956 Achdiat published a collection of short stories,

Keretakan dan Ketegangan, Fissures and Tensions. "The Story of Leader X" was one of several stories that satirised people in the urban privileged class, particularly political leaders who buy bungalows in the mountain resort area of Puncak while their people starve. What is the difference, asked Achdiat, between these leaders and the Dutch? In "Martini's Version" a young divorcee, who is drawn into an affair with a married politician, decides she must free herself from her corrupt lover and take charge of her own life. Achdiat used this tale to link personal and national independence. Other stories took the viewpoint of the victims of economic stagnation. In "Sensation at the Top of a Coconut Tree", Achdiat felt his way into the consciousness of a destitute villager, who is told by a *dukun,* a shaman, that he will overcome his troubles if he meditates at the top of a coconut palm.

The book cemented Achdiat's reputation as a master storyteller. The National Cultural Council awarded him the 1957 National Literature Prize, which had been won the previous year by Mochtar for a short story collection which expressed a similar concern for people trapped in poverty. Although subsidised by the government, the Council was an independent, non-political body charged with supporting Indonesian art and culture.

While my father was preoccupied with corruption, poverty and human rights, I took no interest in politics. I was evolving into a self-absorbed teenager, and the only parties I liked were those where I could dance and have fun.

CHAPTER 12
Childhood's End

Heaven lies under the feet of your mother.
—Hadith (saying attributed to the Prophet Muhammad.)

Kiki, an economics student who lived nearby, had become close friends with my mother and often visited our house bringing flowers for Ibu and chocolates for her children. He began to pay attention to me while I was still secretly meeting Cheppy after school. He called me Yen, from Nyenyen, my father's name for me, and I had made up Kiki as a pet name for him.

I prepared a meal one Sunday, and he said, 'Yen, this is the most delicious *opor ayam* I've ever tasted. You're a clever cook.'

My ego soared.

I liked Kiki when he gave me French perfume, sent me orchids or wrote love poems to me. But I did not like him when he tried to tell me what to do. He was a powerful man, ten years older than I was, and I was afraid of him.

He took me to his graduation party and afterwards drove me home in his father's car. It was a time of chivalry and I waited for him to open my door, but instead he moved across the seat and put his arms around me. When I struggled, trying to push him away, he jumped out and ran around to open the door. But then he held me and kissed me on the cheek until I broke free and ran inside to my bedroom in tears.

I heard Kiki thanking my parents for allowing him to take me out. I stayed in my room, crying. Did it really happen or was it a dream? I pinched my cheek – ow! It's true, it happened.

After Kiki left, Ibu came into my room. 'Why are you crying?'

'Kiki kissed me.'

'But why are you crying? Is that all he did? Where did he kiss you?'

I pointed to my cheek. 'Here.'

'Nothing else?'

I didn't know what she meant. 'No.'

'But that's okay. Why did that make you cry?'
'I'm scared.'
'Scared of what?'
'I'm scared I'll get pregnant.'
My mother looked at me. 'It takes more than that.'
She sat on the bed. 'You're sixteen, almost an adult,' she said. 'Now you have to be careful. You must look after yourself. Don't give it away. Don't let anyone touch you below the neck. But a kiss on the cheek from Kiki is okay.'

Ibu did not explain what she meant by 'don't give it away' but I soon found out from my school friends. After I had been reassured that kissing a boy was safe, the idea became quite agreeable. After a party the following Saturday night Kiki and I sat in the car outside our house, and I learnt to kiss on the lips.

When I next met Cheppy after school, we went to his friend's family's house, where he stayed when he was in Jakarta. After we had tea with the family, Cheppy took me into their office to show me a map on the wall. Alone in the office we stood looking at the map but not seeing it. He put his arms around me and we kissed for the first time. I discovered the feeling of a real kiss with a boy that I loved, a kiss tinged with guilt knowing that my parents had forbidden our love.

At Santa Ursula we were taught etiquette and ballroom dancing. Every three months we had a social evening with the boys from Kanisius College, a Jesuit school. During the dancing the Ursuline nuns and the Kanisius priest would monitor us to enforce the no flirting rule. When we danced too close one of these guardians would approach and we would separate to the permitted distance.

I began to get many invitations to Saturday night parties and dances, and Ibu took charge of my party clothes. When she watched a movie she paid special attention to the dresses, such as the one Audrey Hepburn wore in *Sabrina*. 'I can make that,' she said, and had the dress ready for a trial fitting by the following Friday night.

While I tried the dress on, my mother fussed around, and

I wondered if she had made me this dress so that people would admire her through her daughter. Remembering her harshness in Jalan Meranti, I felt like an empty doll being dressed up. But as I danced my way through Saturday night I forgot my reservations and was happy to be wearing such a lovely dress.

Ibu organised a party for my seventeenth birthday, the most significant milestone on the journey to adulthood for Indonesians. She hired a caterer and a famous band, Aneka Nada. A hundred friends and relatives thronged the house, terraces and garden, bringing gifts and flowers and wishing me 'Happy Birthday for Sweet Seventeen.' Such expressions had become popular in the fifties because of the songs and movies from America. Bapak made a short speech and everyone sang Happy Birthday, again using English.

'I'm proud you've grown up to be a beautiful girl,' said Ma Lengkong. 'I hope you'll go to university, marry a rich man, live in a mansion and have a big car. Make sure it's a really big car so that you can take me driving.'

The dancing began with the polonaise and moved on to the waltz, quickstep, jive and even the cha-cha-cha. I spent the evening in a whirl, soaking up the love of friends and relatives. I kept touching the five gold bangles on my arm – the *gelang keroncong* that Ibu had given me. 'I am really an adult now,' I thought. 'I can be independent. I can choose my own clothes. Ibu can't dictate what to wear. My childhood is over.'

During the fifties I felt the closeness that Bapak and I had once shared slipping away. I was sad, but then I accepted that we were both changing: I was a teenager, my head full of school, friends and Cheppy. Bapak's career took up more of his time, especially after he had become the head of the Jakarta Culture Division in the Ministry of Education and Culture. He was often away for conferences or meetings, or out at night for receptions, cocktail parties and cultural evenings at foreign embassies. He also took a second job, lecturing on Indonesian literature at the University of Indonesia.

Ibu usually accompanied him to receptions, but

sometimes she didn't feel like dressing up in kain kebaya, traditional formal wear, so she would ask me to take her place. Once I went with Bapak to the Chinese embassy, and looked longingly at the exotic food laid out in the smorgasbord. The red apples caught my eye. I looked around. Was anyone watching? Could I slip one into my handbag?

I resisted that temptation, but piled my plate with too much other food, and joined Bapak. The writer Utuy Tatang Sontani, whom I hadn't seen since I was a child, was whispering in my father's ear. Suddenly Bapak roared with laughter, put his arm around me, and exclaimed, 'This is Wenny!'

'Oh, Wenny,' said Oom Utuy. 'You grew up so fast.'

'Why are you laughing?' I asked Bapak.

'Oom Utuy asked if you were my mistress.'

At that time, perhaps because of President Sukarno's example, taking a mistress had become fashionable for people in high positions.

I now had two boyfriends, one open and one secret. With Ibu's encouragement Kiki had begun to monopolise me, and everyone now considered us a courting couple, but I did not love Kiki. It was Cheppy for whom my heart raced if he was waiting when I wheeled my bicycle out of school. He would ride alongside on his motorbike while I peddled to Ragusa Ice Cream Parlour, anticipating the loving kiss over our sundaes. But I felt guilty about deceiving my parents and betraying Kiki and eventually told Cheppy we could no longer meet. 'I don't want to keep seeing you behind Bapak's back. I respect my parents too much.'

He agreed not to come to the school and I tried to forget him. Several months later he was again waiting outside Santa Ursula. 'I've left flying school,' he said, 'so now I won't be a pilot. I want to marry you. I want to see your parents.'

'It's impossible. They will never agree to see you. My father is immovable.'

Seeing Cheppy again, I knew that I loved him more than ever, but felt that I had to obey my parents. I was torn and confused.

It wasn't long before I found out how Cheppy left his flying course. My friend Hartini was engaged to a trainee pilot, and they invited me to an outing at Bogor Botanical Gardens which had been arranged by the flying school for the trainees and their girlfriends. Before our meal an instructor gave a talk on the importance of trainee pilots and their partners all acting responsibly. Don't get too involved with your girlfriend, he told the trainees. She is important, but career should have the highest priority. And he told the women to support their boyfriends in their goal of becoming a pilot. To illustrate his point he used a case study about a very bright student whose heart was broken because his girlfriend's parents would not accept him. The student thought they might change their minds if he did not become a pilot, and he deliberately failed so that he would not have to pay back the scholarship. The main black mark against the student was that during training he flew low over his girlfriend's house, to the horror of the instructor with him. I listened to the end of the instructor's talk in shock for I had realised that I was the girlfriend in this story.

Because public service salaries were low, even for those in high positions such as Bapak, Ibu took in boarders to earn money for school fees. Bapak's new position had entitled him to purchase, at a concessional price, a small government house nearby and Ibu used this house for four university students from Singapore. She also fitted two boarders into each of our large spare bedrooms at Jalan Tembaga. Sometimes they overflowed these rooms, and for three months I shared my room with an American, Hazel Chung, who had come to study Indonesian dance. On the first morning, I woke with a start to see her pirouetting around the room practising ballet. Hazel would go on to gain international acclaim as a choreographer and she kept in touch with my parents, later visiting them in Canberra when she went to Australia.

Ibu also set up a business buying quality batiks cheaply in Solo and Yogya then reselling them in Jakarta. She was often away on business, or accompanying Bapak to conferences, perhaps to keep an eye on him. I managed the household and the boarders during such times, planning the menus and giving Bi Uju, the senior servant, instructions and money to buy supplies.

To manage my own savings I made several money boxes out of condensed milk tins and used each for a different purpose. My pocket money was small, but it was an Indonesian tradition for relatives to give money to children, especially on holidays, so when Aki Noor or Ma Lengkong or my great-uncle Aki Sukamah came to visit, my savings received a boost. I hid the boxes in different places – one under the bed, one behind the wardrobe, one under my books – so that if a thief came he would not find all my wealth.

The money in one of the boxes was always for a present for my mother. I would search the shops for the right gift, such as a powder box, and its price became my savings target, which usually took several months to reach. I often struggled within myself between saving money and buying snacks, especially when my fellow students bought treats at the school canteen. When the savings target was reached I prayed that the gift would still be in the shop.

I wrapped the present in crepe paper and put a jasmine flower from the garden on top of it. Jasmine symbolised the purity of mothers.

When I gave Ibu the gift, she said, 'Thank you, Wenny,' and hugged me. She opened it, smiled, and exclaimed, 'It's perfect.'

Twice a year, for her birthday and for Mother's Day in December, I carefully planned a gift for Ibu, and always reached my target.

'I won't,' I shouted. 'And you can't make me.'

'Dear child,' Ibu replied, 'education is the key to your future. It's much better if you study hard now.'

'What for? I'll marry a rich man and live in a mansion, not in a dump like this.'

'Oh my child, I fear for you.' Ibu turned and walked away wiping the tears from her eyes.

'Oh my child, I fear for you,' I mouthed, wagging my

finger at her back. The audience laughed.

The Rebellious Child, a short play I had written, was being performed at a school concert. My friend Mulyati played the loving mother while I was the wild girl who would not obey her. This was opposite to real life where my mother was the wild one and I the obedient child. To play the role, Mulyati had dressed in kain kebaya and made up her face and hair in the style of an older woman. She looked lovingly at me over her glasses, which were perched on the end of her nose, and she patiently tried to help her daughter with good advice. When I screamed that I didn't want her advice, she went to the corner of the stage and sobbed.

It was my dream to have a mother like Mulyati.

Towards the end of the play my character was sitting by herself when a voice came from the background. 'Heaven is under the feet of mothers,' it said.

'What?'

'Your mother has given you life,' the voice continued in the words I had written. 'As she gave birth to you, she struggled between life and death. We must respect what mothers do to bring us into the world. You would not have survived without her milk, and you would not have grown into the person you are without her love. That is how we know that heaven lies under the feet of mothers.'

My character began to cry, and when my fictional mother came I knelt before her and begged her forgiveness. The play ended with our tearful reconciliation.

At senior high school I edited *Serviam*, the monthly school magazine, under the guidance of Pak Buntaran, the Indonesian language teacher. Serviam, the school motto, means 'to serve.' Pak Buntaran had selected *The Rebellious Child* to be performed as our class contribution to the concert. My parents were not at the concert, and I didn't show the script to them because years before I had proudly given my father a short story I had written, and he had itemised all the things that were wrong with it. He could find nothing good to say about it and I resolved then never again to show my father anything I had written.

I broke this rule once. Disturbed by the dirty streets of Jakarta where there were no bins and people threw rubbish anywhere, I wrote an essay: *How to Keep Jakarta Clean*. I showed my father, but only after it had won a writing competition.

CHAPTER 13
Crisis

Mochtar Lubis had become the boldest and the most prominent of the anti-Sukarno and anti-Communist editors. His arrest and long detention – and particularly his determination not to compromise his views in return for leniency – earned him a life-long reputation as a courageous symbol of 'press freedom'.
—David T Hill, *Journalism and Politics in Indonesia*

Mochtar Lubis's report about the government procuring prostitutes for delegates at the Asia-Africa Conference upset not only President Sukarno but also the Foreign Minister, Roeslan Abdulgani, who was Secretary-General of the Conference. When Mochtar published another report in 1956 about an alleged cover-up of corruption by Abdulgani, Mochtar was charged with libel.

Ibu and I accompanied Mochtar's wife, Hally, to the court to hear him defend the charges. The guards made sure people behaved with the respect due to the court, telling us to take off our sunglasses and sit up properly with legs uncrossed. We watched as Mochtar produced documentary evidence of the truth of the articles he had published. Tante Hally was ecstatic when he was acquitted.

Mochtar's newspaper, *Indonesia Raya*, had also reported on dissent by army commanders in Sumatra and published letters from Mochtar's cousin who was allegedly involved in a coup attempt. In December 1956 Mochtar wrote an editorial predicting that the Sumatran rebellion would spread to other areas of the Outer Islands, and he called on Sukarno, Army Chief Nasution and the cabinet to step down. Before the editorial could be published Mochtar was arrested and detained in the Jakarta Military Prison.

'He's not allowed pen and paper,' Tante Hally told us. 'That's the highest punishment for a writer. If he can't eat, that's okay. But not to be able to write is unbearable.'

I could understand that as I knew Bapak would become

frantic if he ever found himself without pen or paper.

'The guards wouldn't search Wenny,' said Ibu.

Blouses and wide skirts were in fashion. Ibu made a small hole in the hem of my skirt and pushed a pen in. She folded paper tightly into a small bundle and hid it in a deep pocket. I was frightened but told myself I must do this because Mochtar was a brave man who was standing up for the rights of ordinary people.

Tante and Ibu carried food for Mochtar into the prison. There were soldiers everywhere, looking fierce. They must suspect me, I thought. I tried to act normally.

At the office, the soldiers asked, 'Who is this?'

'My sister and her daughter,' Tante Hally said. This was untrue, but Hally and Ibu were so close that they did consider themselves sisters.

Only family members were allowed to see Mochtar, and Ibu had to fill out a form stating the purpose of her visit – to see her brother-in-law. Although the soldiers checked the food for prohibited items, they ignored me, and we were taken to a large room. Mochtar smiled broadly as he was brought in by a guard, and he bent down to embrace Hally. The guards did not watch us closely and I soon had a chance to slip the pen and paper into Mochtar's hands.

Two weeks later he was released from prison but put under house arrest. Mochtar and Hally made friends with the four soldiers on guard duty, inviting them to use their lounge room, and giving them meals and snacks. The guards knew that their prisoner had defended the common people against corruption and one of them told Mochtar, 'Bapak, I'm sorry I have to guard you, but this is my job. I only do it because my family needs to eat. Really, my beliefs are the same as yours.' The soldiers were supposed to prevent visitors from entering the house, but they always waved us straight through.

The stress of not being able to go out affected Mochtar's health and he began to suffer eczema. To relax he cultivated orchids, wrote fiction and painted. Although known as a writer, he was also a talented artist and had helped establish the

Indonesian Artists' Association. Hanging in the hallway of his house was a long painting in which he had depicted various faces of Sukarno, each showing an expression of malice, arrogance, lust or greed.

Mochtar's arrest was one of the few events in the wider world which touched me directly when I was a teenager. Absorbed in my busy life of school and friends, I had not noticed that the country was in crisis or that Sukarno was putting into place mechanisms that would allow him to become a dictator. I had forgotten that such shifts in power might have consequences for my family. History has since taught me more about the tumult of those times than I knew when I was living through them.

The 1955 elections had failed to produce stable government and, in his speeches, Sukarno blamed the party system: 'We are afflicted by the disease of parties which, alas, alas, makes us forever work against one another! ... Let us bury them, bury them, bury them!' The Western model of democracy did not suit Indonesia, he claimed, and in early 1957 he proposed an alternative system based on decision-making at the village level where, guided by the village head, everyone in the community discussed an issue until they reached a consensus. He declared that this would work for the nation as a whole, as it was based on the Indonesian virtue of harmony, in contrast to the Western system of 'fifty percent plus one', which he said was based on conflict. He called his proposed system Guided Democracy.

The Sumatran commanders about whom Mochtar had reported now seized control of the administration in their regions, providing Sukarno with a pretext for declaring martial law, further increasing his power. As a first step towards Guided Democracy Sukarno established the National Council to set policy and advise the cabinet. Council members, representing groups such as farmers, workers, women, the military, and religious leaders made decisions not by voting but by consultation and consensus under the guidance of the leader, Sukarno. The cabinet, following the direction of the Council, attended to the day-to-day management of the country. With the intention of sidelining the parties, Sukarno himself selected the cabinet ministers.

Sukarno was able to make these moves because his own power, initially based on his ability to inspire people through his oratory and his prestige as the Father of the Nation, had been boosted by the failure of parliamentary democracy. He used this power to keep the main political forces – the military, communists and Islam – in balance while working to implement Guided Democracy.

Achdiat was an active member of the Indonesian Socialist Party and close to its leader, Sutan Syahrir. Having fiercely opposed Sukarno's plan because of its authoritarianism and the greater power it gave to the communists, Socialist Party leaders feared that Sukarno would retaliate against them. Achdiat watched these developments with increasing dread. He saw Sukarno manoeuvring to become absolute ruler while explosive pressures were building from the army, the communists, and the regional rebellions, which had now spread from Sumatra to East Indonesia, and Achdiat feared that the country was heading towards a cataclysm.

In Sukarno's new cabinet, the Minister for Achdiat's department, Education and Culture, was Priyono, a communist who had won the Stalin Peace Prize. Priyono was a member of a small Marxist group, not the PKI, the main communist party. He soon had the ministry working on his plans to reverse the growth of Western influence and rebuild national culture by teaching people revolutionary songs, reinventing traditional dances to reflect the lives of workers and peasants, and establishing cultural links with the USSR and China. Achdiat had to manage some of these initiatives.

Holland had refused to relinquish its New Guinea territory, and in 1957 Indonesia retaliated by nationalising Dutch enterprises and ordering the 40,000 Dutch citizens still in Indonesia to get out with no more personal effects than could be carried in a suitcase. Unemployment rose as Dutch firms lay idle, and trade stopped as shipping was immobilised. Sutan Syahrir became more outspoken, giving press conferences at which he criticised Sukarno and condemned the takeover of Dutch assets.

In November Sukarno presented prizes at the school his children attended. As he left the building three grenades were thrown at him. Eleven people, mainly children, died but Sukarno was unhurt. His miraculous escape convinced many that he had been protected because he was destined to achieve great things for the nation, and his prestige increased. Those responsible were not caught, but may have been from Darul Islam, the Islamists who terrorised West Java throughout the fifties, although some blamed the rebellious military commanders in Sumatra and Sulawesi.

In early 1958 these officers proclaimed the Revolutionary Government of the Republic of Indonesia, thus initiating a full-scale revolt. They were strongly anti-communist and anti-Sukarno and their major grievances were corruption, mismanagement, the growing power of the communist party on Java, and Jakarta's neglect of the Outer Islands. Several prominent leaders from the Socialist Party, including the country's most distinguished economist, travelled to Sumatra to join the insurrection. Because of the rebels' anti-communism, the United States, Britain and Australia provided them with covert support in the form of weapons and equipment. America's denial of CIA involvement was discredited when a rebel bomber with an American pilot was shot down.

By mid-1958 the Indonesian military had effectively defeated the rebels, although guerrilla warfare continued for some years. The victory strengthened Sukarno's position, and he made plans for the next steps in establishing Guided Democracy and for taking revenge against his enemies, including the Socialist Party and its leader, Sutan Syahrir.

In August 1958 Mochtar Lubis won the prestigious Ramon Magsaysay Award, regarded as Asia's equivalent to the Nobel Prize. Still under house arrest, he was unable to travel to Manila to receive it.

CHAPTER 14
Judgement Days

> No stories left a deeper impression on my immature mind than the graphic ones about the punishments of hell which earthly sinners had to endure.
> —Achdiat Karta Mihardja, *Atheis*

My parents were Muslims but I never saw them practice their religion. My only knowledge of Islam came from Bi Tasiah, the servant at Jalan Meranti who tried to console me when I sat crying under the mango tree. At night, when my parents were at meetings and I was in bed, Bi Tasiah sat on the floor beside me and told Islamic stories.

'On judgement day,' she said, 'we will be brought before the throne of God. There will be no more secrets. If we cheated or lied or did not pray five times a day, these sins will pile up on the left-hand pan of the scales and everyone will be able to see them. Our good deeds will be put on the right-hand pan.

'Then we must cross the hair bridge over the abyss of hell. The bridge is the thickness of a single human hair divided by seven. We must walk across this bridge as the flames of hell roar up around us, and the black smoke blinds our eyes. If our good deeds outweigh our sins, we will reach Paradise on the other side, but only after a thousand years on the bridge, with hell-fire burning away our sins. If our sins are greater than our good deeds, our feet will slip on the hair bridge, and we will plunge down into the flames of hell and suffer unbearable pain for all eternity.'

When I read *Atheis*, I was surprised to find a similar story told by a maid to the main character when he was a child. Bapak once said in an interview that this episode was based on his own experiences when he was small.

I wanted to follow Islam, but was put off by Bi Tasiah's horror stories and the fact that everything was in Arabic, which I could not understand. Kiki tried to turn me into a good Muslim who prayed five times a day, but he was a bossy, impatient teacher who ridiculed my mistakes.

At Santa Ursula I admired and envied the nuns and priests, who had dedicated their lives to God and sacrificed themselves to serve humanity. I felt the beauty and purity of their lives, especially the nuns who seemed almost as sacred as angels. In religious instruction class everything I learned about Catholicism was beautiful – the ceremony, the celebration of saints' birthdays, the prayers for people in other countries, and the Church's help for those who were poor. We prayed before and after classes every day. For special celebrations we prayed in the cathedral next to the school.

In Grade Twelve, the principal, Mere Romana, said to me, 'Your marks in religion are very high. It seems that you're interested in Catholicism. Would you like to learn more about it?'

She arranged for the priest to give me more advanced lessons. Each day after school I went through the back garden to his room in the cathedral. He was a serious young man from Central Java and had two front teeth which stuck out and rested on his lower lip. During his instruction he stared intently into my eyes, and when I answered correctly, he exclaimed, 'Very good. You're a clever girl.'

Kiki, who visited our house every afternoon, wondered why I was now always late coming home from school, so one day he waited at the front of Santa Ursula. He could not find me among the students leaving after classes finished but eventually saw me coming from the cathedral. He rode home on his motorbike.

When I arrived home Kiki and Ibu were waiting. 'Yen! What were you doing at the Cathedral?' he demanded.

'The priest is giving me lessons about the Catholic religion.'

Kiki was furious and ordered me to stop seeing the priest, but I had become a believer and refused to obey.

One day after a lesson with the priest I stood up to leave. The priest also stood and then he was hugging me and pushing his lips against mine. I wriggled free, ran out to my bike and peddled home as fast as I could. In my room I was still shaking with fright and an overwhelming sense of betrayal. I had revered the holiness of the priest and he had betrayed me. I would never go back to him.

A few days later Kiki asked if I was still seeing the priest, and I told him I was not and what had happened. Kiki immediately went to the Cathedral to confront the man. 'Yes, I gave her a hug,' the priest told him, 'but it was a fatherly hug, that's all.'

Later the priest saw me in school and said, 'Your boyfriend came to see me. But you misunderstood me. That was only the hug of a father for a daughter.'

I was teenager with a growing body, and knew that a father does not hug or kiss a daughter in the way he had done. The incident dampened my enthusiasm for Catholicism, but I still prayed to God every day and sought His blessings for others.

My mother liked Kiki and always had a special treat for him when he visited. 'He's such a nice man,' she would say.

She was happy whenever I agreed to go out with Kiki. She took charge and dictated what dress and shoes to wear. 'Wenny, have you brushed your teeth?' she said one night.

'Why ask me that? I'm not a child.'

'But what if Kiki kisses you?'

I had stopped liking Kiki's kisses. He had become possessive and I began to feel trapped. When I was invited to parties he insisted on coming too, and wanted me to dance only with him. In the etiquette of the time, if another man tapped him on the shoulder while we were dancing, Kiki had to surrender me to that man. When that happened he sat by himself sulking.

'You don't love me anymore,' he said one night as we walked home from a party. When I ignored him, he stopped in front of a steel power pole and banged his head on it, so that the pole pinged loudly. I kept walking, feeling scared.

Another night he followed me into my bedroom after we had come home from a party. We argued because I had been dancing and talking with other male friends. 'If you don't love me I'll kill myself,' he said. He always wore a small *keris*, a traditional Javanese dagger, and he pulled it from his belt and slashed it twice across his chest. I screamed, waking my parents and the boarders who all came running and tried to calm Kiki. His shirt was torn and bloody, but he refused Ibu's entreaties to consult a doctor. She applied iodine antiseptic to the cuts, which seemed little more than scratches once the bleeding stopped.

Kiki once told me that, before he started going out with me, he had discovered that a student who boarded with my parents had also fallen in love with me. Kiki had confronted his rival and they played a game of chess, with me as the prize. Kiki won and his rival withdrew.

I was angry. Did he tell me this to establish his ownership? I am not a doll, I thought, to be won in a game.

'You'll be my wife, Yen,' said Kiki. 'So you have to learn how to be a proper wife and obey your husband. You have to learn to be a good housekeeper and a good cook. You must stay away from other men.'

I felt he was trying to mould me into the shape he wanted. Rebellion stirred in my heart.

'Do you have any contact with Cheppy?' Kiki demanded one day.

'Sometimes.'

He was livid. 'How?'

'He writes me letters.'

'Love letters! How disgusting. Show me.'

'No.'

But Kiki insisted and forced me bring out Cheppy's letters and rip them up. The world became darker as I looked at the torn scraps of paper. What was there to live for now that the last connection to the boy I loved had been destroyed?

Kiki was also jealous of Ken, an Australian economist, who had become a good friend of our family. Ken came to Jakarta as part of the Colombo Plan and lived in a unit across the street from us. Each time he returned from leave in Australia he bought Ibu a bottle of brandy, which she used when making strange cakes from recipes in the *Women's Weekly* magazines that Ken also gave her. He often had dinner at our place and, while I liked

Ken, there was no reason for Kiki to be jealous.

When Ken treated my parents and me to dinner at a Chinese restaurant, Kiki, a strong Muslim, questioned me about it. 'You ate pork,' he said.

'No.'

'But all the food and utensils are contaminated. It means that if I kiss you it will be the same as kissing a pig.'

I turned away in disgust. Why did I have to put up with Kiki? I longed for my handsome Cheppy, but knew that if I left Kiki and went back to the boy I loved, my parents would withhold their blessings.

Now every day seemed worse. Kiki was always jealous and there were frequent quarrels or threats to harm himself. I was trying to do well in Grade Twelve so that I could go to university, but my results were falling.

The feeling of being torn apart kept me awake. 'I can't stand it anymore,' I thought. The house was dark and quiet as I crept into the dining room, opened the cupboard and took out the brandy Ken had given us. I sat at the table, put the bottle to my lips and drank quickly in big gulps. It was my first drink of alcohol and it tasted vile but I took more swigs. When the bottle was half empty the world began spinning and I put my head down on the table.

The next thing I knew, someone was shaking me. 'Agan Wenny, Agan Wenny.' I didn't want to wake up. Then I heard screaming – our servant Bi Uju had risen early in the morning and found me collapsed at the table. Her screams woke Ibu, who hurried out as I was trying to sit up, still dizzy and confused.

'What's this?' demanded Ibu, picking up the bottle. 'What have you done, you stupid, crazy girl?'

Then everyone was there – Bapak, my sisters and brother, the three boarders, the servants and Si Belang, our cat. I could not speak. My parents helped me stand up and stagger to my bedroom as I tried not to vomit. Ibu asked Bi Uju to make hot tea.

For several weeks my parents treated me carefully and affectionately and Ibu prepared my favourite foods. No one mentioned the brandy.

My schoolwork was still suffering, I was desperately unhappy and Kiki had become unbearable. When he was angry or wanted to make fun of me he said I had been kissed by a priest with buckteeth.

One night my father sat with me on the terrace as I wept. 'Kiki is a good man,' I said. 'He loves me and says he wants the best for me. But he's trying to change me into a different person. "Wenny do this, Wenny do that." I have no freedom. He wants total control and when he doesn't get his own way he throws a tantrum.'

Bapak nodded. 'I've been worried,' he said. 'Especially after he cut himself with the keris. Just break it off if you are not happy. You are still young. You should mingle, meet different men and observe their personalities. Find out who is of good character. That way you'll have a larger view and you can see which one is most compatible with you.'

'But Ibu will be upset because she likes Kiki.'

'Don't worry about Ibu. You are the person making the decision.'

Because I was afraid of Kiki I had to prepare myself to tell him our relationship was over. He was enraged. 'You are for me,' he said. 'I am for you. You are my ideal future wife.'

'It's finished,' I said. 'I never want to see you again.'

Kiki kept coming back. It was a tradition in our household to have a daily meal with the whole family and the boarders, and Ibu always made Kiki welcome at this meal. Sometimes I left the table and went to my room. Even after Kiki eventually found another girlfriend he continued to visit my family and to watch me from a distance.

Now that I had freed myself from Kiki my life and school results picked up. I was spending more time with Mas Irwan, a boy I had met at the volley ball club in Grade Eleven. Irwan was training to be a diplomat and he hoped to be posted to Germany. At Santa Ursula, German was the language I had most difficulty with so Mas Irwan came to help me every Sunday. He was gentle, not aggressive like Kiki. At first we were like brother and sister, but then I began to notice how attentive and handsome he was, and looked forward to Sundays when Mas Irwan now stayed at our place for the whole day. In the morning I felt excited as I prepared his favourite food – *kue tape singkong*, fermented cassava cakes, and bread and butter pudding.

He invited me to meet his brother who lived in Grogol. We travelled by becak and, when there was a sudden downpour, the becak driver lowered the plastic cover making us invisible to the outside world. Mas Irwan put his arm around me and said, 'I love you.'

With the rain beating down on our private cocoon we kissed. My heart filled with happiness – now I had found the love of my life.

His brother and sister-in-law welcomed me warmly as if I was already one of their family. Later we visited his parents and sister in Yogyakarta, and they also embraced me. They were a refined, noble family, but very natural and loving. My mother now accepted that Mas Irwan was a better choice than Kiki, and accompanied us on our visit to Yogya, combining it with a batik-buying expedition.

Irwan and I planned our future lives together. We would wait until he knew for sure that he was appointed to the embassy in Germany, and then we would marry and honeymoon in Italy. I loved Italy and had always wanted to go there. We would visit the Coliseum in Rome, ride a gondola in Venice then travel through Switzerland to his post in Bonn.

I was proud of Mas Irwan. He took me to receptions at the foreign affairs department and when he introduced me to the Foreign Minister as his future wife I was filled with happiness.

I sat for the University of Indonesia entrance exams and was offered places in three faculties – Law, Letters and Medicine, the latter to study psychology. I couldn't decide which offer to accept, so my father arranged a career counselling session with a professor in the psychology department, who advised letters because I was good at languages. My father also wanted me to study in this field. But by now I had noticed that the law students were a lively lot, and many of my friends from Santa Ursula were enrolling in the law faculty. The people interested in letters and psychology seemed dull. And if I graduated in literature, what profession could I take up? I foresaw a boring future on that path and so decided that I wanted to be a judge, and I enrolled to study law.

Of course, I knew that once we married, I would follow Mas Irwan on his diplomatic postings and would have little opportunity to work in my profession. But my father had always said that I needed a degree so that I would not be forced to depend on my husband. Back in Indonesia between postings, I could work if I wanted to, and if something happened to Mas Irwan I would be able to earn my own living.

At least that's what I told myself. I was much more likely to become a full time housewife than have a career. In that era, the middle-class ideal for women was the same as in Western countries – they were expected to give up their career when they married and devote themselves to managing the household. In reality I was studying for a degree in order to have high status among the embassy wives, which would be good for Mas Irwan in his career.

Yet I still dreamed of becoming a judge.

CHAPTER 15
University

> I aspired to go on to higher education. But because of the world economic situation, my father was unable to send me to school in Jakarta – too expensive. I felt small in comparison to people who had graduated from universities. To get over my inferiority complex, I had the intention, the drive to lift myself up, so that I was never the lesser in any situation.
> —Achdiat Karta Mihardja, *On the Record: Indonesian Literary Figures*

Seniors mixed their brew in buckets, throwing in anything that was noxious – mainly cod liver oil and old eggs. They removed the chairs from the main hall and covered the tiled floor with this slime. Then all the freshers had to 'swim', which actually meant we had to slide from one end of the hall to the other, while the seniors poured more of the vile mixture into our hair.

We were being initiated into IMADA, the Jakarta University Students Association. The president was my cousin Arifin, who had invited me to join. Initiation week was relentless. Every morning at five we gathered in the park for roll call. On the first day we were given our two 'attributes' – a tall cylindrical hat made from light blue cardboard, and a placard to hang around our necks with the name by which we would be known for the week – names like *Pencopet,* Pickpocket, or *Buaya Darat,* Womaniser. I was called *Kupu-kupu Galur,* Butterfly of Galur, our suburb. I hated the name because it sounded like *kupu-kupu malam,* butterfly of the night, a prostitute. Wearing that name every day, being called that name by seniors, was destructive to my ego.

Make-up was forbidden, boys' heads were shaved and girls were forced to make thirty or forty small plaits in their hair, tied with bright green ribbons, in order to look silly. We had to wear our attributes constantly for the week so that the embarrassment could make us stronger.

Interrogation was the most humiliating. The seniors blindfolded us and forced us to squat down and waddle like ducks around the field while they bombarded us with questions and abused us for our answers. '*Kupu-kupu Galur*, would you like to go on a date with me?' Of course both answers were wrong. Not waddling properly, or falling over, drew more abuse, and by the end many freshers were in tears.

We were also given a book in which we had to collect a hundred signatures of seniors. Each time we begged for a signature was another opportunity for more silly questions and humiliation.

Initiation was supposed to eliminate sookiness and make us strong mentally so that we could face future challenges with confidence. The program was rigorous. To get from home to roll call by five o'clock I would have to rise early enough to shower, put the ridiculous plaits in my hair, grab something for lunch, and peddle to the university. We were on the go until nine o'clock at night, and then I peddled back home and fell into bed. Sleep deprived and stressed from continual humiliation, my body eventually caved in, and late on Friday I fainted. An ambulance rushed me to hospital, where a doctor simply prescribed rest. The senior who took me home told me to take Saturday off, but to be sure to return for roll call on Sunday.

On Saturday afternoon Mas Untung, a family friend, visited us. He was a young man who was back in Jakarta after completing an economics degree in Melbourne. By now I had completely recovered and Mas Untung said, 'Let's go to the Yacht Club.' I didn't think my parents would let me go out at such short notice, but they agreed, perhaps because they knew him well and trusted him. I told Mas Irwan, who was visiting our house. 'Okay, have a good time,' he said.

I was taken aback. You should be strong, I thought, and say no, I am your boyfriend, not Mas Untung. But then I remembered that the debonair Mas Untung was good fun, and we spent the night dancing at the Yacht Club.

Someone dobbed me in. The next morning at roll call, my cousin President Arifin described my crime in vivid detail. All the seniors gathered around me, spitting out abuse. 'Traitor,' they yelled. 'Deserting your fellow students, going out with boys. Shame on you! Getting out of initiation to go dancing!' The more they abused me the more I cried, and the more I cried, the wilder they became.

This attack was the hardest thing to accept. I rationalised that much of the initiation was good for me and made me tougher. But the abuse that Sunday morning was too much. The harshness of initiation attracted criticism and my year was the last in which the full program was to be allowed.

On the final evening we gathered in the field in our party clothes, make-up and usual hair style. We stood in front of a bonfire and sang, 'Goodbye to initiation, goodbye to hardship'. As our names were called we took off our attributes – our hat and name placard – and threw them into the fire. This signified not only the end of our humiliation, but also our forgiveness of the seniors for their treatment of us.

'Now it's your turn,' Arifin said. 'We know we treated you badly, so now you can attack us. You can say whatever you like to us, and we won't say a word.'

We didn't respond. Many of us were crying. We had been moved by the ceremony and now it was time to forgive and move on. The president presented each of us with a certificate and an IMADA beret.

A new camaraderie arose between seniors and initiates. People fell in love, with several senior men having met their future wives at initiation. At the party that followed the ceremony everyone was in high spirits, dancing and singing all night long.

Compared to IMADA, initiation into the Faculty of Law was mild. We still had to wear attributes, attend interrogation sessions and collect signatures from seniors and lecturers, but our attribute-names weren't as nasty, there was less abuse, and no cod liver oil.

Lectures had barely started when they stopped again for Dies Natalis, the anniversary of the founding of the University of Indonesia in February 1950, nine years earlier. Dies Natalis was a week of activities – ceremonies, cultural events, parties and sporting contests between the five faculties. I was nominated as the Law Faculty candidate for University Queen and, after we were judged on general knowledge, ballroom dancing and our clothing, I was chosen to be the year's Queen. I now played a role in the celebrations – kicking the ball to start the inter-faculty soccer competition, and later presenting the sporting trophies. The highlight of the week would be a cultural night at Istana Negara, the state palace, and together with the Queen of Initiation, Nurbani Yusuf, I was expected to accompany President Sukarno during the event.

My first experience of Sukarno had been when I was four and we lived near my parents' friend, the painter Basoeki Abdullah. Sukarno often came to Basoeki's house for a meal and to talk about art, and this is when Sukarno and my father became friends. Sukarno was also attracted to my mother – he was attracted to every beautiful woman – and, having an artistic bent himself, once sketched her.

Ibu had sometimes taken me with her when she visited Sukarno's wife, Ibu Inggit, and each time I saw tears on Bu Inggit's cheeks. My mother would send me to another room while they talked. When I was older my mother told me that the tears were because Sukarno wanted to marry their adopted daughter, seventeen year old Fatmawati, while keeping Inggit as his main wife. Feeling betrayed and unable to accept polygamy, she refused. They divorced and Sukarno exchanged a wife who was fourteen years older than himself for one twenty-five years younger. The Indonesian people grew to love Fatmawati.

In 1954, Sukarno married again, choosing one of his many mistresses, Hartini. Fatmawati was enraged and left the palace to live apart from him, while retaining the status of first wife and title of Ibu Negara, Mother of the Nation.

Everyone who heard that I was to have a role at the cultural night warned me: 'Wenny, you'll be in danger. Don't let him hook you.' Sukarno's passion for seducing young women was famous. As my mother dressed me for the evening, Mochtar Lubis and Tante Hally arrived. Mochtar was still under house arrest but the guards now allowed him to leave his house for short trips. 'What's going on?' he asked.

'Wenny's going to the palace to meet the President,' said Ibu.

'Wenny will have an audience with Bung Karno?' Mochtar said. 'Be careful!'

But I wasn't worried about the President. I had already danced with him. A week earlier he had cut the ribbon to open Dies Natalis and then pulled me onto the floor for *Tari Lenso*, a traditional dance that Culture Minister Priyono had instructed my father's office to promote as an alternative to Western dancing. That encounter was brief but now I would spend more time with him and see the inside of the palace.

The palace complex includes Istana Negara, where state events and receptions are held, and Istana Merdeka, the presidential residence which faces the square where I had sat on my father's shoulders and shouted 'Merdeka' when Sukarno returned to Jakarta in 1949. In our role as queens, Nurbani and I accompanied the two leaders of the Student Council through the immaculate gardens between the two palaces to meet Sukarno and his children. I looked around in wonder at the tall ceilings, massive chandeliers and beautiful paintings in the President's home, but I felt emptiness. There was no mother in the palace. Four of Sukarno and Fatmawati's five children were present. Megawati had just turned twelve and the youngest, Guruh, was six. I wondered if they lived in the palace without their mother, or in Kebayoran without their father.

We escorted the President and his children back to Istana Negara for the cultural night. There we sat in the front row to watch the show, Nurbani on Sukarno's left and I on his right. Behind us sat state ministers, dignitaries, and university staff and students.

I admired Sukarno's physique and manliness, his calmness, his engaging smile. As dancers from Maluku filled the stage he put his hand on mine and held it. He asked me about my faculty, and I told him about my plans to be a judge.

'Who is your father?' he asked.

'Achdiat Karta Mihardja.'

He looked at me closely. 'Ah, you are the daughter of Achdiat and Tati.'

Then his eyes became distant. He turned and began chatting with Nurbani.

President Sukarno (centre) flanked by Nurbani Yusuf, Wenny Achdiat and the Student Council leaders

I loved university and somehow fitted the classes in amongst all the social activities.

One day I returned home from lectures to find a visitor waiting to see me. The young woman introduced herself as Lin. 'Wenny, I know about you from Cheppy. Please, I would like you to release Cheppy.'

Surprised, I said, 'I haven't seen him for years.'

'He still loves you. He has never forgotten you and never stopped loving you. He wants to keep waiting for you. Wenny, I've loved him since I was in high school. I can't live without him.'

Tears streamed down Lin's cheeks. 'Please, Wenny, write a letter to him. Tell him there is no hope, no matter how long he waits for you. Tell him it will never happen.'

Now I was crying. Believing that Lin was a good person who loved Cheppy, I took my pad and wrote to him: 'Forget about me. I now have a boyfriend, and I truly love him. We are planning to marry. Lin is a beautiful person. I hope you will be with her.' The letter took a long time to write, but Lin waited patiently. When I handed it to her she hugged me.

That night I prayed for Cheppy and Lin. I admired her for having the courage to come to my home to ask for the letter. A year later my uncle told me they had married.

Initiation parties, Dies Natalis parties, then parties every Saturday night. Dances, dinners, birthday parties. I had become well-known because I was the University Queen, and now I had two or three invitations every week.

The only problem was my parents' curfew. I had to be home by eleven when the party was at its peak, so before I went out I turned the lounge room clock back an hour. But one night as I tiptoed in through the darkened lounge room the light came on, revealing my grim-faced parents. The game was up, and they grounded me for a month.

But my parents didn't know what else I got up to – about Ami, the son of the Minister for Education and Culture who was teaching me to drive in his father's ministerial car. About Eddie, who took us to Puncak – how happy we were, screaming and laughing as we coasted at high speed back down the mountain. And Bagio who invited me home to meet his mother, and his chimpanzee that sat at the table and ate with us. Bagio asked me to christen the boat his parents had bought him, and I pitched the bottle with such force that glass and champagne showered the crowd.

Without a steady boyfriend I could have fun with all these fellow students. But wait – I did have a boyfriend – Mas Irwan. We had been together since Grade Twelve and planned to marry, although he wanted to wait until he knew when he was going to be posted to Germany. Both our families blessed our relationship. We were in love.

But Mas Irwan was not like Kiki who had flown into a rage if I danced with another man. Mas Irwan was not jealous at all. By the time he thought of inviting me out, another man had always asked me first. When I went sailing with Bagio or Ami took me driving in his father's car, Mas Irwan didn't seem to mind. He said to have a good time as he had when Mas Untung took me dancing at the Yacht Club.

Sometimes I thought I had become too independent, and that Irwan should take control and stop me being so wild. But he was not an assertive man. On another night when the always stylish Mas Untung had come to take my parents, Mas Irwan and me to the Yacht Club, he pointed to Irwan and said, laughing, 'You've made your tie too short.' Irwan just smiled. I was the one who felt humiliated. Defend yourself, I thought.

My first year at university was a whirl of partying and dancing and escapades, such as stealing the American, British and Japanese flags from outside an international conference while the guards looked on, perplexed by our ministerial car. And Mas Irwan was slowly slipping into the background of my life.

My year came to a predictable end. I passed only three of my five subjects. I had failed the year.

CHAPTER 16
Exile

> A guling is a pillow … more than one metre long, cylindrical. Its diameter is just right for hugging. It's everywhere on Indonesian beds. You can cry with it and sleep with it.
> —*Sleeping with a Guling* Facebook Page

I began my second year determined to work hard, repeating the subjects I'd failed and studying to do well in the new subjects. One day I was sitting in the law lecture room when I saw my father's driver standing outside. Strange, I thought, usually he waits in the car. When I went out, he said he had to take me to my father's office at the Jakarta Division of Culture.

When I arrived, Bapak was dictating to his secretary who gave me a friendly hello as she went out. My father looked grim. 'Please sit down,' he said politely, as if I was a stranger. There is something wrong with me, I thought. I sat down across the desk from him and waited.

There was a silence. Then he said, 'Ibu and I are very upset that you failed first year.'

I knew that. We'd already talked about it, and I'd promised this year would be different.

'Your mother is very angry,' he went on. 'She worked hard in the batik business and taking in boarders to make money to send you to university. And instead of studying you went out partying.'

'Bapak, I won't do that anymore. This year I will study. I've already started.'

He ignored me. 'It doesn't matter how hard we have to work to send our children to university. My aspiration is for all of my children to be independent regardless of whether they are male or female. To be independent, higher education is essential.'

I strongly believed this too and said so. There was another silence and then he said, 'You will go to Yogya.'

I stared at him in shock. Yogyakarta made no sense at all.

'You'll do the Standard Training Course at the Ford Foundation Teachers' College. You'll be an English teacher.'

A feeling of horror gripped me. Yogya was old-fashioned, no place for a modern city girl. 'Bapak, please, I want to finish law.'

'I've already arranged it, so you have no choice. It's the best college in the country for English teachers. Last night we met with Irwan and he recommended Yogya too.'

'Mas Irwan? He didn't say anything to me about it.'

'In Jakarta there are too many distractions, too many parties and men asking you out. Yogya is a safe city. People are more polite and refined there. You'll stay in the student *asrama* which is very strict, so you won't be going to any parties. It's because you went to all those parties that you failed. You didn't demonstrate that you were serious about study. It was only party, party, party.'

I was crying. This was the worst thing that could happen. 'Bapak, please don't send me to Yogya. I promise you, this year I'll study hard and pass.'

'There's no choice. The decision's been made.'

He buzzed his secretary and asked her to call the driver to take me home.

That afternoon Mas Irwan calmly faced the storm of my anger. 'It's for your own good,' he said. 'It's for the benefit of our future.'

'It's not,' I cried. 'Yogya will be horrible. I'll be lonely and unhappy.'

'But my parents and sisters are there. They'll look after you. You'll be safe in Yogya. People are gentle and refined there. In Jakarta everyone is too aggressive.'

'Why didn't you talk to me about it instead of meeting with my parents behind my back?'

'It's the right thing to do,' he said. 'In Jakarta you have too many admirers.'

'Mas, why weren't you strong? Why didn't you stop me running wild? It all started when I was University Queen. You saw all those boys chasing me. You should have married me instead of sending me to Yogya.'

'I'm being strong now.'

'No, you didn't want to face me so you talked to my parents. Why don't we just get married? We've known each other for three years. That's long enough.'

'But remember our plans. We have to wait until my appointment. Think of us in a gondola.'

'I'm not going to Yogya,' I told myself, so I deliberately used wrong answers in the English language written test for entry to the teachers' college. But in the oral test it was clear that my English was fluent. Surprised by the disparity between written and oral scores, the testers passed me.

I was going to Yogya, after all. I was filled with dread, but nothing prepared me for the shock of the asrama, the student hostel.

I looked at the paint flaking off the walls, the crumbling cement floor, the cramped space between the beds, and the thick layer of dust on everything. For ten years I had cherished my own room, which had been big enough for dancer Hazel Chung to practise her mid-air leg splits.

My mother saw my tears. 'Just be patient,' she said. 'It will only be for three years. Not long.'

'The others haven't arrived yet,' said Ibu Asrama, the manager. 'You have first choice. Which bed would you like?'

On the right was a double bunk bed, but I didn't want anyone sleeping above me, so I pointed to the single bed on the left.

After Ibu caught the train back to Jakarta I returned to the asrama and met my roommates, Liliek and Umi, who seemed happy with the bunk bed. Then Ibu Asrama called the new boarders to a meeting to give us the rules. Curfew was at ten o'clock. No visitors were allowed in the asrama, and instead we were to meet guests on the 'porch', a large, raised open pavilion in the garden between the asrama and the classrooms.

'Every night before you go to bed,' she said, 'Sprinkle

water on the cement floor to keep the dust down while you're sleeping.'

But I didn't sleep that night – the mattress was hard, the pillow thin, my spirit crushed. In the morning Liliek and Umi reported on how well they'd slept.

At the bathroom door we heard voices and knocked. The door opened to reveal Ita, naked and wet, and behind her two other seniors dipper bathing. I took a step back, stunned. It was one large room with no privacy. I had never shared a bathroom before.

Liliek and Umi entered. 'Come in,' Ita called to me. 'Don't be shy.'

I edged in and backed into a corner, away from the *bak mandi*, the open tank that held water for dipper baths. Liliek and Umi undressed and began their baths.

The three seniors turned their attention to me, the only one still fully clothed. They stood in front of me laughing and yelling, 'Come on, don't be shy. We're all women here.'

'This is an asrama,' said Ita. 'We always share everything.'

I pulled my pyjamas off. Ita pushed me side on against the wall and picked up a pen. 'Let's see how you compare.'

There were several lines on the wall shaped like breasts. 'No,' I yelled, and pulled away. The others shrieked with laughter. I quickly took my bath in a fog of humiliation. It felt as if I was being initiated again.

Mr Moody from New Zealand took our first class. Later an American lecturer shocked us with talk of eating 'hot dogs'. The college had a modern, well-equipped language lab, and the lecturers were skilled, but I was not interested. I wanted to be a judge, not a teacher.

After classes Liliek and I walked to Jalan Malioboro and I bought a *guling*, the large cylindrical pillow also known as a 'Dutch wife.' That night I fell asleep hugging my guling.

My spirits did not improve. I hated the backwardness of Yogya. In Jakarta I'd always worn short sleeves, but here people pointed at my bare arms and whispered. Even worse – much,

much worse – than conservative attitudes, run-down rooms and lack of privacy was the food. Ibu Asrama skimped on meals, and every dish, whether salad, stir-fry, soup, sambal or curry, consisted mostly of green papaya, sometimes flavoured by smelly overripe *tempe*, fermented soya bean cake.

By the end of the first week I knew I couldn't put up with the life there anymore so I caught the night train, arriving back in Jakarta at six o'clock on Saturday morning. My parents reacted with fury, and Ibu took me back to Yogya the next day.

I decided that to survive I would have to make the best of it. I felt attacked, with no privacy or freedom, but if I didn't join together with the others, I would become isolated, so I tried to make myself fit in.

It was hard. 'We always share everything,' Ita had said in the bathroom, and I did like sharing food. But I was not good at sharing other things. Being from Jakarta, I had stylish clothes, and other students began to borrow them – blouses, skirts, shoes, handbags, jewellery. They always gave them back, but one by one my fancy knickers and bras disappeared from my cupboard.

I wrote to Mas Irwan every week, begging him to tell my parents to let me come home. He always wrote back saying, 'No, please be patient. It is safer for you in Yogya. Soon we will celebrate our love with a beautiful wedding. And then we will ride in a gondola.'

On Saturday nights boarders were allowed to go out. The others had all found boyfriends but every Saturday night I stayed home and sat with Ibu Asrama on the porch while she embroidered and I wrote to Mas Irwan. I have never known such boredom.

Hariyadi, a handsome second-year student, turned up one Saturday night to see Ibu Asrama – or so he said. He chatted with us and I told him I was writing to my boyfriend in Jakarta. He dropped in for a chat again the following week, and on his third visit, he said, 'Would you like to go to a movie?'

'Just be home by ten,' said Ibu Asrama.

We walked to Jalan Malioboro for dinner and a movie. We

went out again the next week, and the week after that.

On our fourth date we kissed. After Hariyadi left me back at the asrama I sat down by myself at the meal table outside our rooms and wrote to Mas Irwan, telling him exactly what had happened. 'I have betrayed you,' I said. 'So we must end our relationship. It is better to be honest now, and then you'll be able to meet another girl who will be a better wife for you than I would have been.'

I wrote a long letter, tears of guilt at my disloyalty falling on my cheeks. But I thought of kissing Hariyadi and smiled through my tears, feeling the excitement of being with my new, good-looking boyfriend. I forced myself to return to the letter. 'Our relationship was so beautiful and it was blessed by both our families. It was like a perfect crystal. But now I have broken the crystal, and it can never be the same.'

I looked out at the garden and the papaya trees in the shadows. Fresh tears came. What had I done? I was giving up a good man who loved me, whose family loved me. But then I thought of what Mas Irwan had done, and I returned to the letter. 'We are not the right match to marry. I need a man who is strong. You saw that many boys liked me, but instead of marrying me, you met with my parents and sent me to Yogya. You should have acted to bring us together, not to send me away to where I'm lonely and mixed up in an old-fashioned city. I'm with Hariyadi now. There is no future for you and me together.'

Mas Irwan didn't believe me. While I was home for the holidays we talked. 'We can't continue,' I said. 'It's not nice that I went out with Hariyadi while I was still bound to you. We had better go our separate ways.'

My mother was upset that I had broken off with Mas Irwan because she didn't want to lose him as a son-in-law. 'If you don't like him,' said Ibu, 'how about you just give him to Ati.'

Hariyadi made Yogya a little easier to bear. On Saturday mornings we breakfasted on *gudeg*, jackfruit cooked in coconut milk and spices, at the warung near the railway station, then we pedalled our bicycles up to Kaliurang, high on the slopes of

Gunung Merapi, one of Java's most active volcanoes.

Hariyadi was a devout Muslim from Pekalongan, and he taught me how to pray according to Islam. He gave me a small book that showed each movement and the reading associated with it, and often came to the asrama and tested me. Even when we went out to dinner and a movie on Saturday nights, as we rode to Jalan Malioboro in the becak, he assessed me: 'When you make this movement, what do you say?'

I stumbled through the unfamiliar Arabic.

'And what does it mean?'

Hariyadi was a better teacher than Kiki, and eventually I learnt to pray five times a day.

Boarders at the asrama polarised into two groups: big-city girls from Jakarta, Surabaya and Bali who liked to party, and small-town girls, who were conservative and liked to study and who hated the city girls for being too wild. Liliek and I were big-city girls. So was Ita, who had taunted me in the bathroom but was now a friend.

We all complained about the food, especially the never ending green papaya, and the city girls had a crisis meeting. I had a plan and in the middle of the night we crept out and used a bamboo pole to knock all the fruit off the papaya trees beside the asrama.

When we were found out, the whole college was in uproar with everyone talking about us: 'Those big-city girls, how dare they do that. They're too wild.' The College Director told us we would be expelled if we misbehaved again. But I told him that our parents were paying more for us to stay in an asrama rather than a homestay because we had been promised better food, yet Ibu Asrama gave us terrible food. As a result she was also warned, and the meals improved.

Good food is so important to me that I often wrote to my mother, telling her I needed a new book or had lost my pen, and when she sent money I gave it to Ibu Asrama to buy chicken and treats for all the boarders. Ibu Asrama liked this arrangement.

The ten o'clock curfew did not give Hariyadi and me

enough time to see a movie and also relax over a meal at a warung so I had found ways around it. After ten Ibu Asrama looked through each of the windows to check if we were in bed. Before going out I arranged a cover over my guling to make it look as if I was there, and made a time for one of the other girls to let me in the gate. Then I started giving Ibu Asrama gifts and cultivating her friendship, and she became much less strict about the curfew.

During my second year in Yogya I heard that the University of Indonesia had opened a Faculty of Education. I immediately enrolled and fled back to Jakarta. With credit from first year law and teachers college, it would not take long to complete a Bachelor of Education.

Hariyadi visited me in Jakarta and confessed that for years he had been engaged. It had been arranged by his parents together with the family of the girl. 'I'm sorry,' he said. 'I have to get married to her. There's no way out.'

Although he had deceived me I was not too hurt. I'd left Yogya and the asrama behind and was now in Jakarta with my parents, my own room, and my old friends close by. And I knew that marrying Hariyadi and living in the Muslim enclave in Pekalongan would have been impossible. Amicably, we broke off our relationship.

CHAPTER 17
Back to the Revolution

> [In Europe, the United States and Australia] I found myself still in the grip of ... complexes which at times made me feel quite uneasy, as if I was an ugly duckling surrounded by graceful peacocks and ferocious hawks.
> —Achdiat Karta Mihardja, *Another Human Race*

In early 1959, when I had danced the tari lenso with President Sukarno and escorted him to the Dies Natalis cultural night, I was not aware that he was on the threshold of achieving the power he wanted. Then for two years I had been too engrossed in parties and boys, or feeling sorry for myself in Yogya, to notice the changes he was making to the country, changes that would put many people in danger, including my father.

The struggle to find the best way to govern Indonesia dated back to the proclamation of Independence in 1945. The first draft of the constitution gave most power to the President, but subsequent drafts put government in the hands of a cabinet of ministers, subject to the confidence of parliament, with the presidential role mainly a ceremonial one. Efforts to forge a final constitution had reached a stalemate on the question of an Islamic versus a secular state.

With the cabinet and party system in chaos, Sukarno's power had grown. For two years he had continued manoeuvring to implement his concept of Guided Democracy. In July 1959 he struck, restoring the 1945 constitution by presidential decree, thereby doing away with parliamentary democracy and shifting executive power to himself. A month later he presented his political manifesto in his Independence Day address, "The Rediscovery of our Revolution". He claimed that Guided Democracy would rebuild the revolutionary spirit, which had been lost in the past decade. His manifesto would show people how to identify with the Indonesian Revolution, which was not a single event, but a continuing transformation in all spheres – government, economy, and culture.

Sukarno now ruled by decree, referring to himself as "the Great Leader of the Revolution", and "the Mouthpiece of the Indonesian People". He announced that political parties would only be allowed to exist if they upheld the 1945 constitution, and he gave himself the power to abolish political organisations. He dismissed parliament when it rejected his budget, and established the People's Representative Council in its place, selecting members himself who represented the various groups within Indonesian society.

Sukarno developed his manifesto further in his 1960 Independence Day speech, "An Angel Sweeping Down from the Sky: The March of our Revolution". 'Our democracy is not a battlefield of opponents,' he said. 'Our democracy is nothing less than a search for synthesis.' He argued that apparently antagonistic ideologies and religions could sit together within an Indonesian world view, and coined the acronym NASAKOM based on the names of the three major forces of nationalism, religion and communism which, he said, were striving for the same goals of freedom and socialism: '… NASAKOM is a progressive necessity of the Indonesian revolution. Whoever is opposed to NASAKOM is not progressive! Whoever is against NASAKOM in reality cripples the revolution … is even counter-revolutionary.'

'What is he thinking?' cried Achdiat. 'How can he expect religious people to accept the communists as bedfellows? He thinks he can force them to unite, but he's been carried away by his own ego.'

Indeed, bitter hatred divided the three most powerful political factions – the military (representing nationalism), Islam and the Communist Party. But Sukarno acted as a *dalang*, a puppet-master, maintaining the balance of power between the three. NASAKOM was now part of the new national ideology, in which it was compulsory to believe, but the hatreds did not go away, and the factions bided their time.

The political climate became as oppressive as it had been during the Dutch and Japanese periods. Dissenters were imprisoned or exiled, and newspapers offering alternative views censored. The Indonesian Socialist Party had vigorously campaigned against Guided Democracy, but now Sukarno banned the party for its connection to the regional rebellions.

My father did not talk to me about this, but looking back I can imagine him feeling increasingly unsafe in occupying a prominent government position while being a member of the Socialist Party. He may also have worried about the rising power of LEKRA, the Institute of People's Culture, the art and literature arm of the Indonesian Communist Party. LEKRA demanded that all art must stick to socialist realism, supporting the political struggle as defined by Marxism. They attacked writers and artists who did not follow this line and called for their works to be censored. Achdiat had attended LEKRA meetings in the early fifties, but withdrew from the organisation when it became more communist. Although he rejected the idea of "art for art's sake" – his novels and stories engaged with society and politics – he also believed in freedom, and that artists and writers should not be bound to any one ideology. He worried about LEKRA's authoritarianism and the viciousness of its attacks on dissenters such as his friend HB Jassin, the critic and essayist with whom we had stayed during the revolution.

Indonesian society became more restrictive in other ways. Sukarno and LEKRA had long agreed on the need to stop American cultural penetration in the form of movies and music. Sukarno saw the popularity of Western music and dance in the fifties as an affront to Indonesian identity. LEKRA called for the banning of "cultural imperialism" and arranged events at which Elvis Presley records were destroyed.

While my father didn't care for Elvis, he loved ballroom dancing, and he and Ibu often went out and danced all night, or invited their friends for dance parties at our house. Whenever Bapak or one of his siblings had a birthday they held a big party in Bandung, with my grandmother enjoying the music and watching her children and grandchildren dancing the waltz, quickstep, foxtrot, jive and cha-cha-cha. How would it look for Bapak if word got out that he had spent the night dancing to imperialist tunes instead of doing the Indonesian social dances his office was supposed to promote?

The trends toward political, artistic and cultural repression worried Bapak to the extent that he began to talk to some of his friends about working in another country. Having enjoyed his second job lecturing at the University of Indonesia, he looked for a similar position overseas. He had known Affandi, Indonesia's foremost Expressionist painter, since they taught together at Taman Siswa school in the thirties. Affandi had a long association with India and through his contacts arranged an offer of a lectureship at a university in New Delhi. Bapak was delighted – it was exactly what he wanted. But Ibu turned up her nose. 'India is still in Asia,' she said. 'We might as well stay in Jakarta.'

Anthony Johns, from the Australian National University (ANU), had visited Bapak in 1959 and this connection led to an offer of a position teaching Indonesian literature and culture in Canberra. Ibu was jubilant, but my father had doubts because he had experienced racism in Sydney when he had spent six months there in the mid-fifties learning English under the Colombo Plan. Australians had also seemed so cold and inaccessible that he felt cut off from human society. He decided he would much rather go to New Delhi, but Ibu would not budge.

'You won't like Australia,' Bapak told her. 'It's full of racists. They don't want coloured people. They've got a White Australia Policy to keep Asians out. We'll be much more welcome in New Delhi.'

'I'm not going to India,' Ibu declared. 'India's dirty. Much better to go to a clean Western country.'

'Look, Tati, can't you see that the way of life will be too strange for us? We'll never feel at home there. Everybody's rushing all the time, like dogs with their tails on fire. You won't have anyone to talk to. No relatives, no friends. People there don't talk to strangers, especially not to foreigners. We will be lonely.'

'No we won't. We can make friends.'

'In New Delhi we can have four servants, same as here. In Canberra there'll be no servants at all.'

'I can cook.'

Bapak spent sleepless nights agonising over the decision.

He later wrote that what really disturbed him was his feeling of inferiority around Westerners which was the result of his education in Dutch schools, and which he had been unable to overcome despite his nationalism and his pride at being Indonesian. He doubted he could feel comfortable in a Western country, but Ibu continued to refuse to go to New Delhi.

Every day Bapak and Ibu argued. 'Don't be stupid,' said Ibu. 'Just take the job.'

In the end, Bapak agreed, mainly because the head of his department told him that he could come back to his old position if he wasn't happy in Canberra.

My siblings and I needed no encouragement. We remembered when Bapak had returned from Sydney with gifts that convinced us Australia was paradise – smart clothes in the latest fashion and four scrumptious apples. To make the apples last, the whole family ate one at a time, Ibu carefully cutting an equal slice for each of us.

I became excited about the idea of studying at the Australian National University, and wrote to ask if I could finish my education degree there. All my clothes and books were packed when a reply arrived. The university would give no credit for the course I'd almost finished – I would have to start again. This meant that I would have to complete the degree at the University of Indonesia before I could join my parents in Australia.

My sister Ati had spent a year as an exchange student in Utah in the United States, and had just returned, ill with pleurisy. The Australian embassy would not grant her a visa until she recovered, so Ibu arranged for her to stay with our uncle and aunt, Oom John and Bi Niek, until she became well enough to fly to Canberra. When, at the last minute, I decided not to go, we couldn't find anywhere for me to stay, and finally a friend of my parents offered a vacant room in their servant's quarters. Ibu had rented out our house.

In 1961 Indonesians seldom went overseas, so on departure day the international airport was crowded with our family, friends, colleagues and neighbours who had come to farewell my parents. I stood on the edge of the melee, filled with dread and regretting my decision to stay, tears running down my cheeks. While Bapak and Ibu hugged and kissed their friends, I kept looking at my watch to see how many minutes remained before my parents would be gone. In the short time I had with Bapak and Ibu, just before they boarded, I clung desperately to them. Then I watched the plane disappear, taking them out of my life.

I was in a daze, as I saw Ati get into Oom John and Bi Niek's Mercedes Benz, and watched them drive away. By then night was falling, but I could not move, until Mas Irwan, who had also come to see my parents off, led me to a becak and escorted me to my new home.

In the room I had been given I lay on my thin mattress and wept. My family had moved to another country and I was living in another family's servants' quarters. I was already vulnerable because my latest boyfriend, a doctor called Ruli, had just broken off with me, making me realise how much I must have hurt Mas Irwan and Kiki when I rejected them. I felt desolate. Why had I decided to stay? I was all alone.

But not quite. Ati would still be here for a few weeks. I could visit her and have meals there with Bi Niek and Oom John. Bi was Ibu's sister and Haji Noor had refused to acknowledge her marriage to Oom John because he was a Christian. But when their first child was born, Haji Noor came to Jakarta and gave his blessing.

Bi Niek and Oom John respected each other's religion. Bi remained Muslim but accompanied her husband to Church, while Oom always went to Bandung with her to celebrate Lebaran, the end of fasting month. Oom was an astute businessman with a large factory and immense wealth. Later I was to need his help.

Bapak wrote with good news – in Australia the family had been warmly welcomed, and their arrival was reported on television and the front page of *The Canberra Times*. The university had arranged a house in Yarralumla and after they moved in, all their neighbours brought gifts – flowers, chocolates, a jar of jam. He wrote that Ibu was happy – she made friends easily and invited them for Indonesian meals. When she woke on the first morning she had called for Bi Uju to bring coffee but, when there was no answer, she sighed, crawled out of bed and made breakfast for the family. Nuy and Fari had settled into their school. Bapak wrote that this experience of Australia was completely different from his previous one. How I longed to be with them!

In Indonesia, Sukarno was continuing the Revolution by planning an invasion of West New Guinea if Holland did not agree to hand over the territory. He ordered all university students to do one month's military training before they could sit for exams so that, if the invasion went ahead, they could be part of a paramilitary force that would follow the army in and provide security. I was appalled – I didn't want to spend a month running around a field in the hot sun. And, while I believed that the Dutch should surrender West New Guinea, I hated the idea of another war.

Each day for a month we drilled in Lapangan Banteng. Only later did I discover that as I marched, crawled, jumped and learnt to shoot, I was being watched from a car parked beside the square.

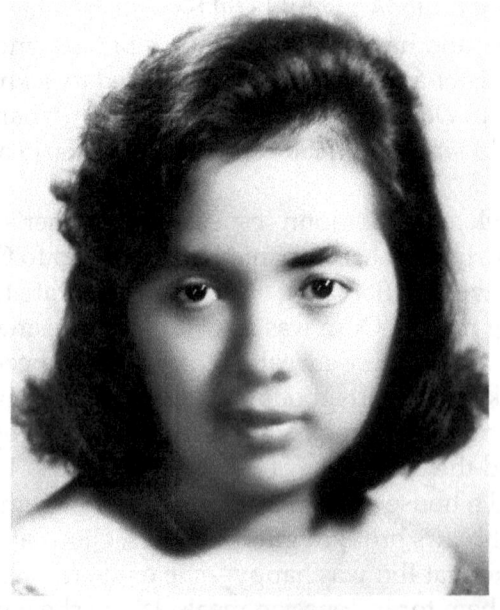

Wenny in 1961

'I can take Wenny home,' Dahlan Thalib told the friend who had brought me to tennis on his motorbike. Dahlan had a car with a driver and knew that I lived near his place.

On the way we chatted. We had only just met but I felt drawn to him. He seemed both self-assured and humble.

'What are you doing tonight?' he asked.

'Studying.'

'Studying? It's Saturday night. You need a break. Let's go to a movie at Garden Hall.'

That evening while I watched the movie, he watched me. 'I've got something important to say to you,' he whispered.

He took me to Trio Chinese Restaurant, which was famous for its fried frog legs with butter sauce. After we ordered he said, 'I want to marry you.'

I stared at him. 'You only met me a few hours ago.'

'I've known you for months.'

'How do you know me?'

'I saw you doing military drill on Lapangan Banteng. At lunch time my driver took me to the square and I watched. My friends at the university told me about you. You are the daughter of Achdiat Karta Mihardja – I studied his novel at school. Now your parents are in Australia. You've just broken up with Ruli. I know that you are my destiny.'

The pain of Ruli's rejection was still raw. I had promised myself that whoever came into my life, I would accept him without investigating his background. I did not care who proposed, I would say yes. And this was the man. Fortunately he was not a gangster. He was not one to pussyfoot around, and I liked that. My previous boyfriends had either been too aggressive, like Kiki, or too humble, like Irwan, but Dahlan seemed to have a good balance of self-assurance and humility. And he was a good prospect for a husband. After attaining a master's degree in economics from the prestigious Nommensen University in Medan he joined Stanvac, an American oil company, rising quickly to the position of sales manager.

'You are free now,' he said, putting his hand on mine. 'Will you accept my proposal?'

'I can't say yes or no.'

'Give me the address of your parents so that I can write and ask them.'

'We can't get married until I've been to Australia. I promised to join my parents after graduating. I'll stay there maybe one or two years and then come back.'

'No,' said Dahlan. 'If you go to Australia you will meet somebody else and forget me. So not one or two years there, not even one month.'

Our next outing was to be a picnic. It was raining when he picked me up and he wore an English raincoat, more stylish than the cheap plastic coats most people wore. 'You look like Sherlock Holmes,' I said.

Dahlan's chauffeur drove us to Bogor where we bought croquettes, profiteroles and *lemper*, chicken in sticky rice wrapped in banana leaf, from the famous Tan Ek Tjoan bakery. At Kebun Raya, the Bogor Botanical Gardens, we spread our picnic mat on the grass under an enormous tree. We unpacked the food and laughed when we saw that we had bought far more than we could eat. Dahlan leaned over and kissed me – our first kiss.

We ate and talked. Then I went into shock. Dahlan had farted – loudly.

'What!' I cried.

But Dahlan didn't apologise. 'Wenny, that's healthy. It's nothing to be ashamed of. We don't have to hold it in.'

'What?' I cried again. I had never experienced such vulgarity before. In Sundanese culture, farting is unforgivably rude, but as a Sumatran, Dahlan would not know that. Maybe, I thought, I should make allowances for the cultural differences. When he kissed me again I responded. But I said, 'If you want to marry me, you must never be rude like that in company. In West Java it's a no-no.'

Dahlan smiled. 'But it's healthy.'

'It's your decision.'

'Okay, I'll listen to you. It's not a big problem.'

A week later we travelled to Bandung and I introduced him to my grandparents, my aunts and uncles, and my dear great-aunt Ma Lengkong. With his engaging style and sense of humour Dahlan impressed them all.

Dahlan had written to my parents, and I had too, telling them I wanted to marry rather than join them in Canberra. Each time we met Dahlan asked if I had heard from them, but it was several months before a letter arrived with my father's approval. Later Bapak told me it had not been an easy decision to allow his daughter to marry a man he didn't know. Bapak had written to friends in Jakarta, including several investigative journalists and a manager at Stanvac, asking them to find out what they could about Dahlan. They had reported that he was a man without blemish, who would be an ideal husband for Bapak's first-born child.

For some time Dahlan had been concerned about my living conditions. He said, 'You have a home. Why don't you move back there?'

No one had yet moved into my family's house in Jalan Tembaga and only a guard was there. I thought Ibu had leased it to the air force but when I contacted the man who had arranged this, the information I discovered disturbed me.

'There's no lease agreement,' I told Dahlan. 'It was just rented privately to a Colonel in the air force. He paid Ibu a million rupiah for a year's rent, and she wrote a receipt. But no other paper work, no solicitor.'

Dahlan knew about such matters. 'Your parents are in danger of losing the house,' he said. 'It happens all the time. The colonel can just say it now belongs to him.'

'Ibu should have known better,' I said. 'But she was in a hurry. Too excited about going to Australia.'

When I wrote to Ibu, she confirmed there had been no agreement and sent me a letter of authority to reclaim the house. At the Air Force Headquarters the Colonel's secretary escorted me into his large office.

As I explained my business he stared at me intently. Then he said, 'You're pretty, aren't you?'

He walked around the desk towards me. 'Sexy. Don't talk about the house. Forget about that. Let's go to Puncak.'

He reached towards me, and I jumped up. 'Don't you dare touch me,' I yelled. 'Are you married? Who do you think I am? I'm not a cheap woman. I'm the daughter of Achdiat Karta Mihardja. I'm a university student, engaged to be married.'

The Colonel backed off retreated behind the desk. 'The million rupiah will have to be repaid,' he said. 'Can you get the money within a week?'

I was startled. How could I find that much in so short a time? But I knew I had to act. Without hesitating I said, 'Yes. But before I pay it I must have the key.'

I was shaking as I left the office.

I decided to ask Oom John if he could lend me the money. Dahlan drove me to his house.

'Okay,' said Oom John, 'I can lend you one million. When are you going to pay it back?'

'Oom, can I pay by instalment? I'll tell my mother I borrowed it from you.'

'You want to pay by instalment? What – a hundred rupiah a month?'

I was humiliated by Oom's suggestion that we wouldn't repay the loan, but I held back my anger and said, 'Oom, I'll do my best. I'll tell my parents to pay as much as possible.'

'Instalments!' Oom snorted as he went to get the money.

In the car I cried. Dahlan said, 'Wenny, just give me a little time. I think I can help.'

I moved back into the house. Our servant, Bi Uju, happily came back to her old job. I took in a boarder, Iyas, a postgraduate economics student. Money was tight, and although Bi Uju was a good cook, the food was monotonous. Dahlan noticed this and sometimes he brought takeaway, or took us to a restaurant. He made sure we had enough cooking fuel – kerosene – which at that time was expensive and hard to get.

Within a month Dahlan repaid the whole debt to Oom John.

CHAPTER 18
A Sundanese Wedding

> Sundanese women play an important role in maintaining and (re)creating rituals and practices, which enables them to nurture and (re)produce the traditional social order in which they have relatively high status.
> —Linda Lentz, *Sundanese Lifecycle Rituals and the Status of Women in Indonesia*

My father's sister, Bibi Neneh, organised our wedding. She formed a committee with each member having an area of responsibility: invitations, transport, hotel bookings, entertainment, bride and bridegroom. As a professional caterer Bibi Neneh would manage the banquets.

Bibi became a substitute mother to me. We had many long conversations about married life. 'Never argue in front of the children,' she said. 'Argue in the bedroom and finish the argument in the bedroom. Stay there until you are lovers again, and come out with a bright face.'

The wedding, on Sunday 13 May 1962, would consist of two functions. The official marriage ceremony, *Akad Nikah*, would be held in the morning in front of family and close friends, followed by Sundanese cultural ceremonies. The reception on Sunday night was to be a bigger event with five hundred families invited.

I took one of the invitations and visited Mas Irwan. He gave me his blessing. 'Dahlan is the lucky one,' he said. 'I still love you.'

'I'm sorry, Mas. You are a beautiful person and I did love you.'

He did not come to the reception.

One afternoon about three weeks after the invitations were sent out Dahlan called in and we chatted in the yard at Jalan Tembaga. He took a sheet of paper from his pocket and gave it to me. 'Wenny, would you like to read this?'

It was a letter from his father in Sumatra. As I read it a

cold terror gripped me. He told Dahlan not to marry me and that he should choose a girl from his own ethnic group. This was completely unexpected.

'Will you obey?' I asked Dahlan, trying not to betray my despair.

'Of course not. I don't want to marry anyone else. I want you. Don't worry about what my parents say. I want to spend my life with you, not with some girl I don't know in Medan.'

'You'll hurt your father and mother,' I said.

'But Wenny, it is decided that I will marry you. The invitations have already been sent.'

Dahlan's parents did not come to the wedding or reception. The only representative of Dahlan's family to attend was his brother, but he would not take on any of the roles of the groom's family during the ceremonies.

A week before the event I moved into the Bandung house of my grandfather Aki Noor and his wife Ibu Gunung, where the marriage ceremony would be held. This week was a period of seclusion, *dipingit*, and during that time I was under the control of Uwa Yayah, an expert on Sundanese wedding culture. She would be the make-up artist, hairdresser, Master of Ceremonies for the cultural parts of the event, and the enforcer of custom. During the week I was not allowed to leave the house or see Dahlan. My diet was restricted – food with salt and certain fruits such as bananas, pineapples or cucumbers were forbidden, and I was given *jamu*, traditional herbal medicine, formulated to prepare the female body for the wedding night.

At the start of the week the bridal bedroom was decorated. The tiled floor was covered with two beautiful Persian carpets lent by Bi Neneh, who kept them for special events. Behind the bed pale pink tulle floated down the wall, blending into a lilac satin bedcover trimmed with gathered ruffles. Jasmine flowers were scattered over the bed and pinned to the tulle. The dressing table was covered with a richly embroidered cloth, its colours matching the satin and tulle, and displayed French perfume, a complete set of make-up and a burner diffusing essential oil.

People admired the room, but I couldn't sleep on the decorated bed. I put a mattress on the carpet each evening and rolled it up in the morning.

One of Uwa Yayah's duties was to lighten my skin, using *bedak lulur,* a yellow powder she made herself, so that the bride would appear to be different from the guests and more attractive to her new husband on the wedding night. I didn't want to be whiter, but I had to submit. Each morning after my bath, Uwa Yayah massaged me and then removed the oil with hot towels. She mixed the bedak lulur with water to form a paste and covered my whole body and face with it. I wore a housecoat over the paste, which stayed on all day. Bedak lulur was made from fragrant plants and flowers but also contained turmeric, so any clothes I wore turned yellow.

The process was repeated before I went to bed – bath, massage, bedak lulur. At night being covered with paste made it hard to sleep. I protested but Uwa Yayah insisted. 'Don't be so difficult,' she said. 'It's only once in your lifetime you have to follow this custom.'

During the entire week Uwa Yayah fasted from sunrise to sunset and prayed to God to help her perform her duties correctly so that the bride would be beautiful and the ceremonies would go smoothly. But her fasting and prayers did not prevent disaster.

Dahlan worked in Jakarta until Thursday, then came to Bandung to stay with my uncle and aunt. I asked my cousin to take a letter to him, because I knew that on Friday Uwa Yayah had another bride to attend to. She instructed me to apply the bedak lulur myself but of course I didn't. Instead, telling Ibu Gunung that I had to buy some hair pins for the wedding, I left the house and had an illicit meeting with Dahlan at the Baltic Ice Cream Parlour.

We hugged tightly. 'Are you learning about Sundanese culture?' I asked.

Dahlan laughed. 'I don't understand a single thing about your customs. I'm lucky your aunt and uncle are teaching me. But there are too many ceremonies so I keep forgetting.' Dahlan had no interest in traditional customs, even those of his own ethnic group. But he was easy-going and readily agreed to wear Sundanese costume for the wedding.

After our ice creams I went to the hairdresser for a cut and perm. I was happy to have escaped from the confines of the house and to have the hair style I wanted for my wedding.

Uwa Yayah was aghast. 'You've ruined the wedding,' she cried. 'Your hair must not be curly. It has to lie flat. And it's too short. I'll never get the *sanggul* on.'

The sanggul is a metre-long length of human hair that is attached to one's own hair and formed into a bun. Uwa was crying. 'Why don't you listen to me?' she yelled. 'You're so stubborn. Just once you could have followed my instructions.'

I had not realised I would upset Uwa Yayah so much. Eventually she forgave me, but she continued to grumble about my hair.

On Saturday, the day before the wedding, flowers began to arrive from family, friends, colleagues and businesses. Arrangements of roses, carnations, gladioli and orchids filled the lounge room, dining room and bridal bedroom. Haji Noor and Ibu Gunung's house was already at its best – as soon as it was decided to hold the marriage ceremony there they'd had it repainted. Now Ibu Gunung supervised more preparation. Servants attached banana plants to each side of the front gate and decorated doorways with palm fronds.

Bibi Neneh had arranged a pre-wedding ceremony called *Ngeuyeuk Seureuh* to be held on Saturday afternoon. This was a Sundanese aristocratic custom, which was supposed to prepare the couple for married life. Only happily married women could be invited to the Ngeuyeuk Seureuh and Ibu Gunung and Bibi Neneh carefully selected about forty guests, excluding divorcees or any woman whose marriage appeared shaky. Children and teenagers were not allowed to attend because of the adult themes of the ceremony. There was an air of secrecy around it.

Before Ngeuyeuk Seureuh I was cleansed in the *siraman* ceremony, in which I was bathed by seven women. I wore a *kemban*, a batik wrapped around the top of my body, and sat on a chair beside a large vessel of holy water into which seven different types of sweetly scented flowers had been added to make it fragrant and pleasant for bathing. Uwa Yayah gave a coconut shell ladle to Ibu Gunung. I suddenly felt desolate. It was my mother's role to be the first to pour the water over me, but my mother was in Australia. In her place Ibu Gunung was the first of the seven women to bathe me, then Bibi Neneh and the other aunts from my father's and mother's families. The water mixed with the tears of longing for my mother.

After cleansing Uwa Yayah took me to the bridal bedroom and shaved all the short downy hair from my face, forehead and neck. She tried to pluck my eyebrows but I resisted, as I liked them the way they were. 'You're so stubborn,' she said, but she contented herself with shaping them a little. She attached the sanggul extension to my short hair with much difficulty and many pins, folding and twisting it into a bun at the back of my head. She applied minimal make-up – the more natural the better for Ngeuyeuk Seureuh – and dressed me in a simple kain kebaya.

Uwa led me to the large dining room. All the furniture had been removed and the tiled floor covered with Persian carpets. Beside the wall were decorated boxes covered with cellophane and displaying all the clothes and jewellery I needed for the wedding. This was *seserahan*, a reverse dowry, provided by the groom to the bride. Usually members of the groom's family would have presented the boxes before the ceremony, and I was saddened by this reminder of their absence.

The women were sitting on the carpet with Dahlan. He stood up when I came in and we faced each other. Uwa asked him, 'Is this the woman you will marry tomorrow?'

'Yes, she is the woman I will marry.'

To me she said, 'Is this the man you will marry tomorrow?'

'Yes, he is the man I will marry.'

Dahlan and I sat down side by side in a cross-legged position. In front of us was a woven palm mat with offerings of vegetables, fruit and flowers, a mortar and pestle, and a betel nut set.

Uwa Yayah sat facing us. She struck the mat with a sapu lidi broom to command attention. 'The purpose of the Ngeuyeuk Seureuh,' she said, 'is to prepare the couple for the roles and obligations of husband and wife.'

Uwa was explaining the ceremony not just to Dahlan and me, but also to the women sitting around us. She knew that some of them, particularly those from my mother's family who were not nobles, may never have attended a Ngeuyeuk Seureuh. 'Every day we must remember,' she said, 'the proper conduct for a husband or a wife. Now let us look at one day in your married life. Wenny and Dahlan, imagine you are already married and that you are asleep in your bed.'

She struck the mat with the sapu lidi. 'Wake up! Dahlan! Wenny! Wake up! It's already late. Time to start the day.'

Uwa instructed us on our duties. After bathing and dressing, the wife must prepare a good breakfast for her husband. The couple eat together and talk about the coming day. Then she gives him a hug and a kiss and wishes him a good day as he goes to work to earn money for the family.

'Do not,' Uwa emphasised, with a swish of the sapu lidi, 'let your husband go to work with an empty stomach, or while you are still asleep or in your pyjamas, unbathed and smelly.'

The wife cannot go back to bed when the husband leaves, but must manage the household and make sure the home is clean and ready for her husband's return. 'You are responsible for managing your husband's salary,' she said as she banged the mat. 'Do not be lazy. Work hard, husband, to earn a good salary. Work hard, wife, at making ends meet. If the salary is not enough, don't grumble. Use your imagination, reduce expenses, simplify meals. And look after yourself during the day. Outside there are many temptations for your husband, especially from his secretary.

'You must both be responsible for your children – the husband by earning money, the wife by caring for them – so that they become strong and healthy and well educated.'

While Uwa instructed us with swipes of the sapu lidi, I thought of my new role as a wife. Yes this is what it will be like from now on. Dahlan will be out in the world working, but my role will be just as important, looking after my husband, children and household. Children! I imagined waking them up in the morning, taking them to school.

The day through which Uwa guided us was a long one and my mind wandered. I thought about my parents, so far away. At least they had given their blessing to this marriage. I thought of the man beside me, a responsible man who would be a good husband. I even thought of my previous boyfriends, the ones I had rejected and the one who rejected me.

'Be ready at the door to welcome your husband home,' said Uwa. 'Ask him how the day was. And Dahlan, ask your wife about her day. Spend time talking together. Communication!' Uwa struck the mat hard with the sapu lidi. 'Communication is the key to successful marriage. Talk to each other.'

She told us that a married couple must *'silih asah, silih asuh'*, a Sundanese expression meaning sharpen (teach) each other, care for each other.

'When you go to bed, you must not sleep back to back,' said Uwa. 'Be like the fork and spoon.' She cupped one hand in another to show what she meant.

Uwa placed a coconut flower, as yet unopened, on the mat in front of Dahlan and gave him a knife. 'Cut it carefully,' she said. 'You must look after it.'

As Dahlan placed the knife on the flower people called out to him, 'Be careful, do it slowly.' He cut lengthways through the green sheath, exposing the masses of white flowers. The guests clapped and cheered, and called to us, 'Yum-yum! Beautiful!'

Dahlan looked at me, shocked. 'Sundanese culture is rude,' he whispered.

Uwa gave Dahlan the pestle and me the mortar, in which she placed betel leaves, lime, slices of betel nut, *saga* leaves and the plant extract *gambir*. 'Husband and wife cannot be separated,' she said. 'The pestle cannot work without the mortar, nor the mortar without the pestle. You must resist other temptations and always be together. Now pound the mixture.'

As I held the mortar and Dahlan used the pestle, people laughed and one called out, 'Be gentle, not too hard.' Another said, 'You're enjoying that too much.'

'This is indecent,' Dahlan whispered.

Next Dahlan and I were in a tug of war, pulling on each end of a rope made of flowers, then scrabbling under the mat for coins and paper money hidden there. Whoever won these games would bring good fortune to the household, but I guessed they had come from the time of arranged marriages, when the bride and groom had not known each other before. In such games they would begin to touch each other and laugh together, and become easier with their new partner. And it wasn't hard to see the educational purpose of other parts of the ceremony.

Uwa had organised the preparation of baskets, each containing seven items: cake, fruit, a flower, a handkerchief, perfume, comb and a mirror, the last item to remind us that we will always see ourselves in the mirror if we do wrong. Dahlan and I presented a basket to each guest to thank them for attending the ceremony. Then we piled all the plant rubbish onto to the mat and carried it to the nearest crossroads, accompanied by all the men, who had been chatting in the lounge room while they waited for their wives. We dropped the mat and rubbish in the middle of the crossroads, in order to throw away the bad luck. In the past the rubbish would serve to let people know there was a party and that they were invited, but nowadays it couldn't be left there, so a servant was dispatched to collect it and put it in the bin.

The ceremony was over and it was time for the smorgasbord, provided by Bibi Neneh. There was much talk about married life prompted by the ceremony. 'At the beginning everything is sweet,' said one woman. 'But after a while we forget our duty and we forget to talk to each other, so the Ngeuyeuk Seureuh is like a refresher course for people who have been married for a while. It opens our minds to correcting our behaviour.'

The other women agreed, and thanked Uwa Yayah for her instruction.

I had to be up early on Sunday as Uwa Yayah needed time to

turn me into a presentable bride for the Akad Nikah, the official wedding ceremony, which would be held at ten o'clock in the lounge room of Haji Noor's house.

When Uwa applied the make-up she began to plaster on foundation that was too pale, and I tried to stop her. 'That's not right for my skin colour,' I protested. 'It's for lighter skin.'

'No, no,' she said, 'I'm using this on purpose. It has to be different from your everyday make-up.'

'But it's two tones lighter than it should be. And you're putting it on too thick.'

'Don't try to tell me what to do. It's the right colour for the wedding. Just remember this is the one time in your life you will wear make-up like this. You are the queen of the day, so you must be different from the guests.'

'Different because I look ugly.'

'Stubborn girl,' Uwa muttered. 'Just leave me alone. I'm the make-up artist. I know what I'm doing.'

She applied powder, a little rouge, lipstick and eye make-up, then tackled my hair. After much grumbling she got the sanggul attached, but gave up on trying to make my curls sit flat. She had sown jasmine flowers together to make a cover for the bun and she attached three long chains of jasmine with a hairpin, so they would fall over the front of the white silk brocade kebaya that my aunt Bibi Ipit had made.

The *Degung* wedding music that we could hear changed to the groom's theme, and the MC, my uncle Mang Babang, announced, 'The groom has arrived. Welcome to Pak Dahlan Thalib.'

'See, the groom is already here,' said Uwa Yayah. 'Your hair and your arguing made us late.'

When Uwa finished fussing I emerged from the bridal bedroom, convinced I looked like a ghost with my white face.

'Here comes the bride,' announced Mang Babang, and camera bulbs flashed. 'Not while I look like this,' I thought.

A path cleared between me and the bridal chair, where Dahlan was waiting. He stood, and I looked at my future husband. He wore a white shirt, a plain black Sundanese

Dahlan and Wenny's wedding ceremony (Akad Nikah)

wedding coat and a kain, which had the same pattern as mine. Richly decorated coats were more popular for weddings but Dahlan did not want to show off. His headdress was a Sundanese *blangkon*, a batik cap, and at his waist he wore a keris. He stood waiting, smiling and relaxed.

Uwa Yayah seated me beside Dahlan on the bridal chair and returned to the doorway of the bedroom, the best position from which to monitor me. Ibu Gunung stood beside me ready to correct any imperfection. The *Penghulu*, the Muslim marriage celebrant from the Department of Religion, sat on the other side of the low table in front of us, with Haji Noor and my father's eldest brother, Bapak Syafei, as witnesses. Near Mang Babang was a large tape recorder, the source of the gamelan music. Bapak Syafei draped a white silk *selendang*, a shawl, across both our heads, to symbolise the two of us becoming one. Ma Lengkong sat nearby, watching me closely. The room was full of people, and through the window I caught glimpses of the crowds in the marquee outside. Everyone was here except the two most important people I wanted at my wedding – my father and mother.

The Penghulu began the ceremony. Dahlan and I recited the *Syahadat*, the Muslim profession of faith. 'Please give the *mas kawin*,' said the Penghulu. Mas kawin is the gift from groom to bride required under Islamic marriage law. Dahlan took a thousand rupiah note from his pocket and put it on the table. The Penghulu gave it to me.

I thanked Dahlan, smiling. Yesterday Ibu Gunung had asked me, 'What will Dahlan give you for mas kawin?'

'A thousand rupiah.'

'No, no,' cried Ibu Gunung. 'Show more. Dahlan is rich, we are rich. Mas kawin can be millions. I can lend you my jewels.'

Many people use mas kawin to display their wealth, giving gold jewellery or the keys to a Mercedes or a house. But I understood Dahlan, and explained to Ibu Gunung that he did not want to show off. A large gift is not required under Islamic law. When I told Dahlan that Ibu Gunung was worried about how it would look, he said, 'You know me. What's most important is our love, not material things. It's all for you anyway.'

So now he had produced the lowly note, not even on a silver plate as was the usual custom.

As the Penghulu continued to conduct the wedding ritual my emotions lurched out of my control. I was taking the biggest step of my life, and my parents were so far away. At least, I thought, the tears are washing away some of the white make-up.

The Akad Nikah was a short and simple ceremony. The Penghulu read from the Koran and took us through the vows. My voice quavered. I found it hard to get to the end of the sentence when trying to recite each vow. Finally the Penghulu pronounced us man and wife and Dahlan kissed my wet cheek. We signed the wedding certificate, and my grandfather and uncle witnessed it. Ibu Gunung removed the white selendang and Dahlan hugged me tightly. He took the wedding ring from my left hand, where he had placed it when we were engaged, and put it on the finger of my right hand. I did the same for him with his wedding ring. We made the sembah, the gesture of respect with palms together and fingertips upwards, to the Penghulu, witnesses and each other. I was weeping freely, and so were many of the guests.

At that moment I heard my father's voice.

The tape recorder! Mang Babang was playing a tape from my father! I sat transfixed, breathing hard.

'Wenny! My heart is full of sorrow,' Bapak said, 'knowing I cannot be with you, my first child, at this great moment in your life. My heart is aching that I have not yet met the man you are marrying, that he is a stranger to me. But my heart rejoices because I know that Dahlan is a man of quality, and will be a good husband to you. Dahlan, even though we haven't met, you are already in our family. I know you will look after Wenny, our dear first-born daughter.'

Then Dahlan was lifting me onto the seat. I had fainted and he had caught me before I hit the floor. Ibu Gunung gave me some water and Dahlan held me as I tried hard to listen to the messages from Bapak, Ibu and my siblings. Now everyone was crying, even the professional photographer. A veteran of hundreds of weddings, he later told us that this was the first one to move him to tears.

I was exhausted. The Akad Nikah was over but the cultural ceremonies still had to go on. First we paid our respects to the elders in my family – Haji Noor, Ibu Gunung, Ma Lengkong, my aunts and uncles – kneeling before each in the position of *sungkem*. We placed our hands at their knees in the sembah gesture, and they leant forward and hugged us. Then Uwa Yayah led us to a table in the dining room for the *huap lingkung* ceremony. In front of us was a dish of yellow sticky rice balls and another plate with a butterfly-cut barbecued chicken surrounded by rice and garnished beautifully with vegetables. She instructed us how to feed the rice balls to each other by stretching our hand around the back of our partner's neck. Then we each took hold of the chicken and when she cried 'Go!' we pulled. Dahlan was left with only a drumstick while I held the rest of the chicken. People laughed, and said, 'Wenny will bring luck to your household.'

Uwa took us outside to the marquee that stretched from

the front yard to the other side of the street, which had been closed off. We sat on two chairs with an uncle holding a large ceremonial umbrella over us. Uwa sang a Sundanese song about marriage, the household, and advice for newlyweds then took the *nyawer*, a bowl of yellow rice mixed with petals, coins and lollies, and threw the contents over our umbrella, showering us with love, wealth and happiness. This was the moment the children and unmarried young people had been waiting for, and excitedly they scrabbled for the coins and lollies.

Uwa directed Dahlan to stand in front of me while I remained seated, and she placed an egg on the ground. 'The bride's girlhood is over,' she said. 'The groom is ready to become a father. Break the egg.'

Dahlan crushed the egg with his right foot, and Uwa gave me a *kendi*, an earthenware jug of water, and told me to wash his foot as a symbol of my loyalty to him.

She gave Dahlan a *lidi*, a dried coconut leaf spine, burning at one end, and he held it while I drowned the flame with water from the kendi. 'If your husband is angry,' said Uwa, 'as his wife you must calm him down.'

That's easy, I thought. Dahlan is always calm.

'Now throw away all the bad luck,' directed Uwa.

I flung the kendi to the pavement, shattering it.

The final ceremony would take place at the front door. As I moved towards it, young girls surged around me, plucking the flowers from my hair and the chains of jasmine, hoping it would help find them good husbands.

It was time for *Buka Pintu*, Open the Door. The front door had been removed from its hinges. I stood inside with a female singer beside me holding one end of a selendang, a shawl, which was stretched across the doorway. Outside the house, a male singer beside Dahlan held the other end of the selendang and sang, 'Let me in. I am your husband now.'

The singer representing me sang, 'Yes, you are my husband now.'

'I want to be with you,' sang the man.

'I want to be with you, too, but on one condition.'

'What is the condition?'

'That you will be a good husband, a loyal husband, that you will help me make a beautiful home and family.'

'I promise to be a good husband to you.'

'And you must recite the Syahadat.'

Dahlan recited the Syahadat, and the woman sang, 'I will open the door now.'

The selendang was removed and Dahlan and I met in the doorway and hugged.

Uwa ushered us back to the bridal chair, and Mang Babang announced, 'You may now congratulate the bride and groom.'

Guests formed a queue, and filed past us, shaking our hands, wishing us well and then hurrying outside for Bi Neneh's smorgasbord.

The meal marked the end of the wedding ceremonies, but there was little time to rest because Uwa Yayah would soon be back to prepare me for the reception. Dahlan and I retired to the bridal bedroom. The door had been removed so that people could admire the gloriously adorned room and the decorated boxes of clothes and jewellery. 'Don't you dare lie on the bed,' Ibu Gunung instructed us, 'You'll spoil it. There are still guests to come who'll want to see it.'

'We have to rest on the carpet,' I told Dahlan.

'What's going on here?' he grumbled. 'We're husband and wife. We don't have to please others.'

But, with no door, there was nothing he could do.

A thousand guests came to our reception that evening at Gedung Panti Karya in Bandung. After everyone else had arrived, my aunt Bi Neneh and her husband Mang Achmed accompanied us to the reception hall. We walked through a guard of honour formed by trainee officers from the local military academy, their swords crossed above us. One of the Karta Mihardja clan was a general.

There was another magnificent smorgasbord from Bi Neneh, followed by entertainment – Sundanese traditional dancers, a gamelan playing Degung marriage music, a western band, a comedian – and the obligatory speeches giving us good wishes and advice in equal measure. With all the ceremonies and cultural activities over I could relax, enjoy the music, laugh at the comedian's jokes, and bask in the attention of family and friends. It was a big party and I liked parties. Only two things weighed on my mind – the absence of my parents and, more literally, the *siger*, the wedding headdress that Ma Lengkong had lent me, made of solid gold and so heavy it gave me a headache. By the end of the night, my lips were stiff from the millions of smiles they had formed. But I was thrilled that I was now *Mrs* Wenny Dahlan.

By the time we arrived home the door to the bridal bedroom had been reinstalled.

With the expense of moving to Australia my parents had been unable to pay for the wedding so Dahlan had paid for everything. On the first day of our married life we were broke, and couldn't go to Bali for our honeymoon. Instead we went back to Jalan Tembaga and Dahlan returned to work while I studied for my final exams.

Dahlan, Wenny, Ibu Gunung and Haji Noor at the reception

CHAPTER 19
The Baby with Perfect Ears

> Since I do not want to dwell on intimate details, I will not describe at this point my happiness ... in the days we spent as lovers in the consummation of all our desires. [We] saw ourselves as the reincarnation of Rama and Sita, or Romeo and Juliet ...
> —Achdiat Karta Mihardja, *Atheis*

Mochtar Lubis had been released from house arrest before my parents left for Australia. He travelled overseas to attend the International Press Institute congress in Tel Aviv, where he spoke of a 'deadly race' between democracy and communism, and the danger to human values from totalitarianism. On his return to Jakarta he was again imprisoned.

The government also arrested and jailed the leaders of Achdiat's political party, the Indonesian Socialist Party, including its chairman, Sutan Sjahrir. Writers and intellectuals who opposed the Communist Party, like my father had, were being forced out of their employment as civil servants or academics.

At the same time as the growing repression of the President's critics, Sukarno ramped up his campaign to liberate Dutch New Guinea, authorising total mobilisation under the command of Major-General Suharto, who began assembling troops, ships and aircraft in Eastern Indonesia for a full scale military onslaught against the Dutch. War was expected to break out at any time. The United States, trying to regain some influence in Indonesia, pressured the Dutch and, in 1962, helped to negotiate an agreement to transfer the territory to a temporary United Nations authority, and then to Indonesia subject to the Papuans choosing whether or not they wanted to be part of Indonesia.

In his Independence Day speech three months after Dahlan and I married, Sukarno proclaimed 1962 to be a year of triumph because of the 'victory' in New Guinea. But with inflation out of control, poverty spreading, and the Communist party organising demonstrations to intimidate their enemies, it did not feel like a year of triumph.

I missed my father but I was relieved that he had read the warning signs early and was now safely in Australia. And with the turmoil in my life as a new wife, I missed my mother. I felt I was without guidance.

In Western countries an idealised version of male and female roles had arisen during the twentieth century, with husbands as breadwinners and wives as being responsible for the domestic domain. Similar ideals developed in Indonesia, not for the majority of people, who were poor and needed both husband and wife working to eke out a living, but for noble and middle class families such as mine. At the Ngeuyeuk Seureuh ceremony before our wedding, Uwa Yayah had admonished us to accept our duties: 'Work hard, husband, to earn a good salary. Work hard, wife, at making ends meet.'

After graduating with a Bachelor of Education I ignored Uwa's instructions and worked at the State High School in Kebayoran. The salary was low and lesson preparation took up my spare time. When I complained, Dahlan said, 'Why on earth do you do it? I'm the breadwinner. I make more than enough money for us, and you'll be busy when we have a family.'

I left the school and devoted myself to managing the household and becoming the dutiful wife Uwa Yayah had envisaged.

One morning Bi Uju, busy at the stove, lifted a lid and the smell of cooked rice filled the house. Without warning I vomited. Later, when I told Dahlan that our doctor had confirmed I was pregnant, he laughed and wrapped his arms around me. We both cried as he whispered, 'You'll be a mother, and I'll be a father.'

Two months later he presented me with a sewing machine. 'But Lan,' I said, 'you know I can't sew.'

Before we married he had told me that in Sumatra it was very important for a wife to be able to sew as well as cook and look after the house. 'No way!' I said. 'Cooking maybe, but I hate, hate, hate sewing.'

'It's easy on this machine,' he now said.

At that time nappies were made at home by cutting them from rolls of *tetra*, special material for nappies, and hemming them. Dahlan tried to show me how to use the treadle.

'It's too hard,' I said. 'Not good for my tummy.'

A few weeks later he surprised me again with a small electric sewing machine. 'It's easy,' he said as he showed me how to use it. 'No treadle.'

When I tried to make the nappies the hems turned out crooked. After a few more failures I gathered up the material, put it in a bag, and took it to the dressmaker.

Dahlan tried to satisfy my strange food cravings. One morning I woke at two o'clock and wanted to eat *jamur kuping*, wood ear fungus. I could see it clearly on a plate of stir-fry and feel it crunching in my mouth. I woke Dahlan and demanded, 'Let's go to a restaurant. I have to eat jamur kuping.'

Dahlan was patient and loving. 'We can't go to a restaurant. They're all closed.'

'No,' I cried. 'In Kota, on Gajah Mada, there's a street stall where they cook it in front of you. I have to have it.'

'No, we can't go. It's not safe at this hour. We'll be robbed.'

I cried like a child while Dahlan held me and tried to pacify me.

The next day when Dahlan came home for lunch he brought two packets of dried wood ear fungus. He had asked all his staff where to buy it, and finally contacted a friend in Bogor. 'But I don't know how to cook it,' I said.

'You have to soak it first. Then you can chop it up and stir-fry it with some chicken or prawn.'

After Dahlan returned to work I tipped one packet into a large bowl of hot water and left it to soak. When I came back, it was full to the brim with black ears. I picked up one with the tips of my fingers and stared at it in horror. I had never seen whole pieces before – in restaurants it was always cut up. I dropped it quickly and ran to the neighbour. 'Mbak,' I called. 'Come quickly. I don't know what to do with the jamur kuping – it grew so big.'

'*Aduh*!' Mbak said when she saw the bowl of jamur. I

showed her the other packet.

'Wenny, you don't use the whole packet. You only need seven or eight pieces to make one dish. And it's so expensive, like gold.'

I could no longer even look at the bowl of ears. 'I don't want to eat it,' I said. 'You have it.'

'We can't eat this much – it's not possible. But I'll share it with the neighbours.'

It would be many years before I could again touch wood ear fungus.

Keroncong means 'the sound of jingling' and is also the name of a style of popular Indonesian music. The jingling of my gelang keroncong, the five gold bangles that my mother had given me for my seventeenth birthday, was part of me, and the bangles had only once been off my arm. Sulastri, one of my fellow students at Yogya, always admired my gelang and asked if she could borrow them for a weekend to wear at a party in her home town. I wanted to say no but I knew that sharing of clothes and jewellery was expected at the asrama and that if I refused I would be ostracised. Grudgingly I took them off for the first time.

Without the gelang keroncong I did not feel complete and I had a sleepless weekend worrying she might lose them. They meant so much to me because they were a gift from my mother marking the end of my childhood. When Sulastri returned them I felt I could live again. Since then they had stayed on my arm.

Shortly after the wedding I received a letter from Ibu in Australia. 'Now that you are married,' she wrote, 'please send the gelang keroncong back to me because I want to give them to Ati.'

After I read the letter I wept until morning. 'Why?' I asked Dahlan, who was trying to comfort me. 'Why does she do this to me? What did I do wrong?'

I relived the beatings and tongue-lashings Ibu had given me as a child, and the emptiness I had felt as a teenager when she dressed me up in her creations, showing off through me.

'Don't worry,' said Dahlan. 'Just keep your gelang. Tomorrow we will go to the jewellery shops in Pasar Senen and buy another set to send to your mother.' I agreed but could not stop crying.

Next day Dahlan came home from work during his lunch hour and we went to the goldsmith. We selected a heavier set, with a different design – I didn't want to give an exact copy. I knew she would be happy with the substitute bangles because they were more valuable than the ones she had given me. Later I would see Ati wearing them.

I kept asking myself why Ibu had done this, and why she had beaten me in Jalan Meranti. Did she hate me? Had I been so bad that she needed to punish me? But I knew such questions were futile, because I would never find the answers.

The gelang keroncong stayed on my arm, but the wound to my heart never healed.

Every month Dahlan handed me his pay packet, leaving it to me to decide how the money was to be used. If he wanted to buy cigarettes he asked me for the amount he needed.

As a fourteen-year-old I had learned to budget when I saved my pocket money in condensed milk tins. Now I budgeted just as carefully, even though Dahlan had a well-paid job. I divided the salary into envelopes for each type of expense to be paid in the coming month, and invested the surplus in gold jewellery. With inflation at over a hundred percent per year and banks untrustworthy, the only safe store of value was gold. I became a regular customer of a Chinese gold dealer, visiting him every month, building up our reserves, sometimes returning previous purchases and replacing them with heavier pieces. As I had once concealed my money tins in different places around my bedroom, I now hid the jewellery and cash in secret niches throughout the house, such as enclosed spaces under cupboards and heavy bookcases. A burglar might find one hiding place but the rest of the gold would be safe.

I made additional income in many ways. Whenever we travelled to Yogya or Pekalongan, I bought batiks and resold them in Jakarta for a profit. Like many others, I acted as an informal broker. If someone had a house, car, land or jewellery for sale, I would ask around to see who wanted to buy. Introducing a buyer and seller would earn a commission if the sale proceeded.

Dahlan provided no advice and left all the decision-making to me. One day as my neighbour and I rode a becak to the market she said, 'I don't understand. Your husband is an economist, but you are the one always finding extra ways to make money. You're the driver of the household economy.'

Sometimes I wished Dahlan would take the reins. But I enjoyed exercising my skills at dealing and brokering.

Dahlan was a good husband. He was also a good son and brother to his family.

When I told Dahlan, before our marriage, that I hated sewing, I said little about cooking. Although I had learnt to prepare food when we were refugees, and as a teenager had cooked meals for the family, they were all simple dishes. I knew I should broaden my repertoire to include more complex recipes, especially from Dahlan's homeland of Sumatra. He gave me a recipe book with sections for each of the main cuisines of Indonesia.

When Dahlan's brother came to stay I wanted to make a good impression, so I opened the book for the first time and turned to the Sundanese section. *Sambal goreng udang*, fried prawn sambal, looked tasty with lots of different spices. I didn't want Bi Uju to know I couldn't cook, so I kept the book in the bedroom. In the kitchen, I began the preparation with Bi Uju, but kept forgetting what was in the recipes, and had to run back and forth to the bedroom to find out which of the spices I'd forgotten and how much of them to put in. We worked all afternoon preparing the sambal and the other dishes, which included *semur daging*, sweet spicy beef; *sayur asam*, tamarind vegetables; and *tumis*, stir-fry.

That evening, after we had eaten, the two men lit cigarettes and Dahlan's brother said, 'Sundanese food is completely different from Sumatran food.'

'How is it different?' I asked.

'Sundanese food has no taste. It goes through your mouth

without making an impression. If you eat Sumatran food, you will still remember its taste when you go to bed.'

When I was alone with Dahlan I told him I was angry about his brother's insult.

'Don't worry,' he said. 'I like your cooking. He can say whatever he wants.'

'No. You have to defend me.'

But Dahlan never defended me against his family. He had ten siblings and our house became their headquarters. They would arrive without notice and stay for weeks. Dahlan was the only sibling earning a high salary and the others flocked around him, always asking for money. In Sundanese families, one's obligations are to children and parents, but Sumatrans have a wider extended family, embracing siblings and their children. I felt like an outsider, with Dahlan's family trying to push me away from him.

Dahlan's sister and brother, Emelya and Iskandar, were sent by their father to live with us. Rather than work or study they only slept and went out. They left mess everywhere and, if I asked for their help around the house, they each turned up their nose and ignored me. Emelya did not accept that I managed the household finances. If I bought new shoes she would say to Dahlan in front of me, 'Abang, Kak Wenny got new shoes. I want a new pair too.'

Dahlan always said, 'Later, okay?'

Why, I thought, doesn't he tell her to ask me?

They made a lot of extra work for Bi Uju so I helped her. Cleaning Emelya's untidy bedroom I found a scrunched up sheet of paper on the floor and as I read it I realised it must be a draft of a letter from Emelya to her parents.

'I am suffering,' she wrote. 'Kakak Wenny is too harsh. She is mean. She buys things for herself but doesn't give us any pocket money. She doesn't feed us properly. She is not a good wife. She doesn't look after Abang Dahlan.'

That evening at dinner I was quiet, controlling my fury. When Bi Uju removed the plates and Dahlan lit a cigarette, Emelya and Iskandar began to get up, and I said, 'No, sit down!

Stay there!'

I unfolded the letter and put it in front of Emelya. 'Read this letter,' I said.

Emelya pushed it away. I took it and read it aloud, then banged my fist on the table. 'Dahlan, your brother and sister live here as parasites in this house that belongs to my parents.' I pointed at Emelya. 'We accommodate you. We feed you. You never help us in the household. How dare you belittle me with these lies? I don't want you in my house. You must leave tomorrow. Dahlan, please organise somewhere for them to go. I want nothing more to do with them.'

Prompted by Dahlan, Emelya apologised but it was too late. The next day they moved to their sister's house.

When it was time for the birth of our baby I wanted Dahlan with me, but the obstetrician would not allow it, as she was worried about how a man would cope. Dahlan said later that it would have been easier to be with me than waiting outside hearing my screams.

Inside the nurse laughed as she said, 'Oh, you're crying now, but you were happy when you were making the baby.' I grabbed her uniform and ripped it, popping the buttons down her front.

'Sorry,' she stammered as she tried to cover herself. 'Just a joke.'

'Not funny at all,' I gasped out between screams.

When the baby was born, the doctor announced that we had a boy. 'I want to look in his ears,' I cried.

'Why?' asked the doctor.

I told her how worried I'd been. After the wood ear fungus episode I couldn't stop thinking of the superstitious belief that if you don't satisfy a craving when pregnant there will be something wrong with the baby. But my child's ears were perfect.

Dahlan came in. 'A big beautiful boy. Thank God,' he said.

He held the baby. 'Little Cheddy,' he murmured. We had decided that if we had a boy we would call him Cheddy, the name of a person Dahlan admired.

I stayed at the private birthing clinic for a week and my room filled with orchids and other gifts from friends and family. Haji Noor and Ibu Gunung came to see their first great-grandchild and, after I returned home, Ibu Gunung stayed to help.

After giving birth women were expected to wear a *gurita*, a type of corset, and to stay in bed for forty days. During that time we hired a nurse to come to our house every day to look after the baby and me.

Each morning after bathing I lay on the bed while Dahlan tied the gurita tightly around me. It was made from one piece of strong cotton cloth, with each end cut into strips. Gurita means octopus, and wearing it felt like being squeezed by the arms of an octopus. The discomfort was extreme but I believed that it was needed to keep my stomach small and to help the uterus recover.

I also accepted the traditional beliefs that bed rest, a special diet and daily doses of jamu, herbal medicines, would promote recovery and produce good milk for the baby. We bought a jamu 'birth pack' which provided a dose for each of the forty days, with a different formulation each week. My diet was managed by Ibu Sasmita, the wife of one of Dahlan's colleagues. She was a slim and fit woman who had given birth nine times. Every day she brought me the prescribed food, a small village chicken boiled in rice wine and ginger. I had to eat the whole chicken and drink the wine. It was nice for a few days but after that I felt like vomiting. I managed to eat some breast and gave the rest to Dahlan. After a week he said, 'Enough!' and passed it on to our servant Bi Uju, who never tired of it.

Forty days in bed was so boring it almost killed me.

At the end of this period we arranged a Sundanese purification ceremony, *Cukuran*, to welcome the baby and to give thanks to God. Friends, neighbours and my relatives from Bandung gathered around me as I held Cheddy. Nearby was a pair of scissors with a gold necklace and rings threaded through the handle, and a copper bowl of holy water containing seven different types of flowers. While praying, Haji Noor took the scissors, cut a small piece of Cheddy's hair and placed it in the holy water. Dahlan repeated this, then Ibu Gunung and Ma Lengkong. In all, seven people took a snip of Cheddy's hair and placed it in the bowl.

The ceremony was followed by a smorgasbord meal. After the guests left I held Cheddy while Haji Noor shaved his head completely with a razor, making me nervous. He placed all the hair in the bowl of holy water and took it outside, where Dahlan dug a hole. Praying, Haji Noor poured the contents of the bowl into the hole. This symbolised cleansing the baby and getting rid of bad luck.

Ibu Sasmita and her husband recommended their niece, Sene, as a *pengasuh*, nursemaid, to look after Cheddy. I liked Sene immediately. She was a pretty teenager, humble, quiet and eager to work for us.

Before she left, the nurse had taught Sene about caring for Cheddy – how to change his nappy, bathe him, and put a gurita on him. Babies as well as mothers wore a gurita to stop them getting a big tummy and to keep them warm.

Sene learnt when to feed the baby and how to sterilise the bottle and, when Cheddy started on solids, Sene knew what food he needed, preparing spinach, carrot, tomato and rice. Chicken livers were considered ideal for Indonesian babies, good for their blood, and every day we bought two from the butcher who went from house to house. Sene boiled them, added a little salt, and scraped them through a strainer. For morning tea she mixed mandarin juice into mashed bananas, insisting that only Cavendish bananas were good enough for babies. For afternoon tea she crushed Marie biscuits into milk.

Cheddy spent most of his time with Sene. When we visited friends or family or went on picnics she came with us to look after Cheddy. If we went to Bandung to stay with Ibu Gunung and Aki Noor for a weekend, Sene packed up everything the baby needed. Ibu Gunung was upset when Sene was strict and insisted on using the utensils she had brought. 'Don't you think we are clean?' Ibu Gunung demanded of me.

'Of course,' I said. 'But even at home we keep everything

for Cheddy separate. Sene is very particular. She knows better than me what the baby needs.'

In managing the household my mother had ignored Bapak's egalitarianism and kept the servants on a lower level than us. As a child I had rebelled against hierarchical customs among family members, but had not questioned Ibu's insistence on preserving a hierarchy between family and servants. Now I followed her practice and asked Sene to call our child Gan Cheddy.

Dahlan soon put a stop to that. 'Oh no, no, no,' he said. 'There will be no aristocratic titles in this house. Everyone is equal here.'

Dahlan's reaction jolted me, and made me see how inconsistent I had been. I realised how badly Ibu had treated our servants, and resolved to follow Dahlan's lead in treating everyone with respect. If we were watching TV our servants sometimes came in and sat on the floor so as to remain below us. Dahlan always insisted they use a chair. Bi Uju was never comfortable with this, but if Sene came in after putting Cheddy to bed she accepted. I was happy to have her sitting on the same level as us. She was like one of our family.

CHAPTER 20
Guests and Ghosts

> Anwar said … "We must free our people of all superstition straightaway! A revolution of the mind! A revolution against stupidity and obscurantism, a revolution aimed at knowledge and enlightenment."
> —Achdiat Karta Mihardja, *Atheis*

The car looked new, an orange Opel. I saw it stop and noticed the number plate, B555, like the cigarette brand. A slim, handsome man got out and came to our house.

I opened the door. 'Wenny!' he exclaimed.

This familiarity startled me. 'Who are you?' I asked.

'Of course, you don't know me, but I'm one of the Karta Mihadja clan. Allow me to introduce myself. I am Kang Herman, a distant cousin of your father. Last week I met Pak Achdiat in Australia.'

'You've seen my father? Where?'

'In Canberra, at an embassy reception. Your mother too.'

'How are they?'

'Very happy. In good health.'

Dahlan joined me at the door. 'You're family,' he said. 'Come in, come in.'

'My wife and child are in the car,' said Herman. 'We've just arrived back in Jakarta. We've been looking for a hotel, but they're all full.'

'You must stay here with us,' said Dahlan.

Herman's heavily pregnant wife and five-year-old daughter came in. 'Oh, no,' he said as our servant picked up his briefcase to take to the guest room. 'Don't touch that. Just the suitcase.'

We sat in the lounge room and chatted. Kang Herman knew my father's brother, Mang Agus, my cousin Arifin, and my Grandmother. He talked about his travels in Australia and about meeting my parents. While we talked he kept his briefcase close, and when we went to the dining room for dinner he took it with him and put it under the table beside his feet. His daughter was cute, with curly hair, but she seemed scared. She cringed away when Herman tried to touch her and I saw tears in her eyes. After dinner her mother took her to bed. Herman, Dahlan and I stayed at the table for hours, engrossed in conversation.

Next morning over breakfast we talked about luxury imports such as television sets and tape recorders. He told us he had bought a lot of goods in Australia to resell at a profit in Jakarta.

'Wenny has always wanted a tape recorder,' said Dahlan.

'I've got one,' said Herman. 'Still at the airport. They won't release them until we pay the tax. You need a tape recorder?'

'Yes,' I said. 'I've been saving up. They're so expensive in the shops.'

'How much?'

'About 80,000 rupiah.'

'You can have mine for 40,000.'

'Really?'

'Sure. I won't make a profit, but that's okay. You're family.'

That's half price, I thought. And I had that much saved up. But I hesitated. It was still a lot of money.

'I can collect it this morning,' said Herman.

'Wenny, that's too good to miss,' said Dahlan. 'Just give Kang Herman the money.'

I went to the bedroom and got 40,000 rupiah from one of my hiding places. When I gave it to Herman he put it in his briefcase without counting it. As he opened the case I saw that it was full of cash. He must be a really rich man, I thought.

The airport wasn't far away. 'I'll bring the tape recorder before lunch,' said Herman as he and his family left.

Dahlan went to work. Alone, I dreamed of my tape recorder. Less than an hour later I rushed to answer the door. But it was Mang Agus, my uncle from Bandung. He spoke quickly. 'Wenny, has a so-called Herman been to see you?'

I told him that Herman stayed overnight and was now at the airport getting my tape recorder.

'I'm very sorry, Wenny. I gave him your address. But I found out he's a con man.'

I began to tremble as Mang Agus told me Herman had been in Bandung, not Australia. He must have researched the Karta Mihardja clan, and convinced my uncle he was family. He had offered Mang Agus a car for 700,000 rupiah, and my uncle trusted him, and had given him the money – the cash that was in the briefcase. Mang Agus told Herman all about me and about my cousin Arifin, who was now a successful businessman. Before he came to our place, Herman had visited Arifin, who was taken in as well but luckily did not have any cash to give him straightaway.

I was scared and crying. I didn't know what was worse – having a robber stay in my house, or losing the money. Mang Agus tried to console me. 'The money is gone,' he said. 'We just have to accept it, and not worry about it anymore.'

'But I saved so hard to buy a tape recorder.'

When Dahlan came home, he also told me not to worry. 'We can start saving again. Mang Agus lost a lot more than you.'

We knew there was no point reporting it to the police – they would do nothing. But Pungki, who had been my good friend at university, was the daughter of the Minister for Police. Early next morning Dahlan dropped me at her place, and I talked to her father before he left for work.

'Leave it with me,' he said.

The next day Pungki visited me. 'Bapak found out all about Herman,' she said. 'He's a member of a gang, like the mafia. They operate in all the big cities, but their head office is here, on Jalan Sunda. Bapak's staff raided it and closed them down. They arrested Herman.'

Mang Agus and Arifin testified at Herman's trial and he was sentenced to prison. The briefcase was an exhibit – there was no longer any money in it, but it held a pistol. The woman who had been with him was also in court, and she admitted that she had worn padding to make herself look pregnant. They had hired the child to act as their daughter.

The pistol undid me. I imagined Herman pulling it out

and shooting me. I began to have nightmares and couldn't sleep properly. Even a little noise would wake me and I would lie in bed shivering with fright. I didn't want to see anybody and never went out. If a car stopped outside our house I would peer through the curtain and, if there was a knock on the door, I would go to my bedroom. I was glad Sene was there, looking after Cheddy. I would have been lost without her.

Mrs Quinn rescued me. The Quinns had been friendly with my parents in Canberra, and now lived in Jakarta where Mr Quinn worked at the Australian Embassy. Mrs Quinn visited to invite us to an Australian barbecue and I told her about Herman and how I couldn't go out because I was so frightened.

'You can't lock yourself away in the house all day,' she said. 'You'll just get more and more depressed. You must get rid of that fear. You weren't harmed. You are safe.'

Mrs Quinn did community work. With other Australian women she visited health centres in the kampungs of Jakarta to give people information about family planning. She persuaded me to go with her and I began to enjoy this work. I saw how important it was for women to know about birth control. It wasn't long before I had fully recovered.

Members of Dahlan's family continued to disrupt our lives. Emelya and Iskandar had left, but Dahlan's brother Arman often arrived without notice with his wife Tina and their six unruly children. They would stay for one or two weeks whenever his work brought him to Jakarta. Arman ignored me as if I didn't exist. He invited his friends to our house, raided our pantry for food, and gave orders to Bi Uju to bring ice and beer. He never asked me if he could have anything – he just took it. If they came when Bi Uju had returned to the kampung for a few days, I cleaned and cooked and managed the water. At that time the town water had stopped flowing during the day and only dribbled at night, when we had to save and store it for the next day. Tina never helped, lying around while her children ran wild.

I complained to Dahlan about their behaviour. 'Your brother and sister-in-law are free-loaders.'

'They're our family. We have to accept them,' he said.

'No, we don't. Sumatran culture might be like that, but you're married to a Sundanese woman. You have to meet me half-way.'

Dahlan did nothing and over time I bottled up more resentment. I was still learning to be a wife and mother, and these outsiders were always here, making no secret of their hatred of me, taking advantage of our hospitality, not trying to help or contribute. Dahlan made them welcome but I was lonely, feeling that I was by myself in my parents' house.

One day I was standing by Cheddy's cot feeling overwhelmed when Dahlan arrived home for lunch. He came into our bedroom and handed me his pay packet. I flung it back at him. 'I don't need this,' I sobbed. 'I need you. I need you to be my husband, my friend. You don't care about me. You only care about your family. You don't understand what's happening. You don't want to understand. Why is your family always here, sponging off us?'

Dahlan stared at me open-mouthed as I gasped for breath between my sobs. 'I want to be a wife to you,' I cried. 'I want to be a mother to our baby. But all these parasites are pushing me under. They hate me. I have to do everything. The burden's too heavy.'

Dahlan was trying to hold me. I grabbed his arms and shook him. 'I can't stand it anymore,' I screamed.

I felt myself falling, slipping from his grasp. Then I was floating, feeling light. I could see my body lying on the floor in my blue check housecoat. I drifted upwards past the cot and my baby, up to the ceiling in the corner of the room. The feeling of peace was blissful. There was no burden.

Then, with a sudden heaviness I was back in my body with Dahlan's mouth clamped over mine and I realised he was trying to revive me.

As he held me, my head on his lap, I felt completely drained, with emptiness replacing the serenity of a few moments before. Then I saw Tina beside Dahlan, laughing. 'Wenny,' she said. 'That looked so funny. When you were unconscious Dahlan was crying. It's so funny to see a man cry.'

Nothing changed. Dahlan's family continued to visit and Dahlan continued to tolerate them. Years later another of his brothers explained the Sumatran way to me: 'In the extended family what's yours is mine, and what's mine is yours.' Maybe so, I reflected, but Dahlan's family only followed half of this custom: what's yours is mine.

When Stanvac promoted Dahlan to the position of West Java Manager in Bandung, I was delighted because most my family – Aki Noor and Ibu Gunung, Ma Lengkong and most of my aunts and uncles – lived in the city, along with many of my friends. We moved into a company house in Ciumbuleuit, a fashionable suburb in the hills overlooking Bandung.

A nearby high school offered me a teaching position but Dahlan said, 'Cheddy's still a baby. It's better for you stay home and look after him.'

I turned down the job offer and accepted the wifely duties that Uwa Yayah had instructed me to follow. But Sene continued to look after Cheddy, so there was little for me to do. Bored, I enrolled for a six-month beautician course, and when I had qualified I opened a small business in a room of our house, providing beauty treatments to friends and relatives.

As Britain withdrew from its South-East Asian colonies, it proposed that the Borneo territories of Sabah and Sarawak be combined with Malaya and Singapore to form a new country. Sukarno objected. He saw the plan as a British plot to maintain colonial power and protect economic interests in the region and he expressed his anger that Indonesia had not been consulted about the proposal.

In September 1963 Malaysia was established and, when Indonesia withheld recognition of the new country, Kuala Lumpur severed diplomatic relations. Sukarno announced a campaign of *Konfrontasi*, confrontation, to 'crush Malaysia.' British firms were seized and rioters sacked and burned the

British embassy in Jakarta. The Communist Party supported the Konfrontasi campaign and began organising militias to protect Indonesia against British imperialism.

Meanwhile, the culture war had escalated, polarising writers, artists and intellectuals. On one side were members of LEKRA, the cultural wing of the Communist Party, who called for the banning of all books and works of art that were not ideologically correct. On the other side an anti-communist grouping, to which many of Achdiat's friends and colleagues belonged, published a Cultural Manifesto, a declaration against the politicisation of art. This provoked intimidation of the manifesto's signatories by the communists, and eventually the manifesto was banned, some of the signatories arrested, and many of their books censored.

Mochtar Lubis, who remained in detention, had been shifted to a prison in Madiun, 800 kilometres away in East Java, a full day and night journey for Hally when she visited him. This was a dire time for Hally, raising their children by herself with little income, but she never showed her fear and desperation. In prison Mochtar kept a diary, wrote four novels and many short stories, translated children's books, and made art through painting, ceramics and wood carving. He wrote frequent letters to Hally, expressing his passionate love for her.

This period of repression was at its worst when Achdiat made his first visit back to Indonesia in February 1964 to attend a symposium and visit family and friends.

'Bapak!' I yelled and ran to my father, throwing my arms around him. We held each other tightly. It had been nearly three years since I watched my parents' plane disappear in the direction of Australia.

'This is my husband,' I cried, wiping away tears. 'This is Dahlan.'

My father embraced the son-in-law he had now finally met. Arm in arm we walked out of Arrivals to where our driver was waiting. 'I'm so happy,' I cried as we got into the car. 'You're really here.'

'It's only for a month.'

'You'll be at Cheddy's first birthday.'

'My first grandchild – I can't wait to see him. And you're in the smart set now, living in Ciumbuleuit with all the big shots.'

'Bapak, don't tease. You'll love our house – it's high on a hill, and you can see the whole of Bandung. It was built for Americans so it's got chandeliers, Persian carpets, even a bathtub. But I still have a dipper bath. You can't get clean sitting in dirty water. Everything came from America, even the doorknobs. And it's got so much land, full of fruit trees – avocados, papaya, mangoes.'

We stopped at Puncak for a meal and Bapak delighted in his first genuine Sundanese food for three years: *pepes ikan emas*, steamed carp in banana leaf, *sayur asam*, tamarind vegetable soup, and *lalap*, vegetable salad with a spicy sauce.

'I'm glad to be back in Indonesia,' he said. 'The food is tastier. The way of life is better. In Australia people are too individualistic – it's not like the close-knit family life here. But Ibu has made lots of friends and is so happy in Canberra that she never wants to come back here.'

He told us how much my siblings enjoyed living in Australia. Nuy and Fari were quickly fluent in English and liked going to school. Ati was at university and in love with an Australian man.

Night had fallen when we arrived in Bandung, and Sene had already put Cheddy to bed. For a long time my father watched his first grandchild sleeping. 'It would be a good idea,' he whispered, 'for Cheddy to live in Australia with Ibu and me, and go to a good school there.'

'No way,' I said. He and Ibu had already suggested this in their letters.

We had much to tell each other, and did not notice time passing until the servants began preparing breakfast. That day we took Bapak to visit his mother.

A few days later two men called on Bapak and took him away. He was distraught when they brought him back. He had been interrogated by BPI, the intelligence agency, and they had threatened to stop him returning to Australia. In Canberra he had given a speech to the Australia Indonesia Association, criticising government corruption.

'Ibu warned me not to talk freely,' he said to Dahlan and me. 'But I can't pretend to believe something that is not true. I never thought anyone at the meeting would report it. Now I could end up like Mochtar.'

We made a hurried trip to Jakarta for Bapak to meet with the Indonesian Ambassador to Australia, who fortunately was holidaying at home, and then with Mr Quinn, his friend at the Australian embassy. Bapak decided to return to Australia immediately and spent a sleepless night praying. Next morning he boarded a flight to Sydney without incident. He missed Cheddy's anniversary, and did not see most of his friends and relatives, but he had left Indonesia safely.

On the day of Cheddy's first birthday, family and friends crowded into our house to celebrate. In the evening, with Cheddy in bed and only a few guests left, I pulled out our hidden long play records. After I'd closed the windows and drawn the curtains tightly, we danced to the forbidden sounds of Elvis Presley and Chubby Checker.

During the sixties the state oil firms, Permina and Pertamin, progressively took control of the assets and operations of foreign-owned companies. General Ibnu Sutowo, head of Permina, managed the takeover of the part of Stanvac in which Dahlan worked. I became anxious that Dahlan would no longer have a job but, although Ibnu Sutowo let many other managers go, he asked Dahlan to become the district manager for Central Java, based in Semarang. I was relieved but Dahlan was unhappy because he did not want to work for a state firm, especially one in which the military was so heavily involved.

Employees at Dahlan's level who had been living in a house provided by Stanvac could buy their home for a nominal price unless Permina wanted to keep it. In that case the employee would be given equivalent compensation. I desperately hoped that Sutowo would not want our house on the hill, and for the first and only time in my life consulted a *dukun*, a clairvoyant, for supernatural help.

He was Chinese, and sat in a cross-legged position surrounded by offerings, candles, incense sticks and brightly coloured statues. I could see only the whites of his eyes and felt a bit scared. But he said, 'You will have the house. Ibnu Sutowo will not want it.'

When I told Dahlan he laughed, 'Dukun magic doesn't work. I'm 99.9 percent certain Ibnu Sutowo will want our house.'

He was right. When Sutowo inspected the house he immediately claimed it for Permina. I began to pack.

We began our journey to Semarang as Bandung was waking up below us, lit by the rays of the rising sun. My eyes prickled with the sadness of leaving our beautiful house and the city of my birth but at least Sene was coming with us, and I felt comforted to have her beside me in the back seat, holding Cheddy. Dahlan sat in the front next to our driver.

We reached Semarang late in the afternoon and drove up into the hilly suburb of Candi, where we turned into a steep driveway. As we came to the top of the rise the city appeared below us, stretching out to the ocean, and a two storey mansion loomed ahead.

A welcoming party waited on the front terrace. The Permina logistics officer introduced three servants and two gardeners, who had been with the house since Stanvac bought it for their American manager. He told us it had been built a hundred years previously for the Dutch Governor.

'The Japanese killed all the Dutch in the bedrooms upstairs,' one of the gardeners said, pointing to the second storey. 'They cut off their heads and piled them up in the office, then threw the bodies into the bathtubs.'

'Their ghosts are still upstairs,' the cook continued. 'Sometimes we hear footsteps and voices, people laughing, things rolling along the floor.'

I shivered but said nothing. I didn't want to show the

servants I was frightened.

Dahlan laughed and said, 'Don't believe that, Wenny. Let's have a look.'

An open-plan lounge and dining area took up much of the ground floor. 'What do you think?' asked Dahlan.

'Good for dancing,' I said.

The floors were marble, and a grand marble staircase curved upwards to the haunted rooms above. Dahlan took my hand and led me up the stairs to the office. 'Beautiful,' Dahlan murmured, caressing the broad teak desk. 'Come in, come in.'

But I stayed at the door.

Each of the immense bedrooms on the second floor had its own en suite. In the master bedroom I stopped at the door of the spacious bathroom and looked at the marble tub that had supposedly held the bodies. My skin went cold.

We walked out onto the balcony. In front of us parkland ran down to a stream where water rushed over rocks. The garden was full of big trees – mango, avocado and jackfruit. To our left were the servants' quarters. To our right, the view of the city. 'Look,' said Dahlan. 'You can see the ships sailing into the harbour.'

But I kept looking back into the bedroom.

'We're sleeping in the guest room downstairs,' I told him.

From then on I lived on the ground floor, only occasionally allowing Dahlan to take me upstairs to see the view from the balcony. I preferred the view from the ground-level terrace, where we sat in the evening watching the city and harbour lights.

The first time my grandfather Haji Noor visited, he arrived late in the evening, and after a quick meal he retired to a bedroom upstairs. We did not mention the ghosts.

At breakfast he said to us, 'There are residents upstairs. Did you know?'

I told him about the Dutch who had been killed.

'Yes, I saw them,' he said. 'But don't worry, Wenny and Dahlan. This morning I walked around the house seven times, praying to God and communicating with the ghosts. I asked them not to disturb my family. We know there are supernatural beings, but remember, humans are above all other creatures. The ghosts won't disturb you as long as you don't disturb them. They live in their own world.'

Our neighbours included company directors, heads of government departments and the Governor of Central Java, all of whom lived in old Dutch houses. Soon after we arrived I was invited to join the local *arisan*, a group of women who have regular social gatherings at which they contribute money and take turns in winning the amount collected. The next meeting was at the house of Yati, wife of the Director of Agriculture.

Our driver took me to Yati's place. As we stopped in front of her house, I noticed a man sitting on the terrace with a cup of coffee, reading the newspaper. Then fear gripped me. It was Herman the con man. 'Go!' I cried to the driver. 'Go back!'

At home I rang Dahlan. I was still shaking as I told him about Herman. 'Just be calm,' he said. 'He can't hurt you.'

'He's out of prison, and it's not even two years,' I cried.

'Did he see you?'

'No.'

'Just stay in the house. You'll be safe.'

I rang Yati and told her I couldn't come because I was unwell. 'It's a pity,' she said. 'All the other ladies are here. My nephew Herman is staying with me too.'

My anxiety returned and I told Sene and the servants to keep the doors locked and not let anyone in unless they could see who they were. A few days later Dahlan brought home a newspaper and pointed to the headline on the front page: *Central Java Governor Conned*. Herman had been busy. 'See?' Dahlan said. 'He's been caught again now, so you don't have to worry about him. No need to lock yourself inside.'

We had been in Semarang less than a year when Ibnu Sutowo transferred Dahlan to a head office position in Jakarta. This was not a good move – after being the boss in Semarang Dahlan would now be working in the same office as his superiors – but I was pleased to be leaving a house in which I had never felt comfortable.

We moved into a company apartment in Kebayoran and I set up my small beauty salon in one of the rooms, working there until the day our second child, Shanti, was born. By this time old customs were being discarded, and I did not spend forty days in bed being squeezed by the gurita.

In Jakarta my husband became more and more unhappy working for Permina. Pay and conditions had deteriorated since the Stanvac days, and he hated the corruption and military involvement that now blighted the nationalised company.

Dahlan had received a large payment from Stanvac, which was partly severance pay and partly compensation for being unable to buy the house we had lived in at Bandung. We disagreed about how to use it. Dahlan didn't want to continue working for someone else so he planned to set up his own business.

'I don't believe in business,' I said. 'Especially when the economy is unstable. It's much better to have a regular salary coming in.'

'I've got a lot of contacts.'

'I don't believe in contacts.'

So we argued. In the end he said, 'We can divide the money. You do whatever you like with your half, and I'll do what I like with mine.'

'Good. I'll buy a house with my half.'

'Why a house?'

'A house is a good investment,' I said. 'Better than a business.'

Dahlan established a business with several former Stanvac colleagues who had not been employed by Permina. His aim was to resign from Permina as soon as the business was strong enough but within a year the business collapsed and Dahlan lost his investment and was forced to stay with Permina. Meanwhile I had bought a cheap, rundown house near the centre of Bandung, with the aim of fixing it and reselling for a profit. My aunt, who lived in the same street as the house, had told me not to buy it. 'It's been for sale for a year,' she said. 'It's haunted. That's why it's so cheap.'

'No problem. I'll become friends with the ghost.'

But I didn't. I hired a builder and he fell from the roof on the first day.

'That's the ghost,' said my aunt, and after that, when the work had to be inspected, I stayed in the car and sent Dahlan in.

One weekend, on an early morning walk with Dahlan in Bandung, I was intrigued by a house being built in Jalan Talaga Bodas. With a front wall that was mostly glass, it was very modern. But I was really attracted by a cluster of dwarf banana plants in the front yard with masses of easily picked fruit. Most banana plants in Indonesia were four times as high and I had not seen any as small as these before.

'I'd like to live here,' I said. 'I think I'll sell my house and buy this one.'

'You can't afford it,' said Dahlan. 'This one's much bigger than yours, and it's got twice as much land and a better location. And we don't even live in Bandung.'

'No, I think I will get it.'

The guard, who was warming himself at a fire in front of the house, told me the builder was Pak Heri from the nearby city of Cimahi.

Later that morning I asked my husband, 'Lan, can you drive me to Cimahi?'

'What for?'

'I'm going to see Pak Heri.'

'Are you serious? You can't afford that house.'

'Leave it to me. It's my money – I can do what I like with it. Your money's already gone.'

Pak Heri told me that he and his family planned to move into the house when he finished building it. I said I had fallen in love with it because of the short banana plants and proposed a swap, that he take my house. At first he refused but I mustered all my powers of persuasion, and explained how he, as a builder, could renovate it properly, sell it for a profit, and build another house for his family. Finally I convinced him. We bargained and agreed on the amount I would have to pay him in addition to giving him my house.

When we left Dahlan said, 'Wenny, I don't understand. You haven't got that much money.'

'I'll get it.'

During the two months until Pak Heri's house was finished I was busy, making extra income from dealing and brokering and calculating the worth of my gold reserves. At that time cash or goods were used for transactions rather than cheques, as banks could not be trusted, so I sold some of the gold and put the rest aside, together with the goldsmith's certificates, to include in the payment to Pak Heri. I even used my personal gold jewellery – everything except my wedding ring and gelang keroncong.

Dahlan just shook his head. 'I didn't think you'd give up all your jewellery,' he said.

On settlement day, we needed four airline bags to carry all the Rupiahs and gold to Pak Heri. As I held the title deeds I felt proud of my achievement. This was a house I would keep. We often came to Bandung on weekends to meet my relatives, and Talaga Bodas could be our second home.

CHAPTER 21
Departure from Chaos

> Who'd expect the Old Order and the Communists to crumble like a paper tiger? How strong their power and status had been in the past! What a mess everything was in now! And how dark the future was!
> —Achdiat Karta Mihardja, *The Scattered Dust of Love*

As I was not interested in politics I had no opinion about the Konfrontasi campaign, but it was all around us, with huge banners everywhere in Jakarta urging us to 'Crush Malaysia'. President Sukarno declared 1964 the 'Year of Living Dangerously' in his Independence Day speech in August, and we began to hear more reports of our forces engaging the enemy. As 1965 began, Sukarno announced that Indonesia would withdraw from the United Nations because Malaysia was about to take a seat on the Security Council.

The Communist Party was becoming even more powerful, organising demonstrations, occupying land to give to peasants, and setting up a worker-peasant militia to fight Malaysia and resist invasion by imperialist forces, particularly Britain. Dahlan and I were frightened that the communists would soon take over. There were continual rumours about army or communist coup attempts. Jakarta was plagued by robbery and violence, and I always felt scared.

Organisations and companies had to demonstrate their patriotic zeal, and now Ibnu Sutowo ordered all employees of Permina and their spouses to do two weeks military training so that they would be ready if needed to defend their country. First the men, including Dahlan, did the training, then their wives. It was shortly after Shanti's birth, and I was still breastfeeding her, but Dahlan's request that I be excused was refused. There were to be no exemptions – Sene would have to bottle feed my baby during the day.

Dahlan was in the upper echelon of staff, which meant I joined the first group of wives, with Mrs Ibnu Sutowo as our

Commandant. Under instruction from army officers we were given drill and physical training and taught to shoot. By the end of the day the shirt of my uniform was saturated with my milk. I struggled home exhausted and fed Shanti.

The two weeks ended with a ceremony at which Ibnu Sutowo presented us with our certificates. Mrs Sutowo had prepared us by giving instructions on how to behave, and told us we must be in full uniform with no jewellery apart from a plain wedding ring.

At the ceremony we gathered in front of the dignitaries. As Mrs Sutowo gave parade commands all her diamonds – rings, earrings and bracelets – sparkled in the sun.

General Nasution, the Armed Forces Chief of Staff, lived in Menteng just around the corner from my aunt and uncle, Bi Niek and Oom John. Early in the morning of the first of October 1965, armed men, apparently soldiers, forced their way into Nasution's house. He escaped over the back fence into the Iraqi embassy garden. As the troops searched the house for him his five-year-old daughter was fatally shot, and the soldiers left with the General's adjutant, mistaking him for Nasution. The adjutant and six other kidnapped generals were killed and thrown down Lubang Buaya (Crocodile Hole), a disused well at the air force base.

Suharto, the Strategic Reserve Commander, assumed control of the army and quickly put down the coup attempt. Those responsible became known as the Thirtieth of September Movement. I do not know whether it was an internal army affair as some believed, or instigated by the communists as Suharto claimed, but over the next six months at least half a million people accused of being communists were killed. Under Sukarno we always had to watch what we said, but now we had to be even more careful. If we said the wrong thing it would be easy to be labelled communist. I became more afraid of leaving the house, especially after student demonstrations against supposedly communist ministers turned violent.

In March 1966 Suharto forced President Sukarno to

delegate most of the presidential powers to him, but the chaos and uncertainty continued and in August I was happy to leave on my first trip overseas, taking Cheddy to visit my family in Australia. Shanti was now eighteen months old, and while I was away she and Sene would stay with my aunt Bi Ipit in Bandung.

To gain approval to leave the country I had to be interviewed by the military to show that I was not a communist trying to escape. The officer questioned me about each member of my family.

'Why is your father in Australia?' he asked.

'He was invited by the university to become a lecturer there.'

'Is he a communist?'

'No, of course not.'

He asked about my grandparents, uncles and aunts.

'Who is your mother's father?'

'Haji Noor of Bandung,' I replied, stressing the word 'Haji'.

'Ah, Haji. So, not a communist.'

'He's a very devout Muslim.'

I signed a statement swearing that there were no communists in my family, and the officer approved my travel.

It was illegal to own foreign currency, let alone take dollars out of the country, so when immigration at the airport asked if I was carrying any, I did not mention the hundred US dollars concealed in the hem of my skirt as an emergency fund.

During Konfrontasi, when Australia supported Britain and Malaysia, Sukarno cancelled flights between Indonesia and Australia, and they had not yet been resumed, so we flew to Manila before catching a flight to Sydney.

At three and a half years old, Cheddy had never met his grandmother and did not remember Bapak's visit when he was a baby. But we had often told him about his grandparents and showed him their photos. He already loved them for the gifts they sent, and his excitement mounted as we neared our destination.

My parents had driven from their home in Canberra, the inland capital city of Australia, to Sydney airport to meet us. As we emerged from customs Ibu ran to Cheddy and scooped him into her arms. Bapak and I embraced and then the four of us hugged together.

As Bapak drove us into the city I felt exhilarated to be with my parents, and at first I couldn't stop talking. Then I began to notice Sydney, especially the clean streets, and I remembered my essay about the rubbish in Jakarta. The traffic was heavy, but mostly cars – there were few bicycles or motorbikes, and no pedicabs, buggies or people on foot pushing food carts or pulling wagons piled high with goods. There were no soldiers or military vehicles. Pedestrians walked on the footpaths, not on the road. Most of the men wore suits and ties, and everyone was white. I looked at everything, taking it in, feeling how strange it was.

And how beautiful. I gaped at the massive bridge and the half-finished sails of the Opera House, above which three tall cranes stood guard. How fortunate, I thought, to live beside such a harbour and go for ferry rides. There was no comparison to Jakarta's small polluted river.

We went to Chinatown for lunch. 'Let's have the Peking Duck,' said Bapak.

'No,' said Ibu. 'It's too expensive.'

'We only live once,' said Bapak. 'This restaurant is famous for its food and I want to enjoy it.'

'The cheaper dishes are good enough.'

'You're always thinking about money. Money, money, money. This is a special occasion – Wenny has arrived in Australia with our grandson. We should pick what we like.'

Ibu's voice rose. 'It's just throwing money away.'

'Don't be so stingy,' said Bapak. 'I'll pay. I can afford it.'

'Have it your way,' Ibu spat out. She looked away, saying nothing more while Bapak ordered, but I could see she was fuming. Dahlan and I both loved good food and never argued about it. If a town several hours away was famous for a particular dish, we would drive there for lunch and enjoy it together.

The waiters filled the table with the dishes Bapak had

ordered. 'Look at all this beautiful food,' he said, 'in honour of Wenny and Cheddy from Jakarta. See, it's worth paying a bit more. This will be a meal to remember all our lives.'

Ibu grasped the table cloth with both hands and pulled. All the dishes crashed to the floor. The noisy restaurant became suddenly quiet, except for the sound of Cheddy crying.

'Look, now Cheddy's upset,' said Bapak calmly.

Ibu walked out of the restaurant. I picked Cheddy up and comforted him, feeling more embarrassed than I had ever been, while Bapak apologised to everyone and negotiated to pay for the damage.

Outside we found Ibu window shopping as if nothing had happened. 'Let's go,' said Bapak.

On the way out of Sydney we stopped and bought hamburgers – the first time I had eaten one. Cheddy loved his but I didn't feel very hungry. Ibu, now in a good mood, chatted with Cheddy. 'Would you like to live with us and go to school here?' she asked him.

'No, he wouldn't,' I said.

Cheddy and I had a good time in Australia. My parents had friends who lived in Toorak Road in Melbourne, and they invited us to stay in their house while they were away for a week. As we passed through towns on the way I noticed banks that were just small buildings on the side of the street with no guards or bars. 'Why do the banks have no security?' I asked Bapak.

'It's safe here.'

An hour's drive after we had been to a service station Ibu realised she had left her handbag, containing cash and jewellery, in the toilet. She panicked and wept, almost hysterical, as Bapak turned the car and drove back. He said, 'Please be calm while I'm driving. God willing you will get your bag. If God doesn't want you to have it, just accept that.'

God was on Ibu's side. A customer had handed the bag in and, when Ibu checked, the money and jewellery were still in it. I was amazed. In Jakarta your handbag can disappear while it is on your shoulder.

I had fun exploring the huge Myer store in Melbourne and learning how to use the escalator. I jumped back in fright the first time an automatic door opened in front of me. Bapak laughed, and this big-city girl felt like a country bumpkin.

Back in Canberra we attended a cocktail party at the embassy to celebrate Independence Day. My parents were esteemed as the senior members of the Canberra Indonesian community, and guests were keen to meet their daughter. A Professor of Economics at ANU, David Penny, introduced himself and his wife. 'The Indonesian economy is my area of interest,' he said in a strong American accent.

'My husband is an economist,' I said. 'Dahlan Thalib. From Medan.'

David was suddenly animated. 'Dahlan! He was my assistant at Nommensen University. He's brilliant. The students loved his tutorials. What's he doing now?'

'He works for Permina.'

'Is he happy there?'

'He hates it.'

'Listen, I want him to work with me at ANU. Can you give me his number?'

Hope surged through me. I had missed my parents so much, and maybe now I could live near them. When I told them, Bapak said, 'That's good news. All our family will be together. And it's better when the political situation in Indonesia is so unstable.'

Later that night Dahlan rang to say David had called and offered him a position as his research assistant. 'Do you want to move to Australia?' he asked.

Yes, I thought, but I wanted Dahlan to make the decision. 'It's up to you, Lan,' I said. 'It's your career. Of course my parents would like us to move here. And I do feel safe in Australia.' I told him about the incident with Ibu's handbag.

On my first night back in Jakarta, Dahlan and I sat up late discussing the job offer. Dahlan was ambivalent because the position was lowly compared to his current one. He said, 'It's up to you, Wenny. What would you like to do?'

'No, it is not up to me. You are the one who is working.'

'I need more time to decide,' he said.

The next morning we drove to Bandung. I had missed Shanti and looked forward to holding her in my arms again. Bi Ipit came out to meet us carrying my daughter, with Sene beside her. I ran to Shanti but she cried and clung to Bi. When I pulled her to me she screamed.

'It's usual,' said Bi, taking her back. 'She's angry because you were gone for so long.'

'I'm your Mama,' I said, touching Shanti's foot. She turned away from me, holding Bi tightly.

I was filled with guilt – my own daughter had rejected me. I felt panic rising and tried to hold it back.

Shanti allowed herself to be passed to Dahlan, who had visited several times while I was in Australia. She sat on his lap sneaking looks at me, but cringed when I tried to talk to her or touch her.

'Don't worry,' said Bi. 'She'll come to you when she stops being angry with you.'

On the way home Shanti clung to Sene and it took several days of encouragement from Sene before Shanti began to accept me again.

Dahlan decided to take the job in Australia, mainly because he was unhappy at Permina and wanted nothing more to do with a company that was so corrupt. He was prepared to resign but Ibnu Sutowo wanted to keep him and granted him three years unpaid leave.

I was excited about returning to Canberra and living near my parents, but I was concerned for Sene – and for Shanti, who had such a close bond with her. I wished that we could take Sene with us, but a servant was unlikely get a visa and, even if she did, we would be unable to afford her wages on Dahlan's lower salary in Australia.

When I told Sene about our plan she said, 'Can I come too?'

I explained why we could not take her. When she finally understood she asked, 'How long before you go?'

'Two months.'

I held her as she cried.

Each morning and night Sene counted the days until our departure. Dahlan and I worried about her, and contacted her family to make sure they would be at the airport when we left, so that she could go home with them. While Dahlan provided generously for her, we could never repay all that she had done for us.

The night before our flight Sene could not stop crying. I stayed up with her, hugging her, stroking her long, thick hair. She was like a sister to me, and I was abandoning her. She was still crying as we drove to the airport the next afternoon. She held Shanti tightly and told her how much she would miss her.

Friends, family, neighbours and colleagues came to the airport to see us off. Many members of Sene's family were there as well. During the four years she had been with us Sene was always quiet, polite and controlled, but now she was transformed, wailing loudly as departure time approached.

Dahlan tried to pacify her. 'Please be calm,' he said. 'We'll write to you.'

When we had said goodbye to everyone and it was time to leave, Sene would not let Shanti go. I tried to take my child but Shanti cried and clung to Sene. Holding Shanti away from me, Sene screamed, 'Don't take the baby! Leave her here!'

Her family crowded around her and finally she loosened her grip on Shanti. I took hold of my child and pulled her to me. Holding Shanti with one arm, I put my other arm around Sene and hugged her. She put her head on my shoulder and sobbed.

As I walked to immigration carrying my tearful child, Sene's desperate cries echoed in my ears. Dahlan put his arm around me. Beside him Cheddy chattered happily, excited at the prospect of grandparents, toys and visiting the zoo again. He had ignored the fuss.

On the plane, Shanti went to sleep on my lap but I could not stop my own tears.

Dahlan said, 'Just forget about what happened. Think about the good life we've had in Indonesia and our future in a new country. We should be grateful.'

I cried until I fell asleep from exhaustion. Early the next morning we landed in Sydney.

CHAPTER 22
Working with White People

> Out of smoke you came walking. Your face
> made a cloud in that cloud-haunted absence
> over the courtyard parterre where our noon
> shadows snagged on our heels, planning to lengthen.
> Then somebody saw the time, and we left for the wake.
> —Lisa Gorton, *Solitaire i.m. Bettina Gorton*

Tears ran down my face and splashed into the sink as I washed the dishes. Upstairs, Dahlan bathed the children. It had been three months since we arrived in Canberra and the move had been a mistake.

How I missed Sene! I realised how much she had done for us, and how hard the other servants had worked. Housework was new to me, and there seemed to be so much of it. Dahlan had to mow the lawn. And with no driver I had to drive Dahlan to work. We were constantly doing things we had not thought about before because servants had always been there, a part of daily life.

Neither of us had imagined our standard of living would have dropped so dramatically. Dahlan's salary had fallen when Permina took over Stanvac but at ANU it was much lower again, and we did not have the house, car and food supplies that Stanvac and Permina had provided. Now I had to budget in earnest and be so careful when shopping. To make things worse, instead of continuing with the Indonesian custom of the wife managing the finances, Dahlan insisted on switching to the Australian way. The first time he handed the housekeeping allowance to me I felt degraded. 'Why?' I asked.

'Australia is different from Indonesia. Australian men give their wives weekly housekeeping.'

'But we're not Australian.'

No matter what I said, he wouldn't change his mind. Before our wedding, Uwa Yayah had instructed us on our duties: Dahlan's role was to go out and earn an income, mine was to stay in and manage the household. Now he had taken over part of my role, while I had become a servant.

Perhaps I could have adjusted more easily if I had not been so lonely. I missed all my friends, especially Yana. Since primary school we had told each other our deepest secrets, which lately had included husband problems. Here there was no one to talk to, not even my parents, who had left on a three month trip to Europe shortly after we arrived in Canberra.

When I told Dahlan how lonely I was he said, 'Why? I'm here. The children are here. I don't understand how you can be lonely.'

And I was pregnant. Meanwhile, in this strange country, Dahlan had turned into a fisherman, and often spent the weekends at Bateman's Bay with his friend Edy, an economic attaché from the embassy, and Edy's wife.

'The kids and I want to go too,' I told Dahlan.

'Too much hassle,' he said. 'We'd have to take two cars, and we can't manage the kids there. It's not good to be up all night while you're expecting. We go fishing from midnight to sunrise. You wouldn't like it.'

When my parents returned from their European trip they gave me a gift of fabric from Mas Irwan who finally had his posting in Germany. They had visited him in Bonn where he was trade attaché. Ibu told me that they saw a photo of me on his lounge room wall and she said to him, 'Forget about Wenny. She has two children and a third on the way.'

I made a mistake, I thought – I should never have left Mas Irwan. It had been perfect with him. All his family, even his uncles, aunts, cousins and nephews, loved me and saw me as already being part of their family. In Yogya his mother had looked after me, cooking good food if I was sick, making special jamu when I had my period. I remembered Mas Irwan taking me to the early morning market on his sister's Ducati. The traders called to us, 'Hey, *Den ngantin*, just married couple, buy from me.' And he was so proud when he introduced me to people, even to Subandrio, the Foreign Minister. Unlike Dahlan, he knew how to communicate, to express his feelings. I should have stayed with him, I thought. I longed to go back in time and start again from Yogya.

One night, while Dahlan slept beside me, I lay awake thinking that I couldn't put up with this life of loneliness anymore. At three o'clock I went to Cheddy's room and watched him sleeping. I kissed his forehead and in my heart said, 'Goodbye, my child. Your father will look after you.' In the next room I kissed Shanti and said goodbye to her as well. I tiptoed down the stairs and out to the car. Then I was driving fast along the deserted streets of Canberra, through the university to Lake Burley Griffin, onto Northbourne Avenue, heading out to the highway. I was on the open road going faster and faster, trees flashing by. Crash into them, I told myself. It's no use going on like this. I just want to be free.

Then there was water instead of trees – Lake George – and I swung off the road and pressed the accelerator hard, heading straight for the lake. 'Mama!' It was the voice of Shanti, clear and strong. My foot hit the brake pedal, stopping the car at the water's edge and I came out of my trance, sobbing. What I'd been about to do was not right, and I prayed, 'Forgive me for acting like this. God, give me strength to face my problems. If I kill myself I kill other life. I have more to do in this world. Please give me strength.'

I drove home filled with guilt just as the sun had risen. At home I lifted the children out of their beds and hugged them, waking them up, first Shanti, then Cheddy. 'Why are you crying, Mama?' asked Cheddy.

In our bedroom I hugged Dahlan. 'Where have you been?' he asked.

I just cried and did not answer. Later I told him what had happened: 'I was lonely and pregnant, and you didn't seem to care. There wasn't another soul I could talk to.'

'Don't worry now,' he said. 'Forget about that. You still have me. Concentrate on the baby.' He put his hand on my stomach. 'The baby needs you.'

Australian nurses did not believe in the Indonesian custom of post-natal bed rest and they got me out of bed a few hours after our daughter was born. I felt like a chicken, laying an egg and running.

On my last night in the hospital, as I searched for a name for the baby, I watched the lights on Lake Burley Griffin through the window of my room, and our third child became Dian, an Indonesian word for light.

After the drive to Lake George I confided in my parents, telling them, 'I want to go home – I can't put up with being so isolated. In Indonesia I had many friends. Here I'm bound to the house and children and I just do housework. And Dahlan can't communicate.'

My parents were sympathetic but tried to convince me that life in Australia was much better than in Indonesia, especially for the children's education. Bapak's support was comforting and Ibu sought help for me from one of her friends, who put me in touch with a nun.

I visited Sister Margaret at the convent and she welcomed me warmly. She showed me her tiny room, in which the only furniture was a bed and a small cupboard containing a few clothes and a comb, nothing else. On the cupboard was a mirror just large enough for her to see her face.

'Is this all you have?' I asked.

'That's all I need in this life,' she said.

We spoke about my loneliness and problems with Dahlan. She led me to think of how I could take responsibility for myself, how I could accept Dahlan as he was and still enjoy our family life. Sister Margaret spoke of balance, of the need for both family and independence.

I was thankful to have found someone I could trust to be my guide but then, before I left, she told me she had cancer and would soon die. 'No,' I cried, my tears coming.

She put her hand on my arm. 'Don't be sad. It's God's will. And I'm ready to be with God.'

I was moved to see her accepting death so peacefully.

With each visit to Sister Margaret I felt myself becoming stronger. 'It depends on you,' she said. 'You can turn away from self-pity, from grumbling. You can choose to study again, or work, or volunteer in the community. While we are blessed with life, we should use our time well.'

My mind opened. It is up to me, I told myself, and set about building a life outside the domestic sphere. To make it easier to find a job I studied shorthand and typing at a business college. When Dian was about eight months old I was offered the position of secretary to the military attaché at the Indonesian Embassy. Perfect, I thought. So why did I hesitate?

One Friday when Dahlan was at work and Cheddy at preschool, I put on some make-up and drove the girls to Kingston for lunch. Side by side Shanti and I pushed our strollers to Seven Seas Café, Dian in mine, a large doll in Shanti's. We took our fish and chips onto the grass of Green Square. When we had finished, as Dian dozed and Shanti fed the leftovers to the pigeons, I noticed an employment office. Yes, I thought, I want to work but not at the embassy.

I gathered the children, went in and told the officer I'd like a job in cosmetics. She wrote down my qualifications and experience as a beautician and sat back, studying me for a while. 'You're young and pretty and have nice skin,' she said. 'I think I have just the thing for you. When can you start?'

When I picked Dahlan up from the university I told him my news – that I had a job at David Jones Civic starting on Monday. He just said, 'As long as the children are looked after.'

'Of course. I can cover child minding fees out of my pay.'

'But why David Jones instead of the embassy?' he asked.

'The women at the embassy always gossip. And I'd much rather work in cosmetics than do shorthand and typing. But I think the main reason is that I want the experience of working with white people.'

On Monday morning the David Jones Personnel Manager said I would be the first Asian woman employed by the firm. He introduced me to Lorna, who managed the cosmetics section and would train me on the job. She put me to work on the general cosmetics counter. One of my first customers was Zara Holt, wife of the then Australian Prime Minister. 'Where are you from?' she asked, peering at my name tag.

'Indonesia.'

'Ah. Sometime my husband and I might visit your country. What present should I take for Mrs Suharto?'

'I'm sorry, but I don't know.'

'But you're Indonesian, you must know. What does an Indonesian lady like?'

'But … I don't know Mrs Suharto.'

'How about Chanel No. 5?' she asked.

'Chanel No. 5 is a beautiful perfume but we don't know if Mrs Suharto likes to wear it. Maybe it's better if you give her something unique to Australia.' I suggested opal jewellery or a quality set of table linen printed with an Australian theme.

'Thank you,' she said, then asked for a bottle of hair fertiliser.

'Excuse me,' I said, 'this is my first day. I have to ask my boss.'

I found Lorna in the reserve room. 'Lorna,' I cried, 'Mrs Holt needs hair fertiliser.'

'Hair fertiliser, dear?'

'Yes, hair fertiliser.'

'Then she must go to a farm.'

I was perspiring freely. 'Lorna, Mrs Holt is waiting. Where is the hair fertiliser?'

Lorna put a hand on my arm. 'Hair *vitaliser*, dear. To use after shampoo.'

I was drenched in sweat. Lorna came out with me to serve Mrs Holt.

Vitaliser later came to be called conditioner, but in David Jones Civic it was often referred to by the name I had given it. Years later when I visited my parents in Canberra, I was riding the escalator down to cosmetics and Lorna saw me. 'Hey, Mrs Fertiliser,' she bellowed. 'Welcome back.'

At the end of that first day I returned home exhausted, having never stood up for so long at one time. But the real shock came the next morning when Lorna handed me a feather duster and I actually had to dust. In public. I forced myself to begin, hot with shame, watching the doors, terrified that someone from the embassy would come in. Later I told my father about the wound to my ego and how, as I held the duster, I had thought of resigning.

'It's the Australian way,' he said. 'Everyone has to dust. Think of it as an honour.'

I recovered from the culture shock and began to love the job. I regularly went to Sydney for training at Elizabeth Arden, Max Factor and other cosmetic houses, and began to accumulate certificates. David Jones staff were friendly and I liked the way people gently poked fun at each other. We often went out to dinner together.

I earned $40 per week, but had to pay $25 for child care. Ibu said, 'I'll look after your children. It'll be cheaper, only $20 per week.'

There wasn't much left after paying Ibu, but it was enough. It had hurt when Dahlan insisted on managing our finances, but now I was earning my own income, and I liked the taste of independence that it gave me.

Later I found out that Ibu provided free child care for her other grandchildren.

The relationship between Indonesia and Australia had been strained since the 1950s, when Australia worried that Sukarno was giving too much power to the PKI, the largest non-ruling communist party in the world. Australia provided covert aid to the regional rebellions and supported the Dutch occupation of West New Guinea. When Sukarno initiated Konfrontasi with Malaysia, Australia, already committed to the war in Vietnam, feared being drawn into fighting Communism on two fronts. Australian soldiers were secretly sent to Borneo to fight Indonesian troops infiltrating Malaysia.

The changes in Indonesia as Suharto took over were met with relief by the Australian government. The New Order stopped Konfrontasi, rejoined the United Nations and reorientated policy towards market-friendly economic development. The massacres of people accused of being communist did not worry Harold Holt who, during a visit to

America in 1966, was reported by the New York Times to have remarked in a speech: "With 500,000 to one million Communist sympathisers knocked off, I think it is safe to assume a reorientation has taken place."

Zara Holt was spared the task of choosing a present for Mrs Suharto. In December 1967 Harold Holt disappeared while swimming at a Victorian beach, and was presumed drowned. Holt was replaced as Prime Minister by John Gorton, whose wife, Bettina, was a colleague of my father at the Australian National University.

Bettina had studied languages at the Sorbonne. In 1960 an official visit to Sarawak with her husband sparked her interest in Asian culture, and she enrolled in Oriental Studies at ANU. With Achdiat as one of her lecturers, she gained a deep knowledge of Indonesian language, culture and literature and graduated with honours. In 1967 she completed her Master's Qualifying thesis on one of Indonesia's regional languages, while working at ANU part-time on a research project to create an English-Malay dictionary, Malay being the source of the official languages of both Indonesia and Malaysia. Bettina and Achdiat had become good friends, and she chose for her Master's thesis the topic of his first novel.

Bettina analysed *Atheis* both as a work of literature and as an aid to studying history, arguing that non-Indonesians, by reading such fiction, could gain the empathy needed to understand Indonesian culture and history. She saw *Atheis* as particularly useful because it took a storyline familiar to Westerners – that of a young man searching for self-realisation amidst conflicting world views – and placed it in an Indonesian social context.

Two days after John Gorton was elected Prime Minister, Bettina made a radio broadcast to Indonesia in fluent Indonesian. Later that year she accompanied her husband on a state visit to Malaysia, Singapore and Indonesia and, as reported in the National Archives, "her speeches and ready conversations with people in their own language had an impact few prime ministerial wives have managed."

The Indonesian Parliament had appointed Suharto President shortly before the Gortons' visit. John Gorton promised aid for reconstruction, and the two leaders agreed to cooperate on major issues such as negotiating the seabed border between the two countries.

After John Gorton was replaced as Prime Minister, Bettina returned to ANU to work on the dictionary and later resumed research for her Master's Thesis, travelling to West Java to collect material on my father's life and work. Sadly, she became unwell and passed away before she could finish her thesis. Another Prime Minister, Gough Whitlam, later said that Bettina Gorton had used her language skills to make a lasting and valuable contribution to Australia's relations with Indonesia. I like to think that her friendship with my father played some part on the path to her achievements.

Suharto had ordered the release of political prisoners including Mochtar Lubis, who initially supported the New Order. Mochtar's international reputation made this support valuable to the regime. He re-established his newspaper *Indonesia Raya*, which combined respect for Suharto with investigation of the corruption and crimes happening under his watch. The paper published evidence of corruption at the state oil company, Pertamina, in particular targeting the head of the company, General Ibnu Sutowo, who was Dahlan's boss.

Dahlan had worked under Ibnu Sutowo at Permina, which had now merged with the other state oil company to become a giant corporation, Pertamina. Dahlan's employment was transferred to the new company. When his unpaid leave neared an end, Ibnu Sutowo sent a long telegram, telling Dahlan that his expertise was urgently needed. Dahlan was unhappy at ANU because of his low position but hated the thought of working for Pertamina because of the corruption, and so he faced a moral dilemma. Finally he decided to return to Indonesia and work at Pertamina until he could find another job.

Although my time in Australia had started badly, now I

would have liked to stay, because Cheddy had settled into the primary school across the road from our house, and I would miss my new friends – the wives of the other lecturers and the white people I worked with. But I was also excited about going home. I felt that Australia had given me the confidence to face the world.

CHAPTER 23
The Scattered Dust of Love

> The world is too heavily covered with what Ina called the *'ubiquitous dust'*, preventing love from being perfect … love doesn't exist if it can't be shown and proven. And in order for that to happen physical presence, or at least the opportunity to communicate, is an important requirement.
> —Achdiat Karta Mihardja, *The Scattered Dust of Love*

In Indonesia we moved into the house with the dwarf banana plants in Jalan Talaga Bodas in Bandung. Dahlan worked for Pertamina in Jakarta, commuting each week.

Shortly after our return, Indonesia buzzed with news of the "wedding of the year" – Ibnu Sutowo's daughter. Dahlan frowned at our invitation, not wanting to go but knowing we would have to. I was curious to find out how rich they really were.

The wedding took place in Central Jakarta at Ibnu Sutowo's family compound, which consisted of several luxury mansions. There were thousands of guests, too many to fit into the main residence where the ceremony was held, so people assembled in the other houses as well. Dahlan and I joined his colleagues in the large parlour of the house reserved for Pertamina staff, while lower status employees gathered in the other rooms. Each room in each house had a TV screen so that the guests could watch the ceremony on closed-circuit television. It was the first time Dahlan and I had seen this new technology.

At other Indonesian weddings it was customary for guests to congratulate the bride and groom after the ceremony and then to mingle over the food, but here each group stayed in their allotted space, each with their own elaborate smorgasbord. Our room was like a reunion of ex-Stanvac managers, and I enjoyed renewing my friendship with the wives after my three years away. One grabbed my hand. 'Come on,' she said. 'Let's go upstairs and check out the swimming pool on the roof.'

But when we reached the staircase, security men barred our way.

The extravagance of the wedding provided *Indonesia Raya* with more ammunition for its series of exposés of corruption within Pertamina. The newspaper published detailed evidence that enormous amounts of cash were passing through the company without being accounted for, much of it skimmed off by Ibnu Sutowo and fellow officers in the military. The evidence demonstrated that, although the company generated revenue for the new regime, Pertamina was paying much less tax than it should.

The newspaper articles prompted large student demonstrations in Jakarta and, in 1970, Suharto was forced to appoint a commission to investigate corruption. The commission confirmed *Indonesia Raya's* allegations, but its recommendations were ignored. Six years later Pertamina was revealed to have billions of dollars of unserviceable debts which the government had to take over, resulting in severe damage to the Indonesian economy. General Ibnu Sutowo was never punished. Suharto dismissed him 'with honour', and later presented him with a state award for services to the oil industry. When he died in 2001, Ibnu Sutowo was buried in the National Heroes' Cemetery.

Suharto's leniency with Sutowo contrasted with his treatment of the former President. Sukarno had been placed under house arrest in the Bogor palace and Suharto denied him good medical care and prohibited visitors, even after he was taken to hospital. Sukarno, "Father of the Nation", died in 1970 and, after a quiet funeral, was buried beside his mother in a simple grave in East Java.

In Canberra when I had cooked and cleaned and washed for my family, I realised how hard our servants in Indonesia had worked. I felt ashamed of the way I had treated them – snapping at Bi Uju if the food didn't meet my standards, wiping my finger on the furniture to show the cleaner she hadn't dusted properly. I know that my mother had terrified our servants when I was growing up and I realised now I must have been almost as cruel.

Housework was hard but by doing it I valued myself

more because I felt independent. I told Dahlan that in Indonesia we would not have any servants, that I would do everything myself. Dahlan smiled, but did not say a word.

At the house in Jalan Talaga Bodas we employed a driver and a gardener but no servants in the house. I prepared breakfast, organised the children to go to school, did the washing, mopped the floors, cleaned the bathroom, went to the market and prepared the meals. I was proud of myself.

One day a neighbour called in. When I opened the door, she said, 'Oh, you're going out.'

'No, I'm in the middle of cleaning.'

'But you're wearing your shoes. In the house.'

'It's more comfortable. I got used to wearing shoes in Canberra.'

As she came in she looked at the mop I'd been using. 'You're mopping the floor? That's no good. Why don't you have a servant?'

'I'm happy doing it. That's what I did in Australia and I like being able to do it myself.'

My neighbour shook her head.

I became famous in the arisan, the neighbourhood women's group. 'Ibu Wenny has a new style,' people said. 'Now she's working in the house with her shoes on.' In Indonesia everyone automatically takes their shoes off when they enter a house.

Another day my good friend Yana dropped in as I was stir-frying vegetables and chicken for lunch. After commenting on my shoes she said, 'Is that all? Only one dish? Where are all the side dishes?'

'It's plenty,' I said.

'But what about Dahlan? There's not enough there.'

'Yan, it's got everything in it – chicken, different vegetables.'

'You're not going to make a fish dish? Or a …'

'No. This has all the nutrients in one dish.'

'Wenny, you've changed. It's like the difference between earth and sky.'

Yana was shocked at my decision to not have servants, as were all my friends, neighbours and family. People often dropped in and I couldn't say, 'Go home, I'm doing the housework,' so I would stop cooking or cleaning to talk with the visitor. By the end of the day there were many things left undone in the house.

After three months I'd had enough! I went to the village near Garut where Bi Uju lived and she agreed without hesitation to come back to work for us again. She took charge of the kitchen, and I hired a second servant to do the washing and cleaning, and a boy to run errands.

I tried to be a good boss. Whenever I was about to criticise our employees I reminded myself how hard I had found their work.

Shortly after we had left Australia, Ibu found work at the Canberra Hospital, delivering meals to patients. Bapak objected to her working, and especially hated her wearing a uniform. 'Quit,' he told her. 'We have enough to live on.'

'No,' she replied. 'I love my job. And it's not harming you. I still look after you at home.'

Bapak retired from ANU in 1971. Ibu had managed their finances well, investing their savings shrewdly, and they also had Bapak's superannuation, but she still worried about how they would survive without his salary, despite the fact that she continued to work.

Now that he was retired, Bapak often spent time with us in Bandung, coming by himself as Ibu did not want to take time off from her job. He wanted to move back to Indonesia, but Ibu refused. For the rest of their lives they argued about where to live, but Ibu never budged. She had sound practical reasons for staying in Australia – their many friends, the better health services as they became older – while Bapak had only his intense longing for his home country.

Dahlan was looking for another job, which I hoped would be nearer our home. The Vice-chancellor of Padjadjaran University in Bandung was a friend, so I invited him to dinner to meet Dahlan. At the table the VC said, 'Dahlan, why don't you help us out? We need a lecturer with your experience in the economics faculty.'

'Thank you, but I must decline. I have a job in Jakarta.'

I looked at Dahlan in surprise. Our guest said, 'But commuting must be tiring, not good for your family.'

'Come on, Lan,' I said. 'Just accept it.'

'I'll think about it.'

But instead Dahlan secured a high position in Jakarta with Esso, plus a second job as Deputy Director of the Management School at the University of Indonesia. I was upset. 'Okay,' I said. 'I will move to Jakarta.'

Dahlan was emphatic. 'No. Jakarta is too expensive. We have a house here and the kids have settled into school. We don't want to disrupt their education by shifting them again so soon.'

'But I don't want to be separated.'

'I'll be here every weekend,' said Dahlan.

I should have packed up and moved to Jakarta, but I didn't. Early each Monday morning Dahlan caught the Parahyangan Express, which took three hours to reach Jakarta, and every Friday evening he returned.

By now I was working too. My training and experience in Canberra helped me obtain the position of manager of the West Java headquarters of a cosmetics firm. Their business was expanding because they had just become the sole agent in the province for Max Factor Indonesia, owned by Ibu Tien Suharto, the wife of the President.

I was based at the firm's store in Jalan Asia-Afrika, where I ran beauty classes for women's groups. I also had a company car and driver, and travelled throughout West Java giving make-up demonstrations and promoting Max Factor products.

After a year I left the firm and set up my own business – the Shandy Beauty School, named after my children, Shanti, Dian and Cheddy. Like many Indonesian houses, ours had a type of annexe known as a *pavilyun* which owners often rented out. I established the beauty school in our pavilyun.

Shandy classes covered make-up, massage, skin care, etiquette, table manners, deportment, fashion and dress codes. Many of the students were wives of men in high positions, and they needed to know the correct combinations of clothes, shoes, bags and make-up for each type of function, depending on level of formality and time of day, and the proper use of crockery, cutlery and wine glasses.

Students in my beautician classes were assessed twice – first by me at the end of the course, and then in government tests. I was sometimes contracted by the education department to be an assessor for students in other schools.

Shandy also had many individual clients who came for facials, manicures and the cosmetics that were produced in partnership with a chemist. I learnt Sundanese and Javanese bridal make-up, and this proved lucrative.

Shandy Beauty School was a success and, in some months, my earnings were higher than Dahlan's. I became active in the industry, serving as president of the Indonesian Beauticians Association for West Java. I was doing what I enjoyed – teaching, using my education degree – in a field I loved.

The New Order regime was now firmly in control. Suharto's party, Golkar, had won 63 percent of the vote in the 1971 election, but this was in the context of intimidation of voters and the arrest of opponents. These tactics ended Moctar Lubis's support for the New Order, and *Indonesia Raya* began to target those closer to the President, questioning corrupt relationships between powerful military officers and their Chinese business partners, and even criticising Ibu Tien Suharto for her plans to build the massive Taman Mini tourist park.

In 1973 Indonesia was beset by unrest. A rice shortage and the resulting high prices caused great suffering among the many still living in poverty. Economic policies favouring foreign capital forced many small Indonesian firms to close and people resented the Chinese businessmen who did well out their connections with the corrupt government.

In August 1973 a car with Chinese passengers collided

with a bullock cart in Bandung, sparking an outbreak of violence with thousands of rioters rampaging through the city, looting and burning Chinese shops and houses, overturning cars and setting them alight. I could see flames and smoke in the city centre, not far from where we lived, and I locked the gate and closed the curtains, anxious because Dahlan was in Jakarta.

That night the children, servants and I cowered inside as we heard a mob approach along the street, sounding like hundreds of people, all yelling 'Smash the Chinese!' Then they were outside the house, rattling our gate. Somebody cried, 'Shandy Beauty School – Chinese!'

'No, stop,' another voice called. 'That's Ibu Dahlan – indigenous Indonesian.'

The mob moved on. A little later the sounds of yelling and breakage escalated and we realised they were ransacking the Chinese restaurant at the end of the street.

The riots continued into the night. The next day we heard that most of the shops in the city centre had been destroyed.

The Information Minister instructed all newspapers to 'refrain from exaggerating the Bandung incident', but *Indonesia Raya* covered the riots in depth. For the rest of the year the paper continued to ignore warnings, and was especially critical of foreign investment from Japan. When the Japanese Prime Minister visited Jakarta in January 1974, there were student protests followed by widespread rioting and looting. The government struck back, arresting student leaders, lawyers, journalists and activists, and banning newspapers, including *Indonesia Raya*. Mochtar was arrested a year later, and then spent two months in prison before the authorities decided not to press charges and released him. But Mochtar's time as a crusading journalist was over. He decided to devote himself to writing, journal editing and advocacy for the artistic community.

In 1974 *Atheis* was adapted into a film by Sjumandjaja, a prominent Indonesian director. The movie provoked a controversy, because on the screen was a man persuasively advocating Marxism, which the New Order regime had outlawed.

The film was banned, but soon more reasoned voices were heard, and the ban was lifted after two days. Ironically, a few years previously, the New Order government had presented Achdiat with the country's highest artistic award for his contribution to Indonesian literature.

After his retirement Bapak remained active in the Indonesian community in Canberra and held various visiting positions such as lecturer at the University of Papua New Guinea. He finished his second novel, *Debu Cinta Bertebaran* (The Scattered Dust of Love), published in 1973. The novel illuminates the clash between traditional Indonesian values, which emphasise family and social obligations, and modern Western values, which give more weight to individual rights and freedom. The protagonist, Rivai, an Indonesian journalist living in Sydney, tries to find a balance that combines the best of both cultures, taking from each whatever makes for a fulfilling life. He observes the consequences of too much individual freedom in some of the Australians he knows – loneliness, alienation, drug use, suicide – but he also believes that people do not thrive where individual rights are overruled by communal responsibilities. He works his way towards a balance of individuality within community.

Bapak used the characters of *Scattered Dust of Love* to portray various modes of loving and ways to strengthen and foster love. A central theme of the novel is the "harsh irony" that humans have been given the capacity to love, but the world is heavily covered with "ubiquitous dust", which prevents love from being perfect – the dust of prejudice, excessive individualism, misunderstanding and resentment.

As my father grew older he became more religious. When I was young I never saw him practice Islam, but after he moved to Canberra he began attending the mosque every Friday. Now, whenever he came to stay with us, he visited a *pesantren*, an Islamic school, near Garut and met with its leader. It was a school that he had known as a child.

Achdiat had been born into a devout family who followed a strand of Sufism, the inner mystical Islamic path, that was taught at the pesantren. My grandparents had often taken their children to the pesantren so they would learn to pray and perform Sufi practices such as reciting God's names while using the *tasbeh*, a string of a hundred beads. The young Achdiat was drawn to Sufi philosophy.

Although the pesantren was a boarding school that provided Islamic education for children, my grandparents had sent Achdiat to a Dutch school because it would give him a better chance of employment in a high position. During the 1930s he returned to the pesantran to study Sufist mysticism, but as he became more involved with other writers and the independence struggle his interest shifted away from mysticism toward the study of humans and their society. Now, late in life, he returned to Sufism.

By the 1970s the school, now known as Pesantren Suryalaya, had become one of the major centres of the Indonesian Sufi revival under the charismatic leadership of Abah Anom, the son of the pesantren's founder. When a drug-taking epidemic had broken out among the children of the political and military elite in Jakarta, Abah Anom gained a reputation for successfully treating addiction and mental illness at the pesantren, using discipline and Sufi practice. Consequently, powerful people became followers of Abah Anom and provided financial support. As well as teaching Islam, the pesantren became a vocational training centre, where students could learn a trade such as carpentry, or study agriculture on a modern irrigation farm.

The Sufi revival spread rapidly in Jakarta. The daughter of one of my devout aunts married a state mining company Director who held monthly meetings in their house for followers of the pesantren, and provided transport to bring Abah Anom to the gathering. Many politicians attended.

I had never heard Bapak mention Sufism previously, but now he talked about it often. He had always been uneasy with conservative Islam's dogmatism and insistence on following rules. Sufism is an interior Islam, and is tolerant of other religious traditions. Bapak was returning to the philosophy that attracted him as a child, but now he began to practice the Sufi path. When he visited Pesantren Suryalaya and met with Abah Anom, he was filling himself, turning his heart towards God. He was never without his *tasbeh* beads, the Sufi method of always remembering God, whether one is happy or sad.

Dahlan and I were not devout. Dahlan had read many books about Islam and other religions but I never saw him pray or fast. I had forgotten Hariyadi's prayer lessons, but I thought it was my duty to raise our children as Muslims, so I employed an Imam to come to our house twice a week to teach them how to pray, and told Dahlan that we had to train the children to fast. During Ramadan we rose early to eat before daybreak and we fasted until sunset.

I was with a client on the second day of Ramadan when I glanced at our house and saw smoke emerging from the louvres of our en suite. I rushed into the house and threw open the bathroom door. My husband was sitting on the toilet, smoking.

'Dahlan,' I cried, 'stop that. We should be fasting. You're giving a bad example to the children.'

'Wenny, I'm sorry. I really tried hard but I can't.'

'Yes, you can.'

'I can't do without it. Smoking is important for me from when I wake up in the morning to when I go to sleep at night. Without it my brain is dead and I can't think. I need my brain to be working.'

I had long been worried that Dahlan would get cancer from his heavy smoking, and many times I had tried to get him to quit, or at least cut down. My efforts had come to nothing, so I knew I would not win this battle either. 'Just make sure the children don't find out,' I said.

Although Dahlan had no interest in any outward show of religion he did believe in its core values. He was generous, always ready to help anyone, refused to take advantage of his position and had left Pertamina because of the corruption. I loved him, and he loved me. But …

Waiting for our meal at a street stall, I flipped through a

Tempo I'd bought from a magazine boy and came across a photo of Dahlan. The article described him giving lectures in Malaysia.

'Why didn't you tell me you'd been to Malaysia?' I asked.

'I was only there a couple of days. At the weekend I'm always in Bandung.'

I was so angry I couldn't eat.

One Sunday after lunch Dahlan called the servant and asked her to clean his shoes and suitcase.

'Where are you going?' I asked.

'Hawaii.'

'What! When?'

'Tuesday.'

'Why?'

'A research project at the university.'

'How long for?'

'Six months.'

I give up, I thought. I can't argue. I just have to accept that Dahlan doesn't talk to me, has never talked to me. We always had our meals together but there was no conversation at the table. I ate more slowly than he did, and he lit a cigarette and waited until I finished before he returned to his study.

One of Dahlan's sisters was less hostile than his other siblings, and when we'd lived in Jakarta I had told her that he didn't talk to me. 'Yes,' she had said. 'That's what he's like. At home he didn't communicate with any of us, not even Bapak and Ibu. He was a bookworm studying all the time. When he came home from school he would say hello to everyone, then go to his room and shut the door. Nobody would disturb him. We all respected him. Actually we were scared of him. He would come out of his room to have dinner, and then go straight back to study.'

One evening after a silent meal I said, 'Lan, why can't you talk with me? You can talk for hours with your colleagues but not with your wife. What's the matter? Is it because the gap between your intelligence and mine is so wide? Is it because I'm stupid and you're brilliant?'

He didn't say a word.

'Do you really love me?'
'Of course.'

The thought came to me that I was part of the furniture. His work was his fulfilment, but for a complete life he needed to equip himself with a wife and children.

When my parents visited us, I told them about my unhappiness. Even though they liked Dahlan, they both said, 'Just divorce him. You're still young.'

But I didn't want a divorce. I wanted us to be soul-mates. I wanted us to be like my parents, but without the arguments. Bapak and Ibu talked to each other constantly. When they went to bed they had a long chat before going to sleep. When they woke they talked for an hour before they got up. Mealtimes were full of lively conversation. That's what I longed for.

Feeling that the love Dahlan and I shared was being choked by the "scattered dust" my father had described in his novel, I became more lonely and depressed, and sought help from a professor of psychology. 'It seems you've tried hard to get him to communicate with you,' he said, 'but nothing has worked. Maybe you can try shock treatment. Go out without him. Go out often. Go out with your friends. Go to the movies.'

One of my clients was married to the Director of Telecom and they planned a big wedding for their daughter. I showed Dahlan the invitation and said, 'I'd like us to go. She's bought a lot of product from me.'

'I'm tired,' said Dahlan. 'Just go by yourself.'

'What! I can't go by myself. This wedding is a big event in Bandung.'

'No, I don't feel like it. I want to sleep.'

So, I thought, time for shock treatment. The nephew of Dahlan's colleague was boarding with us. I asked him if he would like to accompany me to the wedding. His eyes opened wide. 'But – Pak Dahlan? Is it alright with Pak Dahlan?'

'It's okay.'

I was Ibu Dahlan, but I went to the wedding with the boarder. It was what the psychologist meant by shock treatment.

A lot of people were shocked but not Dahlan. The treatment didn't work. Did. Not. Work.

In 1976 Chris, a history professor, stayed with us during a visit to Indonesia. After lunch we had coffee in the courtyard. Chris stood at the fountain, playing with the water and poking at the fish. 'Wenny! I don't understand,' he said. 'Dahlan is in Jakarta and you are here. It's not healthy for the marriage. Why don't you move to Jakarta or he move here?'

'He doesn't want to, Chris,' I said. 'Every day I think about moving to Jakarta but he won't agree because it's too expensive. And he doesn't want to work in Bandung. He was offered a position at the uni here and turned it down.'

'Why don't you go back to Australia?' Chris suggested. 'There's a vacancy at Griffith University in Brisbane. They need an economics lecturer for their Asian Studies Program.'

'He won't do that.'

But the more I thought about it, the more I liked the idea, and the more I thought Dahlan would consider it. After six years he was tired of commuting. Since arriving back in Indonesia he'd been trying to set up an oil business with some ex-colleagues, but it hadn't worked and again he'd lost money.

The children's education was a good reason for going back to Australia. We now had four children – our new daughter Ira was only a few months old. We both worried about the standard of schooling in Indonesia. Cheddy was in high school where the poorly-paid teachers insisted that every student, regardless of ability, needed private tuition after school, provided by them at additional cost. I knew Cheddy didn't need it, but if we had refused he would have received lower marks, or been given a difficult time in class.

A lecturer position in Brisbane would be a lower paid job for Dahlan and I would have to give up my beauty school, but I wanted us to be together. Yes, I decided, I was prepared to sacrifice material wealth so that we could live under the same roof and the children could have a good education.

When Dahlan returned from Jakarta, I held my breath as

Chris told him about the position. 'Okay,' Dahlan said.

Dahlan applied for the job and was offered a five-year contract. He left to start straightaway, while I stayed behind to arrange the move. I leased the house and sold the beauty school stock, cosmetic recipes, our furniture and car, and transferred the money to an Australian bank. I would put it towards buying a house in Brisbane.

Wenny in 1975

CHAPTER 24
Tears and Laughter

> [Pramoedya Ananta Toer] is a tragic figure ... I knew Pram from the Revolutionary era, and experienced myself how he was always short of money. That is the characteristic of an artist.
> —Achdiat Karta Mihardja, Interview, *Syir'ah Magazine*

As for Dahlan and me previously, the lack of servants in Australia was a shock for the children. In Indonesia they had freshly shined shoes waiting for them each morning, a driver to take them to school and bring them home, where a servant met them and carried their bag into the house. Now they were horrified that their mother insisted they help with demeaning chores like vacuuming or cleaning the bathroom. I was strict, and they didn't like it. 'This is Australia,' I said. 'We have to work together.'

Cheddy, now fourteen, went to Canberra to stay with my parents during the Christmas holidays. When it was time for him to come home, Bapak rang and told us, 'Cheddy wants to stay here and go to school in Canberra. He doesn't want to go back to Queensland.'

'No,' I said. 'Cheddy has to come home.'

Bapak put Cheddy on the phone. 'Mama, I want to stay with Nini and Aki. I've met lots of Indonesian friends. Their fathers work at the embassy. I don't have any friends in Brisbane – there're no Indonesian kids at McGregor High. I'm lonely there. I want to stay here.'

'No, no, no,' I said. 'You must come back.'

Bapak asked to speak to Dahlan and I handed the phone over reluctantly, because Dahlan was a good son-in-law who would not want to argue with my parents. He spoke to Bapak, then Cheddy, then Bapak again. I could see that he was upset, but he couldn't say no to my father. 'If Cheddy really wants to stay there,' he said, 'It's up to him.'

Dahlan was very quiet after the phone call.

'Lan, why didn't you say no,' I demanded. 'I said no.'

'Wenny, there's no point. If the child doesn't want to live with us, I don't want to force him.'

'But you're his father. You have the power.'

'No, that child has already decided what he wants. Just let it go.'

I was angry with my parents, who had been trying to get Cheddy away from us since he was born. Now we would not see our child growing as a teenager.

A few days later my mother rang to ask me to send regular money for Cheddy's board. We also had to cover schooling costs – books, uniforms, excursions. In Indonesia, grandparents often bring up their first grandchild, but never ask for money to do so. Ibu had definitely adopted Australian customs.

Bapak and Ibu began to refer to Cheddy as their friend. 'We have a friend in the house,' they said. Before he came they had been lonely. I don't think they considered the impact on Dahlan and me.

Soon after I arrived in Brisbane, the School of Languages at Griffith University offered me a position as a tutor in Indonesian. I was excited, but Dahlan said, 'No, I cannot agree. It's not right for both of us to work at the same university.'

'What! But Lan, I'm sure there are lots of married couples working there.'

'They are them, I am me. And there's no need for you to work at all. I'm the breadwinner. It's better for the children if you stay at home.'

I soon found other things to do – volunteering at Meals on Wheels, teaching Chinese and Indonesian cooking at TAFE, teaching Indonesian at a private language school in the city.

In the 1950s many Indos – people with Dutch fathers and Indonesian mothers – had been forced to leave Indonesia because of their connection to the hated Dutch. A group who lived in Brisbane contacted me shortly after my arrival, asking if I could help them improve their language. They could speak *bahasa pasar*, market Indonesian, but wanted to learn formal *Bahasa Indonesia*.

They cooked Indonesian food at home and craved contact with people from the country they'd grown up in and still loved. I enjoyed working with this lively group who had suffered so much discrimination.

My next project was direct selling of Bessemer Cookware by party plan. At each party I cooked several dishes to demonstrate how the utensils were used and this was a success, especially when my parties became popular amongst the Greek community.

In the middle of this activity our son Ari was born. A year after his birth I took a job in cosmetics at David Jones Garden City.

Initially we lived in a rented house but one day Dahlan told me he had bought a house at Runcorn Heights, close to the university. I was angry. The money I'd brought from Bandung would be needed to cover half the cost of the house. 'Why didn't you involve me?' I demanded.

'No time. It was going cheap so I had to move fast.'

'You could have rung me from your office.'

He did not answer.

The five houses in our small cul-de-sac each had a different design and all had been display homes. The house was too small – it only had four bedrooms, tiny compared to what we were used to in Indonesia, but I grew to love our cul-de-sac community. When we moved in, Myrtle from two houses up held a party for all the neighbours to welcome us. Later Nancy and Jack moved in next door to us and it was my turn to entertain.

Shortly after they moved in Nancy was chatting with the children and me in our front garden when Dian called her 'Auntie Nancy'. 'Oh, no, Dian. Don't call me Auntie,' she exclaimed. 'I'm not that old.'

I told Nancy that in Indonesia we always treated older people with respect by addressing them with a title, and that not to do so was considered rude.

'Oh, Wenny. I still don't want it. Please Dian, just call me Nancy.'

Dian looked uncomfortable and after we went inside she said to me, 'I don't understand. Why doesn't Auntie Nancy want me to call her Auntie?'

I told her that when we moved to Canberra I too had been shocked to hear Dahlan use only first names when addressing colleagues in higher positions such as the Dean. 'How come?' I had demanded of Dahlan.

He had told me about Australian customs, and I now explained them to Dian. She found it hard but eventually managed to drop the titles when addressing our neighbours.

Nancy and Jack, who knew everything about the neighbourhood, held open house every afternoon. They were like grandparents to our children. Nancy always noticed if Shanti or Dian went out and would call them over, pressing fifty cents into their hands.

Dahlan was no more communicative, but we were now living under the same roof and doing things together. While he mowed the lawn, I gardened and tended the four mango trees I had planted in the back yard. We went to the supermarket together. We used any excuse – birthdays, Lebaran, Christmas – to throw a big party, and friends filled our house with stories and laughter. Together with another family we often spent the weekend fishing at the Gold Coast. We left on Friday after work and stayed at Cascade Gardens on the Nerang River at Broadbeach. We fished all night and went back to the units at sunrise to sleep until lunchtime. On Saturday night we fished again. Sometimes Dahlan caught two buckets of fish, and I allowed him to bring them home as long as he cleaned them at the river first.

One of our best friends was Noel, who was frugal and taught me how to make ends meet, taking us to the Rocklea markets to buy boxes of fruit and vegetables to share, showing us the enormous jackfruit tree in front of the pub at Cleveland. Noel and Dahlan climbed the tree and we filled our car with the young fruit, to be blanched, frozen and used for gudeg, the dish of jackfruit in coconut milk and spices that I had enjoyed with Hariyadi on the footpaths of Yogya.

Driving through Redland Bay to a park beside the sea for a barbecue, the car began shuddering. We got out and found nuts scattered all over the road. 'Hey,' Dahlan cried. 'These are candlenuts.' We looked up. A whole street of candlenut trees. It was like a dream. We could only buy candlenuts in Chinatown where they were expensive.

I had become nervous about driving since an accident in Bandung, and the best thing Noel did for me was to help me drive again. Noel was a patient teacher, helping me learn all the road rules so that I could pass the test to get a Queensland licence. Later I was to have good reason to be grateful for the confidence he gave me.

The five years Dahlan and I had in Brisbane were a time of happiness, but also sadness. Every day I thought of Cheddy and tears would come to my eyes. I knew Dahlan was also affected by losing his son, but there was nothing we could do. At least we saw Cheddy when we stayed with my parents during holidays, or when they came to Brisbane. For too short a time, the whole family would be together.

Fishing through the night at Broadbeach, I often thought of catching carp in the farmer's pond when we had taken refuge in the mountains during the Revolution, and the peace of rural life when we stayed at Rancaekek where my grandmother, Haji Noorwati, had owned highly-productive rice fields, which had been in her family for generations.

Haji Noorwati had died from tuberculosis when my mother was nine. After Haji Noor married Ibu Gunung and began a second family, he divided the Rancaekek fields between his first wife's children, my mother and her four siblings.

Then, in the 1960s when Indonesia was in turmoil, Ibu gave me the title deed to her share of the rice fields as a form of security, something that would always have value, and Dahlan paid to transfer the title deed to my name, using a consent letter from Ibu.

Since then Dahlan and I had paid the land tax and seed cost each year and given our share of the harvest – rice, fish, goats, coconuts – to Aki Noor and Ibu Gunung. I valued the connection to the grandmother I had never known, and to the generations before her. This connection was strengthened by visits to my grandmother's grave in the Noor family cemetery in the hills near Garut. Once my father came with me and we knelt on the tiled ledge border of the grave, scattered flower petals over the grave soil, then poured water over it in accordance with custom, silently praying for my grandmother as we did so. Between us, the caretaker prayed aloud. Suddenly there was strong smell of incense, yet no incense was burning. My father and I looked at each other at the same time, both of us surprised. Bapak asked the caretaker if he could smell incense.

'No,' he replied. 'But if you smell it, that is a sign that your mother-in-law and grandmother accepts your prayer. She shows that she is pleased that you have visited her grave and are praying for her.'

I was deeply grateful to Ibu for passing her mother's inheritance on to me.

In 1979 one of Ibu's sisters, Bi Iyat, visited Australia. I took her and Ibu on a tour of the Gold Coast and Noosa and brought them back to stay at our house at Runcorn Heights. When Dahlan and I had decided to marry, Bi Iyat complained to Aki because I told another aunt the news before I told her. Since then I had always felt awkward with her, but I treated her politely.

On the day Ibu and Bi were to fly back to Canberra, the three of us were chatting at the dining table after lunch and the conversation turned to the fields at Rancaekek.

'You and Dahlan have a good life in Australia,' said Ibu. 'So you should give the title deed to the rice fields back to me.'

I stared at her. I felt the gelang keroncong on my arm, the five gold bangles my mother had given me for my seventeenth birthday. I remembered how she had asked for them back because she wanted to give them to my sister.

'Yes,' said Bi Iyat. 'You have a comfortable life. You don't need the rice fields anymore.'

Without replying I went to the bedroom where I kept my files. I retrieved the title deed and held it, trying to control my anger. I thought of the many times Ibu returned from overseas with gifts for my nephews and nieces but not for my children, and how she had charged me for child-minding. She didn't need to beat me anymore as she had in Jalan Meranti, because she had other ways to hurt me. But why did she need to?

When I returned to the dining table I threw the deed down in front of my mother. Her head jerked up and she stared at me with narrowed eyes.

'I was so happy you trusted me with the rice fields,' I said. 'It was my link to my grandmother, to my homeland.'

'But you don't need it anymore.'

'Maybe not. But you gave it to me, and now you want it back. That is what is hurting.'

My mother took the deed and put it in her suitcase.

Dahlan became increasingly dissatisfied with working at Griffith University, and in1981, the final year of his contract, he told me he would not renew it. He was unhappy that he had not been offered a Senior Lecturer position.

'But Lan, what will you do?' I asked.

'Don't worry, Wenny, I want to have a rest. We have enough money in the bank for a year and superannuation as well. I don't want to waste my time with a job I don't like.'

'I'm nervous if you're not working. Will you look for a job?'

'No, I'll just stay home and have a rest. With my CV and experience I know I'll get a good job before the year is up, one that pays more than Griffith.'

'I'll have to work.'

'No, you don't have to. We have enough money.'

But I was worried. I had left David Jones and now was keen to get back to my first field of education. I knew the local Multicap Special School needed Teacher Aides, so I went to see the Principal, Mrs Martin. She looked at me doubtfully. 'Maybe you have never seen how disabled a child can be,' she said.

'I'd like to try.'

She showed me around the school, taking me to each

of the classrooms. By the time we got back to her office I was in tears.

'Mrs Dahlan,' she said, 'I think you won't be able to cope with this work.'

'I want to try.'

'You still want to work here?'

'I can be strong. If I can help the children I'll be happy.'

The next morning I went to the school for a trial day. The time passed quickly as I changed nappies, cleaned up vomit, and massaged the students. Jackie was tiny, six years old, unable to talk or walk, but she had large bright eyes and a beautiful smile. Earl was a sweet boy who liked a cuddle but ran around wildly and would suddenly pull my hair or give me a push as I was feeding someone else. The hardest task was lifting John, a heavy twelve-year-old, from his wheelchair onto the changing table.

At the end of the day I drove home in a daze and staggered into the bathroom, my clothes smelling of saliva and vomit. I stood under the shower for ages, then lay on the bed and wept. Dahlan came in. 'Wenny, what's wrong?' he asked.

'The children. I can't bear to see children suffering like that.'

'Listen to me, Wenny. You don't need to work. Trust me. I'm the head of the family. I'll make sure we have enough money.'

'No, I want to be safe. What if something happens to you and I'm on my own in a foreign country looking after the kids?'

'Well, just find a different job.'

'No, I want to help those children. It's a challenge for me. I want satisfaction for myself.'

For the first week I struggled and each day I came home a mess. But then I began looking forward to going to work and seeing the children again. I felt that I was connecting with them, and they seemed to like me. Each time Jackie saw me her eyes lit up and she waved her arms, giving me a huge smile.

Dahlan told me to open my own bank account. 'I'm the breadwinner. The money you've earned with your sweat and tears shouldn't be going into our joint account.'

After Dahlan finished working at Griffith the School of Languages again asked me to tutor in Indonesian, and I began working there part time two nights a week. I now had two jobs but I was still not satisfied. A friend who had been to my dinner parties and knew I loved cooking told me the local nursing home needed a weekend cook. When the Matron looked at my resume she was doubtful. 'You've got a degree,' she said. 'Why do you want to be a cook?'

'I cook for six people every day,' I said. 'And I often cater for big parties, sometimes more than a hundred guests. I'd like to give it a go.'

She showed me the menu, covering morning tea, lunch, afternoon tea and dinner. The meals were basic, easier to manage than Indonesian cuisine. 'I can do it,' I said.

I worked every Saturday and Sunday from ten in the morning until seven at night, and I liked being able to serve the residents, getting to know them, finding out what they liked, perhaps cheese or fruit, and giving them extra treats. The job became just as satisfying as my work at the special school.

One morning at six o'clock Matron rang. 'Wenny,' she said, 'I need your help. The cleaner is sick, and I can't find anyone to replace her. Can you do some extra work before your usual shift?'

I felt I couldn't say no as Matron was an understanding boss. But when I was there, looking at the row of twelve toilets, I wished I'd refused. After cleaning the first one I closed the lid and, on my knees, leant on it and cried. 'Why?' I asked myself. 'I'm a university graduate, spoiled by my parents, used to having servants. Why am I cleaning up other people's dirt? I was Mrs Dahlan, lady of leisure, *nyonya besar*. But now in Australia, far from my own country, Mrs Dahlan is the cleaner.'

I dried my tears. No, I thought, this is my challenge. It's only one day.

I stood up and cleaned the remaining toilets. Then, at ten o'clock I scrubbed my hands and arms, changed my shoes and put on my cook's uniform. When I got home that night I cried again from sheer tiredness. After my shower Dahlan gave me a massage. 'Wenny, I think it's time to leave all these jobs,' he said. 'We've got enough money.'

'No, I'm only tired because I had to work all day. I'm not giving up any of my jobs.'

My parents were visiting from Canberra. 'Why were you crying?' Bapak asked.

'I'm tired. And I've got a degree but I had to clean the toilets.'

I told my father about the questions I had asked myself as I cried over the pedestal.

'You felt ashamed of doing that work? It was lower than being a teacher?'

'Yes.'

'Wenny, in Indonesia there is a big gap between rich and poor people, and the rich look down on those of a lower social level. That's wrong. In Australia the gap is not so wide. We live in two countries, two cultures. We should pick the good from both and reject the bad. If we take the humane qualities from each culture, we will be very rich in here.' He put his hand over his heart, and went on. 'Don't despise being a cleaner, Wenny. It would be bad if you were a thief, a gambler, or a conman. But cleaning is a praiseworthy, noble occupation. It's doing good for others. The people in the nursing home need your help. Be happy that you can do that for them.'

My father had recently completed a term as Fulbright Visiting Professor at the University of Ohio's Indonesian Studies Summer Institute, where he had delivered a speech on Lebaran Day about the significance of the fasting month. He spoke of the *Jihad Besar*, the great holy war inside us between our humane qualities and our destructive drives. Fasting, he said, is an effective way to win the battle, because during Ramadan we must not only abstain from food and drink, but also from committing bad actions. When the battle ends, the victory should be celebrated with love for our fellow humans at Lebaran, especially by showing a willingness to forgive each other's wrongs. He compared the fasting and Lebaran practises of Muslims to the Educational

Exchange Program instituted by J. William Fulbright, which funded the Summer Institute. Both had the goal of humanising mankind.

Achdiat enacted his belief in forgiveness, as shown by his reconciliation with the writer Pramoedya Ananta Toer. They had known each other during the Revolution and early years of independence, but had moved onto opposite sides of the cultural war that erupted during the Guided Democracy period. Pramoedya had been a prominent member of LEKRA, the cultural arm of the Communist Party, and strongly attacked the anti-communist group of which Achdiat and Mochtar Lubis were members. When Mochtar won the Magsaysay Award, Pramoedya called him an "imperialist stooge."

After the coup of October 1965, Pramoedya and other LEKRA members were detained without trial in barbaric conditions on the prison island of Buru. He was denied writing materials for most of his time on the island but managed to complete four novels by memorising them and reciting them to his fellow prisoners. The novels were published after his release in 1979 and were immediately banned by the New Order. However, overseas Indonesian and English editions established Pramoedya's reputation as one of Indonesia's greatest writers and many saw him as the country's only hope for a Nobel Prize for literature.

When Achdiat heard that Pramoedya had been released, he visited him at his home in Jakarta. The two writers embraced and then talked for four hours, recognising their differences but forgiving each other for past wrongs.

Mochtar was not so forgiving. In 1995, Pramoedya won the Magsaysay Award. Enraged, Mochtar began a campaign to reverse the decision, and when that failed he returned his own award to the Magsaysay Foundation.

CHAPTER 25
Crunch Time

Actually, it was rather difficult for Rivai to imagine what life was really like at home. He had lived overseas for too long.
—Achdiat Karta Mihardja, *The Scattered Dust of Love*

In 1982, when Dahlan had been unemployed for almost a year, his colleagues at the university in Hawaii recommended him for a World Bank position as consultant on the Indonesian economy, and two directors of the bank flew to Brisbane to interview him. It was a Sunday, and the directors were still there when I came home from my nursing home job in the evening.

'Mrs Dahlan,' said one, 'is it okay if your husband moves to Jakarta to work?'

'It's up to Dahlan. He's the one who'll be working.'

'But do you agree, Wenny?' Dahlan asked. 'It's a three-year contract.'

I made myself answer quickly. 'If you want the job, go for it.'

Later we talked. It was the type of work Dahlan wanted and the salary was far higher than he had ever earned before. 'How about if I ask for two years instead of three,' he said. 'You and the children stay here for the time being. If the job doesn't work out I can come back. If it goes well you can join me.'

'When do you start?'

'It's urgent. I've got three weeks to get there.'

I almost screamed. 'What? Lan, it's too soon. What about Ira?'

Ira was on medication for kidney reflux and was booked in for surgery in a month's time.

'I told the Directors about Ira, that I needed to stay here until after her operation, but they can't wait. They need me there straightaway.'

'Please, Lan, I can't do it on my own.'

Dahlan tried to reassure me but I was afraid. That night

I lay awake, worrying. It was bad enough when we lived in Bandung and he worked in Jakarta. Now we would be living in different countries. How could I manage Ira in hospital? Noel had given me more confidence in driving but only in our local area, not through city traffic to the Mater Children's Hospital in South Brisbane.

My whole family seemed scattered. Earlier that year Shanti had begged us to allow her to move to Canberra to complete Year Twelve while living with my parents. We had spent most holidays staying with my parents, and Shanti had made many friends among Indonesians her own age. We reluctantly agreed, but it seemed that Bapak and Ibu were taking our children from us one by one. Now I would have to look after my younger children without the help of my eldest daughter.

Two weeks later at the airport waiting for Dahlan's plane, I knelt before him and cried, 'Lan, don't go, don't go.'

I wrapped my arms around his legs and begged, 'Please don't go.'

He pulled me up and held me. 'It's only for two years,' he said. 'We have to do this to survive.'

I pulled my crying children to me as we watched Dahlan walking to immigration, and in that moment I realised the magnitude of my responsibility as a single mother in a foreign country. I felt utterly alone, and returned home filled with dread.

During the first few months after Dahlan had left I often woke about four o'clock in the morning and drove to Cleveland. I sat in the car watching the ripples of the sea as the sun rose. 'How come my husband lives far away over the horizon?' I asked myself. 'Why am I stranded in Australia?' I thought of Cheddy and Shanti in Canberra. Tears ran down my cheeks. Dian was getting good results at McGregor High and Ira was doing well at primary school, but she would soon have to go to hospital. Ari was in his first year of school. 'It's too much for me,' I thought. 'How can I manage?'

I dried my tears and drove back to Runcorn Heights to get the children to school and go to work at Multicap.

Every month Dahlan sent enough money for the

household and the children's education, so why was I wearing myself out in three jobs? During the Revolution when the Dutch almost captured my father and our city was bombed, I learnt that anything can happen. That feeling of insecurity stayed with me all my life. What if Dahlan should die or remarry? I would have to keep going, educating the children without his salary.

In Indonesia I would not have felt so insecure. If something were to happen to Dahlan I had many friends and relatives there to help me. But in Australia there was no one I could ask for support except my father, and Ibu, who controlled the money, would not allow him provide any assistance. I felt it was up to me to be financially strong, so I saved and invested the income from my work.

Gradually the routines of home and work settled to a manageable pattern.

When it was time for Ira's operation our neighbour Jack took us to the hospital, and each day drove me to visit her. But he wasn't available when it was time for her to come home, so I went by bus. A nurse called a taxi and Ira and I waited outside. It was a cold winter day, windy and raining. When the taxi pulled up, the driver peered at us and drove off.

I stood in the rain, crying and holding Ira, who was still unwell. I felt utterly alone. I looked back at the entrance of the hospital, where it was warm and dry. Then I carried Ira along the street to a phone box and rang for another taxi.

When it came the driver jumped out of the car, took Ira from me and lifted her gently onto the seat. When we arrived home he carried her into the house. Thank you, God, for this kind man, I thought.

A few months after Ira's operation I felt pains in my abdomen. The doctor told me I was having a nervous breakdown. 'You've got depression because your husband has gone away and left you in charge of the children,' he said.

'There's too much on my plate,' I agreed. But I didn't believe the pain was due to depression. He was a locum doctor and who did not know me so I wasn't confident about his quick diagnosis.

A few days later I was standing in front of the stove preparing dinner when I felt I was going to faint. I turned off the gas as a terrible pain gripped my abdomen and I fell to the floor. I called Dian, who was organising the two younger children, and asked her to finish cooking and to have a meal with Ira and Ari.

'Mama,' said Dian, 'you have to go to hospital.'

'No, I just need to lie down. Maybe the pain will go away.'

I crawled to the toilet to be sick. That's funny, I thought, green vomit. I lay on my bed but the pain got worse until I knew I had to go to hospital. In my distress the only way I could think of to get there was to drive. I told Dian and hobbled to the garage, pulled up the roller door, climbed into the car and started it. I sat there trying to find the strength to reverse out. When I looked up the children were standing in the headlights. Dian was holding Ari who gripped his comfort blanket, sucking his thumb. Ira stood beside her clutching Felix the cat, her favourite fluffy toy. Ira called, 'Mama, where are you going?'

'I have to go to hospital.'

Tears poured down Ira's face. 'You're not going to die, Mama?'

I got out of the car and hugged them. 'I just have to see the doctor,' I said. 'I won't be long. Dian will look after you.'

I drove the short distance to the Queen Elizabeth II Hospital clutching my stomach. At the emergency department, a nurse brought a wheelchair, and a doctor saw me straightaway. I screamed at his touch. He arranged an ultrasound, and on the monitor he pointed out the gallstones. 'We have to operate immediately,' the doctor said. 'Can we get your husband to sign the consent form?'

'He's in Indonesia.'

'Who brought you here?'

'I drove myself.'

The doctor stared at me. 'You drove? You could have killed yourself. You could have killed innocent people. Why didn't you call an ambulance?'

I gasped. The ambulance, of course! We were paid-up members of the Queensland Ambulance Service, but I'd been too confused to think of it.

The doctor went on and on. 'How could you be so irresponsible?' he yelled.

While waiting a nurse helped me to ring home and I asked Dian to pray for me and phone my parents.

When I awoke next morning in my hospital room I felt small and alone in the world. When a doctor came, he asked, 'Why are you crying?'

'My husband's in another country. I'm worried about the children at home.'

He asked if I belonged to a church and I told him about the Baptist Church I sometimes attended. A few hours later, the minister came with two women from the parish, bringing flowers. I felt more at peace knowing there was somebody there.

My parents took the first available flight and at lunchtime they appeared at my bedside with the children. Surrounded by my family, I told them how wonderful Dian had been. I felt grateful to have such a capable daughter.

As the end of Dahlan's two-year term with the World Bank approached in 1984 the children became more and more excited, expecting him back in Australia, and I was hoping my time as a single mother would be coming to an end.

He rang me. 'Wenny, I'm not renewing the World Bank contract. The Reserve Bank has offered me a Director position at LPPI,' he said.

LPPI, the Indonesian Banking Development Institute, ran training programs for senior managers in the banking industry. My heart sank.

'Will you accept?'

'I've already accepted. A four year contract.'

He had already accepted. I felt as if I had been hit. 'Lan, we were praying you'd come back to Australia.'

'There's nothing for me in Australia. This position is perfect. It pays twice as much as the World Bank and they'll give me a big house. The campus is new and the first one to use computers. It's a model project.'

I knew Dahlan loved computers. 'I need the family to be together,' I said. 'I'm fed up with looking after the kids by myself, living in this tiny house while you've got a mansion in Jakarta. We'll come back to Indonesia.'

In the end we decided on a trial return during the Australian school holidays over Christmas while the Special School and the University were also on vacation. Indonesia had switched to a July-June school year, so Dian could try attending school in Jakarta to see whether it suited her. A keen student, she had just won her school's top award for mathematics, and was about to start Year 12. Now she was enthusiastic about going to school in Indonesia. She packed up all her books.

When we arrived at Jakarta airport we were delayed as a customs official opened and perused each of Dian's books. At that time many foreign books were still prohibited in Indonesia. Dian became more and more angry. 'Excuse me,' she demanded in English. 'Why are you doing this? I'm not a criminal.'

I was alarmed – Dian didn't understand how easy it was in Indonesia to get into trouble with officials. 'I'm sorry, Bapak,' I said. 'My daughter is rude.'

'It doesn't matter,' he said. 'I like someone who stands up for herself. More Indonesians should be like her.'

I was excited and happy to be back with Dahlan and so were the children. 'Look, Mama,' cried Ari. 'The house is so big I can ride a bike inside it.' Dahlan's driver took them sightseeing and shopping and their aunties and uncles gave them gifts. Shanti had returned to Indonesia after completing a business course, and was now living with her father and working for a private television channel. Apart from Cheddy, who was at university in Canberra, the family was together.

Dahlan took me to the LPPI Christmas party and after the smorgasbord we sat in the front row with the other three directors and their wives for the entertainment and the speeches. I began to dream of again being a nyonya besar, an important lady, like the other directors' wives, with a big house full of servants. And a driver. I would never again have to worry about reversing a car. Dahlan would take me to parties and I would always sit in the front row. I noticed the other wives looking at me. They were the real nyonya besar, dressed in expensive kain kebaya and adorned with diamonds and gold jewellery. When Dahlan worked for Stanvac I was like that, but in Australia my ideas and priorities had changed. Now I just wore a simple dress. No, I thought, the value of life is not what shows on the outside but what you have inside. I was not envious of the other wives.

As the end of the holiday approached, we had to make a decision. One afternoon after Dahlan had come home from work we had tea on the terrace and talked about the children's education. Dian's experience of school in Jakarta had not been as happy as she'd anticipated, not because of the language, which she spoke fluently, but because the teaching skipped shallowly from one subject to the next. In Australia there were fewer subjects and more depth. Dahlan said, 'Wenny, I think you'd better take the kids back to Brisbane.'

I had known this was coming but I was full of resentment all the same. 'In Australia I have to look after the children by myself. I have to make all the decisions, while you go to cocktail parties, get driven everywhere, go overseas.'

'But Wenny, those things are part of my job. Going overseas is no fun – I have to attend conferences and give papers. The main thing is that Australia has one of the best education systems in the world,' he said. 'For the sake of the children it's better they go to school there.'

'Lan, I don't want us to be separated.'

'We have to think of the future of our kids.'

I agreed with my husband – education was number one – but I dreaded returning to Australia. I wanted to stay in Jakarta not to become a nyonya besar, but to be together as a family.

With a heavy heart I took the children back to our tiny house in Runcorn Heights, back to my three jobs, back to being a single mother in a foreign country. My dream of a meaningful family life was over.

John, the boy in the wheelchair at the Special School, was now seventeen and heavier than ever. One day, transferring him from wheelchair to changing table, I felt sudden searing pain in my back. My doctor sent me to an orthopaedist who told me I had a serious injury and must not go back to the school. He could operate, he said, but there was only a fifty percent chance of improvement. Surgery was a risk and might make matters worse.

Five years ago, I had sat in Mrs Martin's office tearfully insisting that I could do the work. 'You mustn't become attached to the children,' she had said, but I had. Now I was in the new principal's office, telling her I couldn't come back, again in tears. I would miss the children so much.

I needed different work. Griffith University increased my tutoring work to full-time, but I would need another qualification if I wanted to work at a higher level. I saw an advertisement in *The Courier Mail* offering positions in a graduate diploma course in second language teaching at the Brisbane College of Advanced Education. It was part-time, two nights per week for two years.

On my first night I looked around at the other students, all young teachers. What am I doing here, I asked myself. I'm the oldest person in the room. English is my second language. How can I do this?

Gary, the lecturer, saved me. Several times over the next two years I said to him, 'Gary, I want to drop out. I can't do it.'

He always talked me into staying. 'We need Indonesian teachers,' he said, 'and I know you can do it.'

For two years I worked weekdays at Griffith, weekends at the nursing home, went to class two nights a week, and spent any spare time studying. Sometimes when assignments were due I slept two hours a night, and felt guilty about giving the children takeaway instead of home-cooked meals.

Thanks to Gary I did keep going and I earned my diploma. Even before my graduation in 1987, I was offered a position as lecturer at the University of Southern Queensland in Toowoomba, replacing the two Indonesian language lecturers who had left at short notice. When my father said he was proud of me I felt that I had finally atoned for disappointing him by failing my first year in law.

Nearly thirty years previously I had fought the decision of my parents and Mas Irwan to send me to Yogya to study the teaching of English. Now I was grateful for that training and where it had led me.

Dahlan continued sending money for household and education expenses but seldom wrote or phoned, and if I rang and left a message for him he did not call back. In my loneliness I had entered a relationship with an Australian man, but that ended after I moved to Toowoomba. The children and I hoped that Dahlan would return to Australia at the end of his contract with LPPI, but in 1988 he signed on another four-year term.

Dahlan visited us in Toowoomba. I said to him, 'I've had enough. I want to move back to Indonesia and live with you.'

'But what about your career?' he said. 'What would you do in Jakarta?'

'I just want to be a housewife.'

'You won't be happy. You're different from the wives of the other directors – they just want to go shopping'

'You don't want me to come because you have someone else.'

He knew I was joking. 'I'm thinking of you,' he said. 'I want you to be happy. And Ira and Ari are still at school.'

Such debates always ran aground on this reality – the better education system in Australia.

Okay, I thought, I accept. I am settled here, he is settled there. We are now leading separate lives.

Wenny and her children in Brisbane in 1982
From left: Dian, Ari, Wenny, Ira (front), Cheddy, Shanti

CHAPTER 26
Standing Up For Myself

[A]ccording to me, religions other than Islam are not infidel. They believe in God ... Hindus, Christians seek God, only the method differs.
—Achdiat Karta Mihardja, Interview, *Syir'ah Magazine*.

'The Christians among us are invited to come and stand with me,' said the Ambassador, 'so that the other guests can give you their Christmas wishes.'

If I stand, I thought, I will hurt Bapak and Ibu. If I don't, I will hurt my God.

I was staying with my parents in December 1988 and we were at the Indonesian Embassy Christmas party. Six years previously I had converted to Christianity but hadn't told my parents. Bapak was a loyal follower of the local mosque, and if I now joined the line of Christians I would embarrass him in front of the Ambassador and the whole Canberra Indonesian community, of which Bapak was a respected elder. Declaring publicly that I was not Muslim would be an insult. And I had to decide quickly, as only a few people at the party were Christian and nearly all of them had joined the line.

I know little about religion but I have always been deeply spiritual, praying to God in my own words, believing that each person approached God in their own way, that God understood every language. I had become a Christian in Brisbane, when I attended a Baptist Church, and had asked the minister to baptise me. Now I had to choose: my parents or my God? God is above everyone, I thought. I stood up and walked to the front, the last person to join the line.

The Ambassador stared at me. Everyone in the line, everyone in the room, was looking at me, surprise on their faces. I glanced at my father and saw tears in his eyes.

The others at the party came and shook our hands and wished us *Selamat Hari Natal*. My parents didn't, but later I noticed them giving their Christmas greetings to the other

Christians. They said nothing to me until we arrived home, then Bapak began. 'You are the granddaughter of Haji Noor, and you converted to Christianity. That makes me very sad.'

The harsh tone of his voice told me he was more angry than sad. Yet he was known for his open-mindedness and his defence of human rights. He followed a Sufi strand of Islam that was tolerant of other religions. 'I'm sorry, Bapak,' I said. 'Please forgive me. But I cannot understand Islam. You and Ibu never taught me. All I heard were the scary stories about hell that the servant told me. In church I don't feel frightened. I feel at peace.'

'You embarrassed me. You embarrassed Ibu. The Karta Mihardjas have always been strict Muslims. Not one has ever left Islam. Until now.'

Meanwhile, Ibu said nothing. She didn't seem to be worried.

Bapak rang me after I returned to Toowoomba. 'I feel very hurt,' he said. 'You insulted me in public.'

'Bapak, please forgive me. I'm sorry I hurt you, but my religion is my decision. I need to hold onto something, and I told you before, I don't understand Islam.'

'You are not my daughter. We must go our separate ways.'

'Bapak,' I cried. 'I beg you, please forgive me. I am your daughter.'

'Yes, by blood you are my daughter, but our way of life is different.'

'Bapak, I love you. You are the most important person in my life. Please don't reject me. I was caught between my duty to you and my duty to God. I can feel how hurt you are, but I need you. You're my best friend, the one person I can really talk to. You always understand me.'

'Of course I love you as a daughter,' he said, but he still sounded angry.

My close friendship with Bapak was the most sustaining thing in my life, and I worried that I had broken our bond. Feeling confused and guilty, I consulted the chaplain at my university. He helped me understand how my father, despite his tolerance, could still be upset by my conversion, but he also reinforced my belief that I was on the right path for me. He talked about being aware of God inside our heart, which is what my father sought in his Sufi practice. In essence, my religion was the same as my father's.

Wenny and Achdiat at Brisbane City Hall, 1995

Bapak soon stopped talking about my apostasy and gradually we resumed our former relationship, mostly through long telephone conversations in which, by tacit agreement, religion was never mentioned. When I stayed with my parents a year later my mother surprised me. On Christmas Eve she whispered, 'Do you want to go to the Midnight Service? Just get ready and wait outside at the gate. I'll make sure your father's in bed.'

    A little later she drove out in the car. 'He's asleep,' she said.

    She dropped me at the nearby Baptist church. After the service a parishioner gave me a lift home and I crept inside. Ibu helped me in this way several times over the following years. Although I was grateful for Ibu's kindness, I couldn't understand why she was being so kind when, so often, she had hurt me with her cruelty. She hid what she was doing from Bapak because, while she ruled the household, she deferred to her husband in the intellectual and spiritual matters which were in his domain.

    One year Bapak found out that Ibu had helped me to attend the service. The next morning he was angry with both of us, giving us the silent treatment.

    The following year Ibu apologised for not being able to drive me to the church. 'I don't agree with your father,' she said. 'I understand why you became Christian. Like you, I went to a Catholic school. I can't take you but our friend Mira will.'

    Before I went to the service she gave me a small plastic Christmas tree. I embraced her. This gesture of acceptance meant a lot to me.

Years later, in 2001, the Canberra Indonesian community organised a big surprise party for Bapak's ninetieth birthday. The next morning the family gathered in my parents' house and relived the party over breakfast. We were not talking about religion but somehow the subject arose. Suddenly Bapak declared, 'Wenny believes in a god whose mother wasn't married.'

    For a moment I couldn't believe what I'd heard. Then a great rage erupted inside me. 'You hypocrite,' I yelled. 'You're famous for defending human rights, and you insult my religion in front of my family. How could you do that?'

    Weeping, I ran to the kitchen. My sister Ati followed and tried to comfort me. 'Don't take it as an insult,' she said. 'Bapak likes to be critical. Just ignore him and follow what *you* believe in.'

But I could not stop my tears. I had thought that Bapak and I had rebuilt our close relationship, but now it seemed that he had never accepted my choice of religion.

I am not a member of any church now, but sometimes I go into the Catholic cathedral in Toowoomba. I sit alone and small in the huge silent space and I pray for forgiveness and guidance.

In 1992 our daughter Shanti, who now lived in Jakarta with her father and worked for a television station, married Eri, a Javanese man. Uwa Yayah was the Master of Ceremonies at her wedding, just as she had been at mine thirty years previously.

When I had married, the cultural meaning of the Sundanese pre-wedding ceremony, the Ngeuyeuk Seureuh, was taken seriously. It was only used by noble families, and attendance was restricted to a small group of happily married women, with no children allowed because of the adult content. All windows and doors were shut so that no one else could see or hear the ceremony.

With passing years it had become fashionable for any Sundanese bride or groom, not just those from noble families, to have the Ngeuyeuk Seureuh, as a way to entertain the guests with an interesting custom. There were no restrictions on attendance and, when the ceremony was held for Shanti and Eri, everyone – men, women and children – crowded into the big living room in Dahlan's house, with doors and windows left open. During her instruction on the marriage relationship, when Uwa Yayah said that in bed the couple should be like a fork and spoon, cupping one hand in another to show what she meant, I overheard Javanese guests complaining that this was indecent, and inappropriate with children present. In past times neither Javanese guests nor children would have been at the ceremony.

When Uwa Yayah had instructed Dahlan and me on our roles as breadwinner husband and household manager wife, I had imagined myself carrying out my assigned duties. Uwa gave the same instructions to Shanti and Eri, but I knew they no longer bore any relation to the real world. My daughter had no intention of giving up her career.

Seven hundred guests attended the reception. 'Who are all these people?' I asked Dahlan.

He pointed out those who were from his office – the governor of the reserve bank, fellow directors and work colleagues, secretaries, drivers, security officers, tea-ladies and messengers.

I was stunned. 'But there's such a big difference in class. Why did you invite them all?'

'Wenny, we are all human beings. And maybe this is the only time some of the guests will be invited to a party like this. I hope it's a good experience for them, one they will remember. The high rankers will soon forget.'

I was moved by how great Dahlan's heart was. He was a good man.

Toowoomba, the "Garden City", is perched on a mountain range and is full of parks. The second largest inland city in Australia and less than two hours by road from Brisbane, Toowoomba is a thriving business and education centre for southern Queensland. My house is in a new suburb near the university. To me Toowoomba is beautiful and vibrant but, when my cousin Nina visited, she was not impressed.

In Bandung Nina, a university student at the time, had often babysat the children. I was busy with the beauty school and gave her pocket money to help the kids with their school work. 'I envy you,' she told me then. 'You have a good husband in a high position, a beautiful house, a good life. I want to have a life like yours.'

Nina married a businessman and found her own good life, wearing diamonds and gold, living in a luxurious Jakarta mansion and travelling the world. Her husband gave her generous birthday presents such as a 5 Series BMW.

I met Nina at Brisbane airport and took her to the Gold Coast for lunch and sightseeing, then brought her to Toowoomba. On the way she looked out at the farming land and said, 'There are no people or houses. You seem to live in the middle of nowhere.'

When we arrived at my place and walked inside she hesitated, looking around at my neat, lowset new home. 'Is this your house?' she asked in a shocked voice. 'How can you live like this?'

'I'm proud of this house,' I said. 'I built it with my own money.'

I told her how Ira and I had seen the block of vacant land for sale as we were walking one Saturday afternoon. I had bargained with the agent to get him to sell it for a much lower price. I told Nina about choosing the house plan, altering it to suit my needs, selecting the bricks, paint, curtains, and light fittings, and fighting with the carpet man because he had tried to con me. 'I did it all myself,' I said. 'I didn't have to rely on my husband.'

Over the next few days Nina continued to be surprised at my lifestyle. 'In Indonesia, you had so much. You went to all the cocktail parties. Now you have to drive Ira and Ari to school. And go to the supermarket and do your own shopping. What sort of life is that?'

'I have a cleaning lady once a week.'

'Once a week! That's not enough. How many hours?'

'Three.'

'Three hours a week! Oh Wenny, I don't know how you do it. And how can you stand Toowoomba? It's like living in a village.'

'Nina, don't criticise the way I live,' I said. 'Sure, in Indonesia my life was glamorous, but that was because of Dahlan's position, not mine. Here I make my own decisions and raise the children myself, without servants. I love my teaching job. I buy and sell real estate and manage my own investments. I've experienced so much more than I would have if I'd stayed a lady of leisure in Jakarta. I can wear jeans wherever I like and there's no need to go to the hairdresser every day. If my house is a mess it's okay. My life is richer in Australia.'

Nina was unconvinced. I took her to Brisbane the day before her flight and booked into the Chancellor Hotel. She turned up her nose. 'It's only four stars.'

She lay on the bed. 'Oh Wenny, this is so uncomfortable. Why didn't you book a better hotel?'

Later she was upset about the service. 'The staff are rude,' she complained. 'I could buy this hotel. Then they would learn how to look after their guests.'

Nina and I had a good time together, but I was pleased to return by myself to the home I loved. The lifestyle of a nyonya besar was not for me.

But I hadn't told Nina the whole truth – that I was lonely, and would give up all my independence for a loving bond with another person. That is what my parents had, and what was missing from my life. Although I had not followed Uwa Yayah's instructions to be a dutiful wife, and was proud that I had run my own business, worked in the disability field and was now a lecturer, I still deeply missed my husband.

During the 1990s Ira and Ari became adults, so I no longer needed to stay in Australia for their education. But my parents and four of my five children lived here – Cheddy in Canberra, Dian with her husband Tim in Sydney, and Ira and Ari in Toowoomba. If I returned to Jakarta I would miss them and I would miss the job I loved. I would have to give up the life I had made for myself in Australia. I was torn in two directions, and in the end I stayed in Toowoomba, proud of my independence, but regretting what it had cost.

CHAPTER 27
Dahlan

> One of the most significant attributes of Allah is 'Love'. And one of the most beautiful characteristics of Love is the 'willingness to forgive'.
> —Achdiat Karta Mihardja, Speech on Lebaran Day, Athens, Ohio, 1981

Indonesia was the country hit hardest by the Asian economic crisis of 1997-98. Rising prices and unemployment provoked demonstrations, and when student protestors were killed by the military, rioting and looting broke out in Jakarta. Suharto's power collapsed, and after 32 years as leader he stepped down in May 1998. His Vice-president, Jusuf Habibie, became President. *Reformasi,* the Reformation Era, had begun.

Throughout this time of economic collapse and political unrest, Dahlan continued carrying out his usual duties. LPPI had become the Indonesian Bankers Institute, but Dahlan remained a Director, and in late 1998 he led a group of senior bank managers on a study tour of Australia. I met him in Sydney and was shocked to see how much weight he had lost. When he came to dinner with Dian and her husband Tim, he kept leaving the table to use the toilet.

'Lan, you're not well,' I said. 'When you finish the study tour let the group go home. Stay in Australia and have a medical check.'

'I can't do that.'

'Number one is your health. Don't worry about getting a medal.'

'No. I'm responsible for the group until we're back in Jakarta.'

Dian, Tim and I tried hard to persuade him to have a check-up, without success. He returned to Jakarta, and a few weeks later Shanti rang. 'Mama, Papa's in hospital. He's got prostate cancer. He's having an operation.'

I flew to Jakarta and spent a week with Dahlan after his

surgery. He recovered quickly and looked healthier than he had in Sydney. He's going to be okay, I thought.

Several months later Dahlan rang and cried as he told me he was about to have surgery for bowel cancer. Immediately I arranged leave without pay and returned to Jakarta. I went straight to the hospital from the airport. He was skin and bone.

After the operation the oncologist told me the prognosis was not good. 'He's had the bowel cancer for maybe two years,' Dr Manap said, 'and the doctor who operated last year missed it. Now it's too late.'

'How long has he got?'

'Hard to say. Anywhere from two to twelve years.'

Dahlan stayed in hospital a month for chemotherapy and radiation treatment, and I stayed with him. The Gatot Soebroto Army Hospital had been established by Ibu Tien Suharto, the wife of the previous President, and Dahlan's room in the Kartika Pavilion was directly above the one in which she had died three years previously. His suite was like a luxury apartment, with a kitchenette, lounge area and balcony. Every night I slept in a fold-up bed beside him.

I worried about the number of people who visited Dahlan – all his work colleagues, from his driver to the governor of the reserve bank, and the many members of his extended family. He had about twenty visitors a day, the first arriving at seven in the morning when his secretary came for her instructions. I felt he needed more peace to recover and asked Dr Manap to authorise a sign limiting visitors to immediate family.

'We can't do that,' he said.

'But he's seriously ill.'

'Ibu Dahlan, you've lived in Australia too long. Perhaps you've forgotten how different it is here. We can't say no to his extended family. And Bapak Dahlan is proud and happy that his colleagues want to visit him.'

I did see how much my husband's staff respected him. One day, while a nurse was with Dahlan, I chatted with the Logistics Manager. 'If Pak Dahlan passes away, he will go straight to heaven,' he told me. 'He is a man of principle.'

'I know,' I said. 'One time I nagged Dahlan to take me overseas with him but he said, no, if he went to Germany he had to work. The wife only goes for leisure. It would be wasting government money.'

When we returned to Dahlan's bedside the manager said, 'Bapak, Ibu never went overseas with you, but there are funds allocated for directors to take their wives.'

'If other directors want to do that, that's their business,' said Dahlan. 'I have different principles.'

'Bapak's driver complains,' the manager said to me. 'The other directors get a new car every two years, but he's had the same BMW since he started sixteen years ago.'

'That car is still good,' said Dahlan. 'It can take me from A to B. It'd be a waste of government money to replace it.'

During the month in hospital, Dahlan and I became closer than we had been for many years. In the evening I wheeled him onto the balcony and we looked at the street scene below as we reminisced about our life when we were young, courting, getting married, our children being born and growing up.

'Remember Pelabuhan Ratu?' I asked, holding his hand.

'Yes, we took Cheddy to the beach,' Dahlan said. 'He was so excited about the water. He'd just started walking.'

'And remember the restaurant on top of the cliff. We listened to the waves and watched the sun setting over the ocean.'

'Ah!' Dahlan smiled. 'I will never forget the fish cooked on charcoal. I can still taste it.'

I felt as if we were two young lovers, speaking to each other from the secret places within our hearts.

'I'll give up my job and move here to look after you,' I said.

'No, go back to Australia, stay in your job. I'll follow you when the treatment's finished.'

We still had our house in Runcorn Heights. 'If you don't like Toowoomba, we can live in Brisbane,' I said.

'Toowoomba's good – there's no pollution. I can look after the garden. And we'll go fishing. I'm always dreaming about going back to Fingal Head.'

We planned our future. We looked at our finances, and

decided that we would have enough. I asked Dr Manap if it was safe for Dahlan to fly, and he said it would be no problem. He may not have many years left, but they would be good years. These were our dreams.

After a month Dahlan was discharged, and I helped him settle into the home he shared with Shanti and her family. He planned to return to work while he was having further treatment, then move to Australia. I had used up my leave and needed to get back to my students. When it was time to go, I dragged my suitcase out to the terrace where Dahlan was sitting in his dressing gown. He cried and hugged me. 'Wenny,' he said, 'I'm sorry that I can't take you to the airport.'

I held him. We would soon be living together.

During Dahlan's illness, enormous changes were happening in Indonesia. President Habibie had initiated many reforms including decentralising government and removing limitations on political parties. He lifted censorship of the press and freed political prisoners. However, economic decline continued, and he became more unpopular when, in 1999, he agreed to give East Timorese people a referendum on whether or not they wanted to stay in Indonesia. Many Indonesians felt humiliated by the Timorese vote for independence and the subsequent presence in the territory of Australian troops leading the international peacekeeping force.

In June 1999, free general elections were held in Indonesia for the first time since 1955. In October the Assembly elected Abdurrahman Wahid as President and Sukarno's daughter, Megawati Sukarnoputri, as Vice-president.

Dahlan had gone back to work after his month in hospital. In September he celebrated his sixty-fifth birthday at a small party that Shanti arranged. Then, two months later, Shanti rang me. Dahlan was in hospital again, seriously ill. Dian, Ira, Ari and I took the next available flight and rushed from the airport to the hospital. Dahlan looked much worse than when I'd last seen him but he said brightly, 'I'm so glad you came. How was the trip?'

Shanti said, 'Mama, the whole day Papa's been waiting for you, always watching the door.'

In the following days I stayed at Dahlan's bedside. We did not talk about death, but once when we were alone, he began to cry, holding my hand tightly. 'Wenny, please forgive me,' he said. 'I loved my job, my career, more than anything else, more than anyone.'

Finally, I thought, when it's too late. I could not stop my reaction from showing on my face, and he gripped my hand and said, 'Don't be angry with me – it was already written above. It was your fate to marry a workaholic. We can't change.'

Now I really was angry. It's not written above, I thought. It's up to the individual.

'I'm sorry for the way I treated you,' he said. 'Please, can you forgive me?'

My anger vanished as I was overwhelmed with love. 'Of course I forgive you,' I cried. 'Can you forgive me? You know I had an Australian boyfriend. I'm sorry I was unfaithful to you. Please forgive me.'

'I forgave you long ago,' he said. 'I understand. I wasn't there for you. I gave everything to my job.'

Two days later a doctor asked Dian and me to meet with him. 'Pak Dahlan won't last long,' he told us. 'It's in God's hands, but medically I think he only has a few hours left.'

'No,' I screamed. 'It can't be. He's so alert.'

'Everything depends on God, but the cancer has invaded his whole body.'

He drew a sketch to show how the disease had spread from one organ to another. I could not stop crying.

'What would you like to do?' he asked. 'Leave him in the room, or shift him to the Intensive Care Unit? ICU is fully equipped, but it's much more expensive.'

'Of course the ICU. I don't care about the expense.'

As we left the doctor I told Dian we must dry our tears and try not to show our feelings. Dahlan watched me come into the room. 'Am I really bad, Wenny?' he asked.

'You need to go to Intensive Care.'
'Why?'
'They have more equipment there. Here there is nothing.'
'Oh,' said Dahlan. He understood.

After he was transferred to ICU, he began drifting in and out of consciousness. I held his hand, with Ira and Ari beside me, and Dian and Shanti on the other side of the bed with Shanti's husband, Eri. Cheddy arrived, having come straight from the airport. 'Papa, it's me,' he said.

Dahlan opened his eyes. 'Cheddy! What are you doing here? You're supposed to be sitting for exams.'

'Don't worry, Papa. I deferred.'

'No.' Dahlan sounded angry. 'You should have stayed and finished your study.'

'I want to be with you, Papa.'

'Study is number one. Promise me you'll finish your Master's.'

'I promise.'

Dahlan closed his eyes again.

Dahlan's brothers and sisters and their families now filled the room, crying, screaming and praying loudly. It sounded like a marketplace. The families of my father and mother had arrived, but they waited quietly in the hallway outside. More of Dahlan's extended family pressed up against a large window, as if watching a performance. Ira closed the curtain, but Dahlan's brother opened it again. There were now dozens of people milling around in Intensive Care.

When Dr Manap arrived, I pointed to the notice on the wall stating that only immediate family was allowed in ICU. 'With all this noise it's not peaceful for Dahlan,' I said. 'Can you ask everyone to wait outside in the hallway?'

'I can't do that,' he said.

In the middle of the melee Dahlan lay still, his eyes closed. His brothers and nephews now began to shout at him to recite the Syahadat, the Muslim profession of faith: "There is no god but Allah, and Muhammad is His Messenger." They crowded around the bed, yelling, 'Say the Syahadat!' They pushed past our children to get close enough to shout it into his ear. 'Say *lâ ilâha illallâh, Muḥammadun rasûlullâh,*' they screamed.

Through all the commotion, Dahlan's eyes remained closed.

Watching him, I felt a strong voice in my heart saying, 'Wenny, help him to say it.' An equally strong voice said, 'No, you can't. You are Christian.' An urgent debate unfolded inside me.

'You must help him. Islam is his religion, even if he didn't practise it.'

'If you help him you will betray your Christian God.'

'No, God is always One. God will understand.'

I believe in one God, I thought. I have to help him. I held his shoulders and whispered into his ear, 'Lan, say this: *lâ ilâha illallâh, Muḥammadun rasûlullâh.*'

He opened his eyes wide and looked at me. Then he recited the Syahadat loudly and clearly, and the room fell silent.

A few minutes later Ari, who was watching the monitor, screamed. Dahlan had taken his last breath.

CHAPTER 28
Ibu and Bapak

> Rivai thought [a couple who had been married 60 years] seemed to suit each other perfectly, like the keris in its sheath ... their love would now be pure – no longer disturbed by the 'dusts of love' ... All that was left was love and affection.
> —Achdiat Karta Mihardja, *The Scattered Dust of Love*

The mango tree in Jalan Meranti had been my refuge after my mother's beatings. In the gardens of each of my houses, in Bandung, Brisbane and Toowoomba, I planted mango trees. Whenever I felt upset, I sat under one of these trees or looked at them as I watered the garden, and slowly peace would fill me.

In Toowoomba I spoke with a psychologist about my painful relationship with Ibu. He asked me to imagine returning to Jalan Meranti, walking through the house and out the back door to the huge mango tree. As I pictured this, I felt as if I was entering a trance. 'Can you see little Wenny?' he said.

I looked down and saw a little girl quietly crying as she sat under the tree. She was wearing a light brown *celana kodok*, the type of playsuit with big pockets which I had worn for most of my childhood.

'Take her to a beautiful park and play with her,' said the voice of the psychologist.

I took the child's hand in mine and led her away from the tree. A large park with lush grass and gardens of bright flowers appeared around us. Little Wenny smiled up at me, her tears gone, her shining hair tied into two pigtails with green ribbons, her white dress patterned with small green flowers and red edging, feet clad in black shoes with white socks. I bent down and, with our heads together, we breathed in the scent of a rose. We both laughed and began dancing around the park. Little Wenny was happy.

And I was moving past the memory of the hurt.

I had two mothers, one cruel and one kind, and I will never understand how they could have been the same person.

The pain of the beatings by my cruel mother was rekindled each time she favoured my siblings over me, or their children over mine. When she had asked me to return the gelang keroncong so she could give the five gold bangles to Ati, when she charged me for child-minding but looked after her other grandchildren for free, when she demanded I give back the title deeds of the rice fields at Rancaekek, when she returned from overseas with gifts for my nephews and nieces but not for my children, then I was wounded. I tried to forget and move on, but I couldn't, so I became determined to mould the hurt into motivation.

The kind mother loved and cared for me. She worked hard to pay school fees and send me to university, and stayed up with me all night when I studied for exams. She fostered my love of cooking, trusting me to choose recipes and prepare meals for the family. I was depressed in Canberra, and she comforted me and asked her friend to help. In Bandung I was unhappy in my marriage, and my mother supported me during her visits. When Bapak was angry about my religion, kind Ibu was understanding.

I wish I could have talked to my kind mother about my cruel mother, but any attempt to do so would have flipped her from one persona to the other, and she would have responded with a tirade of abuse. Instead, I changed the weeping child in celana kodok into a laughing girl in a white dress. I no longer need to seek solace under the mango tree.

My father had always wanted to die in Indonesia. Now, in his nineties and aware of his failing faculties, he became desperate to move back to Jakarta before he was too frail. But Ibu would not hear of it – she loved Australia too much. Whenever they visited Indonesia she was always pleased to return home to Canberra. Thirty years previously she had bought a plot for Bapak and herself in the Islamic section of a Canberra cemetery.

They often argued about returning to Indonesia. Bapak would bang his walking stick on the floor and say, 'I need to go home.'

'What are you going to do there? You can't look after yourself.'

'The family will look after me.'

'That's what they say. But when you get there, big question.'

'I don't care. I want to die at home.'

'Okay, you go,' she said. 'Just go by yourself.'

'Right, I will. I can look after myself. I can cook.'

Bapak had never cooked in his life. If he wanted a cup of tea, Ibu made it.

Bapak and Ibu

My father longed for the greater sense of community that he had experienced in Indonesia. As he had written in *The Scattered Dust of Love* he felt that individual freedoms in Australia often went too far and overrode social responsibilities, leading to loneliness. He believed that one need never be lonely in Indonesia – you could always visit a friend without notice for an idle chat, and stay as long as you wanted.

Unlike Bapak, I now felt more at home in Australia and experienced reverse culture shock when I went to Indonesia, resenting the attacks on my privacy. 'How much do you earn,' friends asked me. 'What assets do you have?' When I stayed with relatives, everyone wanted to know what I'd been doing. Even the servant asked me where I'd been and what I'd bought.

Despite their arguments about where to live my parents were becoming even closer as they grew older. Ibu had not been interested in books and I had never seen her read one. But now she volunteered to be her husband's eyes, and every night in bed she read to him, often from one of his own books. Even during the day, if he lay down on the bed, she lay beside him and read to him. My father told me how good this felt. Finally his wife was reading his books, becoming interested in them.

The English translation of *The Scattered Dust of Love* had recently been published with the dedication, "To my lovely wife of more than sixty years, Tati".

Around this time, the relationship between Indonesia and Australia, which had deteriorated because of East Timor, began to improve. The two countries cooperated in the aftermath of the 2002 Bali Bombing, and then Australia provided a large aid package for the rebuilding of Aceh after the 2004 Boxing Day Tsunami. New President Susilo Bambang Yudhoyono spoke of the need for the two countries to work together. A Presidential visit to Australia had been arranged for March 2005, but two days before Yudhoyono was due to arrive in Canberra, an earthquake devastated the island of Nias off the west coast of Sumatra. The visit was postponed while Yudhoyono dealt with the crisis. Then, on 2 April, an Australian Navy helicopter crashed while ferrying a relief medical team to Nias. Nine people on board were killed. President Yudhoyono arrived in Australia a day later.

Bapak and Ibu were invited to two meetings with the President: a breakfast at the Embassy, and a luncheon at Parliament House. I was staying with them at the time and, as Ibu didn't want to dress up, Bapak asked me to go with him. I had not brought the traditional kain kebaya that the breakfast invitation specified, so I only accompanied him to the luncheon.

When we arrived, the Great Hall of Parliament House was filled with row upon row of tables and packed with people. At our table were several journalists, and Bapak introduced one, from the ABC, who was a friend of his. The President and the Australian Prime Minister sat at the front table. In his speech, President Yudhoyono paid tribute to the nine Australians killed in the helicopter crash, and thanked Australia for its aid. He spoke of the need for the two countries to be strong partners and good neighbours.

Afterwards the ABC journalist said to me, 'Your father is a brave man.' He had been at the breakfast and told me what had happened. He said that, by the time Bapak arrived, everyone else was seated, and the President and his wife had risen to greet Bapak and to pay their respects. Later, during the question and answer session, Bapak publicly told Yudhoyono, 'You, as President, as leader of the Indonesian people, must wipe out corruption. That is your task.'

'Yes, Pak,' replied Yudhoyono. 'I understand. There is a lot of work to do.'

The next day the President was at Sydney Airport for the arrival of the bodies of the Australian medical personnel. On each casket he placed the Medal of Valour, Indonesia's highest honour.

Because of his failing eyesight, Bapak used a cassette recorder to complete his third novel, which was transcribed by a typist provided by the embassy. In June 2005, Bapak and Ibu travelled to Indonesia for the launch of the novel.

Manifesto Khalifatullah portrays the confrontation between secularism and religion. The central character sets out on a philosophical quest, meeting the founders of the ideologies that influence us today. His spiritual need is not met by Marxism, which denies the existence of God, or the capitalist and secularist thinking of Adam Smith and Francis Bacon, which he feels belittles God. Finally he meets the leader of a pesantren, who delivers a sermon about the commission that God gave

Adam and Eve – to be His representatives on earth, not the representatives of Satan.

Achdiat described the novel as the answer to *Atheis*. Since he was a child he had questioned everything, testing belief systems against each other. Now he had a core of belief that said God created human beings to act as His agents on Earth and the purpose of religion was to empower people to follow God's commission by becoming good. His novel emerged from his own experience and contemplation, but was also shaped by the Sufism of Abah Anom, the leader of Pesantren Suryalaya, the Islamic school that Achdiat always visited when he was in Indonesia.

In the media interviews that followed the launch, Achdiat was forthright. He said that he rejected the idea of an Islamic state based on Sharia law, and maintained that democracy was compatible with Islam. He criticised the secular West, using the example of the church-going George Bush who ignored God's commands when he went to war. Achdiat condemned fanatics such as the Bali bombers who said they are right to kill infidels. He said that people of other religions believed in God just as Muslims did and therefore were not infidels. In his view the real infidels were those who commit terrorist acts.

Bapak returned to Canberra exultant about the reception he had received. He told me he had wanted to stay in Indonesia, but Ibu wouldn't hear of it. 'The medical care is much better in Australia,' she said. 'You need more treatment as you get older.'

Over the next few years, Bapak became progressively frailer. During my visits he spent most of his time in his rocking chair, his fingers moving around the beads of his tasbeh. When I took him out, he used a wheelchair.

Then Ibu changed. Overnight she became forgetful, confused and more volatile, and was diagnosed with dementia. For a while, Bapak feared her angry outbursts and worried about her refusal to eat, but eventually her mood improved and she accepted food and medication, and became less confused. Sometimes she was even able to read to Bapak. For a short time their routine was re-established.

CHAPTER 29
Achdiat Karta Mihardja, My Father

> You are a person who never stops seeking. And what you're looking for I'm looking for too – love, the meaning of love, the significance of love, *without its dusts*, for you, for us, for mankind, for life, for Him … so knowing you is a source of happiness and strength for me.
> —Achdiat Karta Mihardja, *The Scattered Dust of Love*

The day after his ninety-eighth birthday, my father and I talked quietly as my mother dozed nearby. We reminisced about the Japanese occupation and the Revolution.

'When I listen to you, I also remember,' Bapak said. 'I can visualise it.'

When I told him about working with Bryce on my memoir he said, 'To a writer there are no secrets. You must be honest as long as you don't hurt people. And now it is time to be honest with each other. How have I been as a father to you? Tell me if I have done anything to hurt you.'

'Oh, Bapak,' I said. 'Let's not talk about that.'

'I would like to know how you felt as my daughter.'

'That's all in the past. Let's talk about something else.'

'Wenny, I don't have long to live. If we don't open our hearts now, we never will.'

'Bapak, if I answer you honestly, will you do the same? Will you tell me how I have been as a daughter?'

'Of course.'

At first I could not speak. There were so many things I wanted to say but I feared they would hurt him. 'Oh Bapak, when I was small, I was so happy that you were my father.'

'Tell me what has caused you the most pain,' he said.

'There are two things.'

'Yes?'

'I am sorry to say this. Please forgive me if it hurts you.'

My father watched me closely, his eyes bright. I pictured him, over fifty years ago, leaning on the bottom half of the Dutch door of our house in Jalan Tembaga. His eyes had blazed when he saw me arriving home on the back of Cheppy's motor bike. Now I said, 'The first thing is what you did to Cheppy.'

'Who is Cheppy?'

'You know Cheppy. You abused him. You threw him out for no reason. He was innocent. It was so unfair.'

'I can't remember any Cheppy.'

I had thought my father's memory was still excellent but it held no trace of my first boyfriend. I took a deep breath to calm myself and told him the whole story.

He was surprised. 'Really? Was I that bad?'

'You have forgotten it. But I was the one who was hurt, so I have always remembered.'

'Please forgive me.'

'I forgive you, of course.'

'You said there is a second thing.'

'The morning after your ninetieth birthday party you insulted my religion. You made a joke about Mary being an unwed mother. You studied all the religions, you are famous for what you have written, preaching acceptance of other faiths. Why did you ridicule my religion in front of other people?'

'Did I do that? Was I so thoughtless? I can't remember it.'

'It has always stuck in my mind. Please forgive me ten million times, Bapak, if I'm too honest with you, if I have hurt you.'

'I hurt you, Wenny. That was wrong of me. Please forgive me. We must always pray for each other. I will pray for your peace and I ask you to pray for mine.'

'I pray for you and Ibu every day.'

I had said there were two things, but now I had started I could not stop. I told him about the beatings Ibu had given me at Jalan Meranti, how I had cried under the mango tree. 'Maybe you didn't know, or didn't want to know,' I said. 'You were always busy with your writing. You write, write, write, you only think about your books. You didn't see what Ibu did to me.'

'Really? She beat you? I didn't know that.'

'Yes, Bapak, she beat me many times. And you didn't care

what she was doing to the children. I'm sorry but you asked me be honest. I do love you. I always remember our walks in Menteng when I was a little girl, just the two of us, my hand in yours. You told me legends and stories about Si Kabayan, and brought us treats when you came home from work. But you are a writer. You are very egocentric – you don't want to know about other things. I had to enrol myself in high school. You never checked my homework, you never came to my school, you were not interested in what I was doing.

'You left everything to Ibu. She was the strong one. You're famous as a champion of human rights, but you didn't stand up for rights in the home. You were the henpecked husband.'

'No, no, I wasn't henpecked.'

'Yes, you were. You were selfish. Always thinking about writing, your career, your fame, not about your children. I'm sorry, Bapak, but you wanted me to tell you.'

'Wenny, I did not know I was like that. Please, can you forgive me?'

'Of course I forgive you. The past is past.'

I told Bapak about Ibu's demand that I return the gelang keroncong after I had married so she could give it to Ati, about how she asked me to give back the title deed to the rice fields, and about all the ways Ibu had discriminated against me and my children.

'Are you jealous of your siblings?' he asked.

'What?' I snapped. 'Jealous? Me? You don't understand. I only wanted equal treatment. If she wanted to treat me differently, okay, but not my children. She should have treated them the same as your other grandchildren.'

'Wenny, Ibu is galak towards everyone but she is still a gorgeous woman. People are scared of her but she is renowned for her kindness.'

'She may have been kind to everyone else but not to me and my children. Oh, Bapak, I'm sorry to talk about her like that. I do love her.'

'I'm sorry, Wenny. I have made many mistakes. I have not done the right thing by you. Please forgive me.'

We hugged.

I dried my tears, and said, 'Bapak, you agreed to tell me how I have been as your daughter.'

'You are a good daughter, Wenny. You have done well in your life. But do you think that sometimes you are oversensitive? Easily offended?'

This was a shock. 'No, I'm not,' I said, sitting back. 'I only get offended if there's a good reason for it – if someone says something hurtful.'

But when I thought about it I knew he was right. 'I do get hurt easily,' I said. 'Sometimes my tears come out straightaway.'

'But I am proud of you,' said Bapak. 'I was upset when you failed your first year at university, but in the end you succeeded and became a lecturer.'

'That's only because you sent me to Yogya for teacher training, Bapak. So, thank you for doing the right thing for me. At the time it hurt, but not now. I remember you telling me you wanted your children to be independent, regardless of whether they were daughter or son. And all your daughters did become independent – we didn't cling to our husbands.'

We were silent for a while, and then he said, 'We are both blessed, to have talked like this. I still suffer from the time my father ordered me away from his deathbed. I had not made my peace with him. Now I will die soon, and I'm grateful that we have opened our hearts to each other.'

'Bapak, what do you believe happens when people die? Is there life after death?'

'I don't know.'

'What do you think you will experience?'

He laughed. 'Beautiful angels. But I have not yet experienced death, so I cannot know.'

He still has doubt, I thought. He is a devout Muslim, but he is also the young man who questioned everything. In his last book he wrote that the purpose of religion was to guide our actions as God's representatives on earth, and he saw obedience to God's commandments as more important than rituals and creeds. He had identified what for him was the essence of religion, but this conviction coexisted with doubts about the details.

Bapak and I talked for hours. I apologised for calling him henpecked. 'But Ibu did bully you. Remember when she dumped all the food on the floor at the Chinese restaurant? I admire you, Bapak. You are so patient. You are a strong man to put up with so much bad behaviour and to still be loyal to her.'

'Maybe she had to put up with a lot from me too.'

I smiled. 'Like the woman in the Netherlands who called you her darling Didi?'

He laughed. 'I was young and silly. Men do that when they're far from home. It was just a fling. But Ibu is very kind. She forgave me.'

'I remember her making your life hell for a long time before she forgave you.'

'But she is really the only one, the love of my life.'

'I do admire your relationship. You have been together for over seventy years, and you are still inseparable, talking all the time, complimenting each other, always touching, holding hands, hugging. You fight like cats and dogs but then you're like love birds.'

'Yes, Ibu and I are already one soul.'

My tears came again as Bapak said that. Tears of wonder at this bond between my parents, tears for the lack of such a bond in my own life.

When I returned to Toowoomba, I felt at peace. My father and I had opened up to each other, and had spoken of what was in our hearts. I felt that he had given me a great and precious gift.

Three months later, Bapak and Ibu moved to an aged care home in Canberra. In Indonesia, where letting old people live in residential care is considered cruel, Ibu's brother called a meeting of family members, including Cheddy and Shanti. Cheddy told me they had all agreed that Bapak and Ibu should be brought back to Jakarta, where there were many family members who would care for them. 'It's impossible,' I told Cheddy. 'Bapak's too frail to travel and Ibu has never wanted to leave Australia.'

When Dian and I visited my parents, the sight of Bapak sleeping, slumped in his wheelchair, pierced my heart. But their unit was spacious and bright, with two beds, ensuite, lounge area, a dining table big enough for the four of us to share dinner, and a flower garden just outside.

While Bapak often slept, Ibu was busy, bossing the other residents around and entering their rooms and ensuites to clean them. 'I don't understand why your father brought me here to live in this big hotel,' she told me. 'You will have to come and stay with us. We have lots of rooms.'

Ibu, Bapak and Wenny in 2009

Bapak told me he was bored. As we sat together, he sang a Dutch song. 'Do you often sing?' I asked.

'Yes, since I've been in this prison I've been depressed, so I have to sing.'

Then he surprised me by singing a French song.

'How come you can sing in French?' I asked.

'Oh, that is a love song.'

'Bapak, let's sing *Es Lilin*.'

Together we sang a traditional Sundanese song about a peddler pushing his cart along the street, selling paddle-pops. A passing nurse stopped at the door. 'Your father makes us happy when he sings,' she said.

My parents had been in the residence for twelve months when Bapak became critically ill and was taken to hospital in a coma. Ira, Ari and I flew to Canberra as soon as we heard. When I saw Bapak in the bed, so small and fragile, I wept. 'Bapak,' I said. 'It's Wenny.'

He opened his eyes, looked at me and groaned softly. I hugged him, and stood beside the bed, holding his hand and praying hard, 'God, if you want him to come home, please give him the easiest way. If he still has more life, please make it good life.'

'Bapak,' I said. 'When you get well, I will read to you from my life story – what we have written about you.'

His eyes opened again, and he murmured, 'Bagus.' Good.

For three more days he drifted in and out of consciousness and sometimes, while I sat with him, he spoke softly but clearly. 'There is no meaning at all,' he murmured, gripping my hand. 'It doesn't mean anything. Where is God?'

I held my head close to his so that I could hear what he was saying. 'Oh, I found … there's a light. Hot. There is water. Cool.'

He slowly enunciated his own name: 'Cece Ach … diat Kar … ta Mi … hardja.'

He spoke so softly that the others around the bed could not hear him, and I repeated his words to them. 'I have two keys,' he said, and I wondered if one was to leave this world, and the other to open the next.

'Emak! Emak is giving me a plate of rice. Apak is here.' Emak and Apak were his mother and father.

'Babang has come.' Babang was his brother. He recited the names of his siblings who had already passed away. Then he said, 'Ati is here. How is your husband, Ati?'

My sister Ati had died from cancer several years previously.

'Ayo, ayo, let's go,' he said. 'Okay, I'm coming.'

'He wants to leave this world,' said Dian.

'Tati, Tati,' cried Bapak.

'He does not want to leave Ibu,' I said. 'His heart is heavy for her.'

During those three days, friends and family came and sat quietly around the bed. My sister Nuy brought Ibu from the residence each day. Bapak's former Dean, Tony Johns, arrived with his wife Yohanni. It was peaceful, not at all like the melee around Dahlan when he lay dying.

'Bapak,' I said. 'Can you say the Syahadat: *lâ ilâha illallâh, Muḥammadun rasûlullâh.*'

He opened his eyes. 'You don't believe that.'

'No, Bapak, because I am Christian. But you are Muslim, and the Syahadat is your way.'

He recited the words so quietly I could barely hear them.

'Wenny,' said Yohanni Johns. 'Tony would like to hold Aki's hand.'

I realised I was monopolising my father, and quickly made room for Tony.

'Where is my tasbeh?' asked Bapak. In recent years he had never been without his prayer beads, his fingers moving over them as he remembered God.

We had thought Bapak was dying, but he improved, regaining full consciousness. He would soon be ready to return to the residence. But it seemed to me that he had been on the border, glimpsing the next world. This strengthened my belief that there is something after death.

I spent more time with Bapak before we left Canberra, asking his forgiveness for all the times I had wronged him and thanking him for everything he had done for me.

On the way to the airport we called in to the residence to see Ibu, as Nuy had not yet brought her to the hospital for the day. She was in a common room with about twenty other people, but she stood out. At 93, she was still fit and strong, and looked radiant. We hugged, and my heart filled with love and sadness for my mother.

My father, Achdiat Karta Mihardja, died on 8 July 2010. He was 100 years old, although he is reported to have been 99 because the young Achdiat had changed his birthdate in his determination to obtain the best education possible.

Many people, including the Indonesian Ambassador, attended the funeral, which took place on the afternoon of the day he died, in accordance with the Islamic requirement for burial as soon as possible after death. I will always regret that I was notified too late to be there, but I treasure the time I had spent with him at the hospital three weeks before.

At the grave side, Tony Johns delivered the eulogy. He said that Achdiat Karta Mihardja was a great man, a great Indonesian and "a great writer, who contributed much to the development of a modern Indonesian literature… He dared to lead it along paths it had not ventured on before."

Ibu was at the service for the man who had come to the restaurant where she worked over 70 years earlier. A former colleague of Bapak told me that Ibu looked at the wrapped body and asked, 'Who is that?'

'Your husband,' said the colleague.

Ibu said, 'Achdiat is a really good man.'

Achdiat Karta Mihardja was also the father whose hand I held as we walked together through the darkening streets of Jakarta, the father I looked up to as he smiled and said that the moon loved me.

Glossary

Abang	elder brother
Agan	aristocratic title
Ajengan	community leader, Islamic teacher; term of respect for older man
akad nikah	official marriage ceremony
Aki	grandfather; respectful form of address for elderly men
ampun	forgive me
Bahasa Indonesia	Indonesian language
bak mandi	open tank holding water for dipper baths
Balai Pustaka	state-owned publishing house for Indonesian literature
Bandung	capital of West Java province, and Indonesia's third largest city
Bapak	Father; form of address to an older man
Batak	ethnic group from North Sumatra
becak	pedicab
Belanda	Dutch
Bi	shortened form of Bibi

Bibi	Aunt; form of address for an older woman, usually as Bi
Bu	shortened form of Ibu; form of address to older women
bung	brother; often used as title for leaders, as in "Bung Karno" for President Sukarno
Ciumbuleuit	an upper class residential area in north Bandung
congklak	game in which tokens are moved between holes in a wooden board
degung	Sundanese gamelan (gamelan = Indonesian orchestra)
delman	horse and buggy
Dies Natalis	anniversary of the founding of an institution (from Latin: "day of birth")
galak	fierce
Gan	short form of Agan, an aristocratic title
Garut	city in West Java
gelang keroncong	series of bangles
goreng	fried
gunung	mountain

Gunung Telagabodas	volcano near the city of Garut
Ibu	Mother; form of address for older women
Indo	Eurasian, usually with Indonesian mother and Dutch father
Istana Negara	State Palace, where state events and receptions are held
Jakarta	capital city of Indonesia
jalan	street
jamu	traditional herbal medicine
Jepang	Japan
kain	cloth, in particular, a length of cloth worn on the lower part of the body
kain kebaya	traditional clothes for Indonesian women, a tight fitting blouse (kebaya) coordinated with a length of cloth wrapped around the lower part of the body (kain)
kak	short form of kakak
kakak	older sibling; form of address for older sibling or for a somewhat older person, especially as kak
kampung	village
Kang	elder brother

kebaya	traditional female garment, a tight fitting blouse
kemerdekaan	freedom, independence
Konfrontasi	Indonesia's campaign against the formation of Malaysia 1962-1966
keris, kris	traditional Javanese dagger
Lebaran	day of celebration at the end of fasting month
lotek	Sundanese vegetable salad with spicy peanut sauce
Mamih	mother (Dutch); Wenny's name for her mother when she was a child
Mang	term of address for parents' younger brother
Menteng	a suburb of Jakarta
merdeka	freedom, independence
Minangkabau	ethnic group from West Sumatra
Nini	Grandmother; respectful term of address for elderly women
Nyonya besar	important woman
Om, Oom	uncle; term of address for older man
opor ayam	chicken cooked in coconut milk

Padang	capital and largest city of West Sumatra, the home province of the Minangkabau ethnic group.
Pak	shortened form of Bapak; form of address for older men
Pakuwon	suburb of Garut inhabited only by nobles
Paman	Uncle
Papih	father (Dutch); Wenny's name for her father when she was a small child
Parahyangan	mountainous area of West Java
Pekalongan	city on the north coast of Central Java, famous for its batik
pesantren	Islamic boarding school
pisang goreng	fried banana fritter
Ramadan	Muslim fasting month
rendang	beef cooked in spices and coconut milk for several hours
sambal	chilli based sauce, usually very spicy-hot
Semarang	city on the north coast of Java, capital of Central Java province

Sundanese	Ethnic group native to West Java, the second most populous Indonesian ethnic group after the Javanese
Syahadat	Islamic profession of faith: 'There is no god but Allah, and Muhammad is His Messenger.'
Tante	aunt; form of address for older women
Tempo	Indonesian weekly news magazine
tukang	worker specialising in a particular skill or trade
warung	small shop or stall
Yogyakarta	City in a Special Region within, but not part of, Central Java; often referred to by its shortened form, Yogya. One of the main centres of Javanese culture. Capital of Indonesia during the revolution.

Appreciation

From Bryce Alcock

Stories poured from Wenny during our first session to record her life: the frightened little girl clinging to her mother while Dutch soldiers searched for her father; learning to cook for her family when they fled to the mountains; an encounter with a huge python. Wenny was still telling stories as we walked out to my car after the session, and as I listened I regretted that I was no longer recording.

These events had been fixed in Wenny's memory by the drama of the times and by the emotions they had aroused in the little girl. Yet Wenny and I are aware of how unreliable memory can be. While I have recreated events and conversations based on Wenny's recollection and understanding of them, we acknowledge that others may have different memories of the same occasions. The names and identifying details of some people have been changed to protect their privacy.

I am extremely grateful to Wenny for entrusting me with the task of writing the story of her life and that of her father.

Thank you to the Australian Society of Authors for their Annual Mentorship Program for Emerging Writers and Illustrators, and to the Copyright Agency Cultural Fund for supporting the program, which provided a mentorship for the manuscript of *Daughter of Independence*. My thanks go to the mentor, Judith Lukin-Amundsen, whose guidance and encouragement resulted in a manuscript that finally felt like a book.

That the manuscript reached a high enough standard to attract the mentorship was due to my participation in a small group of writers who act as mentors to each other. I have learned much about the craft of writing from their kindly yet merciless critiques of my drafts. For their great generosity, I am indebted to group members Kate Fawns, Ruth Francis, Jan Silcock, Michelle Stigwood, Danae Sweetapple, Jillian Watkinson and Claire Wood. I am especially grateful to Jillian, a prize-winning author whose editorial work greatly improved the manuscript, and to Claire for detailed comments on parts of the draft.

Thank you to Lisa Gorton, who provided a copy of her grandmother's unfinished thesis on Aki Achdiat; to Professor Anthony Johns for information about Aki Achdiat; to Professor David Hill, who answered my questions about Mochtar Lubis and whose biography of Lubis was very useful in writing the historical background to the story of Wenny and her father; to the authors of other works that I consulted, which are detailed in a separate list; to the welcoming staff of Museum Basoeki Abdullah in Jakarta; and to Lucy Robertson-Cuninghame for cover and layout design.

I am grateful to those who have fostered and supported my passion for Indonesia: Wenny herself; Junedi Ichsan, former Lecturer in Indonesian Language at the University of Southern Queensland, who has sadly passed away; the staff of the Salatiga Program, the intensive course in Indonesian language and culture at Satya Wacana University in Central Java; and my Indonesian friends, some of whom I have known since my first visit to the country in 1973.

Most of all, I am deeply grateful to Ann for her loving support.

From Wenny Achdiat

As my father and I reminisced in his later years, our memories sparked off each other, and he urged me to tell my story for a wider audience. He inspired this book, and I regret that it was not ready for him to read before he died. *Daughter of Independence* is not just my story; it is also my tribute to the loving father who never stopped guiding me. I am deeply grateful for the principles and values he instilled in me, especially the importance of independence.

My mother used her businesses to fund my education and then supported me while I studied at Santa Ursula and the University of Indonesia. In these ways she fostered my independence, and I am extremely grateful.

My husband Dahlan was a good man who taught me much about kindness and generosity and encouraged me to keep my independence. I feel blessed to have shared my life with him.

I am indebted to my children for their support and understanding while I was a single mother. I regret that I was sometimes too busy working and studying to spend more time with them.

If it had not been for Senior Lecturer Gary Birch, I would never have achieved my diploma in second language teaching and joined the teaching staff at the University of Southern Queensland. Whenever I went to Gary crying and convinced that I could not go on, he gave me the strength to continue. Thank you, Gary.

My thanks go to photographer Ann Alcock for restoring the photos used in the book.

Bryce Alcock spent many hours interviewing me, patiently drawing out my story, recreating the scenes and people of my life, and capturing how it felt to experience those events. Our collaboration was enjoyable and productive, and I am especially grateful to Bryce.

Permissions and Credits

Our thanks go to the following publishers and writers who kindly gave permission to use material for the chapter epigraphs.

Lontar Foundation: epigraphs to chapters 1, 6 and 15 are from *On the Record: Indonesian Literary Figures, Volume 4*. Copyright © 2004 Lontar Foundation, Jakarta.

University of Queensland Press: epigraphs to chapters 3, 10, 14, 19 and 20 are from *Atheis* by Achdiat K Mihardja. Copyright © 1972 R J Maguire and Achdiat K Mihardja.

Australia Indonesia Association ACT: epigraphs to chapters 5,7,21,23,25,28 and 29 are from *The Scattered Dust of Love* by Achdiat K Mihardja, translated by Pam Allen, edited by Lois Carrington. Copyright © 2002 Pam Allen and Achdiat K Mihardja.

Barry Turner (Adjunct Professor, RMIT University): the epigraph to chapter 11 is Dr Turner's translation of an excerpt from a short story by Achdiat Karta Mihardja. The excerpt is from Dr Turner's PhD Thesis, *Nasution: Total People's Resistance and Organicist Thinking in Indonesia*. Swinburne University of Technology, 2005.

Taylor and Francis Books (for Routledge): the epigraph to chapter 13 is from *Journalism and Politics in Indonesia: A Critical Biography of Mochtar Lubis (1922-2004) as Editor and Author* by David T Hill. Copyright © 2010 David T Hill.

Lisa Gorton: the epigraph to chapter 22 is the first verse of the poem 'Solitaire i.m. Bettina Gorton', from *Press Release* (Giramondo). Copyright © 2007 Lisa Gorton.

Credits: The sources of epigraphs to other chapters are:

Chapter 2: the Indonesian Declaration of Independence is reproduced from *Indonesia 1987 An Official Handbook*. Jakarta: Department of Information, Republic of Indonesia.

Chapters 4, 17 and 27: articles by Achdiat Karta Mihardja in *Pelangi*, a magazine published from 1985 to 1999 by the University of Southern Queensland to provide materials for the teaching and learning of Indonesian (see *Works Consulted*).

Chapter 8: *SMA Santa Ursula* Facebook page.

Chapter 9: Museum Basoeki Abdullah brochure.

Chapter 12: The Hadith (sayings attributed to the Prophet Muhammad).

Chapter 16: *Sleeping with a Guling* Facebook page.

Chapter 18: *Sundanese Lifecycle Rituals and the Status of Women in Indonesia*, a PhD Thesis by Linda Lentz, abstract available on the Oxford Centre for Mission Studies website at http://www.ocms.ac.uk/abstracts/pdf/2011_llentz.pdf

Chapters 24 and 26: from an interview with Achdiat Karta Mihardja reported in Syir'ah Magazine, July 2005. Syir'ah is a biweekly Indonesian magazine focussing on Islamic issues, published by Yayasan Desantara, Jakarta.

Works Consulted

Anggraeni, Dewi. "Indonesia's Pancasila Democracy Exists in Name Only." (Interview with Achdiat Karta Mihardja.) *Jakarta Post* 22 March, 2001.

Brown, Colin. *A Short History of Indonesia: The Unlikely Nation?* Crows Nest, NSW: Allen & Unwin, 2003.

Cribb, Robert. "The Nationalist World of Occupied Jakarta, 1946-1949." *From Batavia to Jakarta*. Ed. Susan Abeyasekere. Clayton, Vic.: Monash University, 1985. 91-107. Available at: http://works.bepress.com/robert_cribb/15, accessed 10 March 2013.

Cribb, Robert. *Digital Atlas of Indonesian History*. Copenhagen: Nordic Institute of Asian Studies, 2010.

Cribb, Robert and Colin Brown. *Modern Indonesia: A History Since 1945*. London: Longman: 1995.

Feith, Herb. *The Decline of Constitutional Democracy in Indonesia*. Ithaca: Cornell University Press, 1962.

Fitri, Emmy. "Achdiat Karta Mihardja: Not of an age but for all time." *Jakarta Post* 13 June, 2005.

Gorton, Lisa. *Press Release*. Sydney: Giramondo, 2007.

Hill, David T. *Journalism and Politics in Indonesia: A Critical Biography of Mochtar Lubis (1922-2004) as Editor and Author*. London: Routledge, 2010.

Johns, Anthony H. *Cultural Options and the Role of Tradition: A Collection of Essays on Modern Indonesian and Malaysian Literature*. Canberra: Australian National University Press, 1979.

Johns, Anthony H. "Former Faculty Lecturer Passed Away" (graveside tribute). *Asia-Pacific Culture, History and Language, News from the School of Culture, History, and Language in the ANU College of Asia & the Pacific* 12 July 2010. Available at: http://arktos.anu.edu.au/blog/?p=1308, accessed 10 March 2013.

Johns, Anthony H. "Writer was at forefront of modern Indonesian culture." *Sydney Morning Herald* August 20, 2010.

Johns, Yohanni. "Gorton, Lady Bettina Edith (1915–1983)", *Obituaries Australia*, National Centre of Biography, Australian National University, http://oa.anu.edu.au/obituary/gorton-lady-bettina-edith-434/text435, accessed 10 March 2013.

McDonald, Hamish. *Suharto's Indonesia*. Blackburn: Fontana, 1981

Maier, Hendrik M. J. "I felt like a car without a driver: AKM's novel Atheis." *Identity in Asian Literature*. Ed. Littrup, Lisbeth. Abingdon, Oxon: RoutledgeCurzen, 2004. 129-150.

Mihardja, Achdiat Karta. *Atheis*. Jakarta: Balai Pustaka, 1949. English translation by R. J. Maguire. Brisbane: Queensland University Press, 1972.

Mihardja, Achdiat Karta. *Keretakan dan Ketegangan*. Jakarta: Balai Pustaka, 1956.

Mihardja, Achdiat Karta. *Debu Cinta Bertebaran*. Singapore: Pustaka Nasional, 1973. English translation by Pam Allen, *The Scattered Dust of Love*. Edited by Lois Carrington. Canberra: Australia Indonesia Association ACT, 2002.

Mihardja, Achdiat Karta. "Puasa and Lebaran." *Pelangi* 4.3 (1988): 17-18

Mihardja, Achdiat Karta. "Another Human Race." *Pelangi* 6.4 (1990): 10-12.

Mihardja, Achdiat Karta. "Martini's Version: Introduced and translated by D. M. Roskies." *Review of Indonesian and Malaysian Affairs (RIMA)* 26 Winter (1992): 21-41.

Mihardja, Achdiat Karta. *Manifesto Khalifatullah*. Bandung: Arasy Mizan, 2005.

Museum Basoeki Abdullah. *R. Basoeki Abdullah (Sebuah Biografi dan Pengabdiannya dalam Bidang Seni Lukis)*. Jakarta: Departemen Kebudayaan dan Pariwisata, 2009.

On the Record: Indonesian Literary Figures: Achdiat Karta Mihardja. DVD videorecording and transcript. Jakarta: Lontar Foundation, 2004.

Penders, Chr.L.M. *The Life and Times of Sukarno*. Oxford: Oxford University Press, 1974.

Rankin, Stephen. *From Dichotomy to Difference: The Australian Literary Construction of Indonesia*. Perth, Australia: Murdoch Univerity PhD Thesis, 1999.

Smail, John R. W. *Bandung in the Early Revolution 1945-46: A Study in the Social History of the Indonesian Revolution*. Jakarta, Equinox Publishing, 2009.

Sukarno. *Sukarno: an Autobiography, as told to Cindy Adams*. Indianapolis: The Bobbs-Merrill Company, 1965.

Syir'ah Magazine. "Achdiat Karta Mihardja: Khalifatullah Bukan Khilafah Islamiyah." Jakarta: Yayasan Desantara, July 2005.

Teeuw, A. *Modern Indonesian Literature*. The Hague: Martinus Nijhoff, 1967.

Turner, Barry. *Nasution: Total People's Resistance and Organicist Thinking in Indonesia*. PhD Thesis, Swinburne University of Technology, Melbourne, 2005.

van Bruinessen, Martin. "Shaykh `Abd al-Qadir al-Jilani and the Qadiriyya in Indonesia", *Journal of the History of Sufism* vol. 1-2 (2000): 361-395.

Vickers, Adrian. *A History of Modern Indonesia*. Cambridge: Cambridge University Press, 2005.

www.ingramcontent.com/pod-product-compliance
Lightning Source LLC
Chambersburg PA
CBHW070729160426
43192CB00009B/1373